C. S. LEWIS

THE CROSSROAD SPIRITUAL LEGACY SERIES

The Rule of Benedict: Insights for the Ages
by Joan Chittister, O.S.B.

Ignatius Loyola: Spiritual Exercises
by Joseph A. Tetlow, S.J.

Francis de Sales: Introduction to the Devout Life *and* Treatise on the Love of God
by Wendy M. Wright

Teresa of Avila: Mystical Writings
by Tessa Bielecki

St. Francis of Assisi: Writings for a Gospel Life
by Regis J. Armstrong, O.F.M. Cap.

Augustine: Essential Writings
by Benedict J. Groeschel, C.S.R.

Thomas Aquinas: Spiritual Master
by Robert Barron

Hildegard: Prophet of the Cosmic Christ
by Renate Craine

Karl Rahner: The Mystic of Everyday Life
by Harvey D. Egan, S.J.

C. S. Lewis: Spirituality for Mere Christians
by William Griffin

C. S. LEWIS

SPIRITUALITY FOR MERE CHRISTIANS

William Griffin

A Crossroad Book
The Crossroad Publishing Company
New York

Acknowledgment is gratefully extended to quote from the following:

C. S. Lewis, "In Praise of Solid People" from *Spirits in Bondage* (copyright © 1984) and "Deadly Sins" from *Poems* (copyright © 1966). Used by permission of Harcourt, Brace.

C. S. Lewis, *The Pilgrim's Regress,* copyright © 1933, 1943 by Clive Staples Lewis. Used by permission of the Wm. B. Eerdmans Publishing Co.

Noel Coward, "Twentieth Century Blues" (copyright © 1931 by Chappell & Co., Ltd.); copyright renewed, published in the U.S.A. by Chappell & Co., Inc.: international copyright secured; all rights reserved. Used by permission of Chappell/Intersong Music Group.

The Crossroad Publishing Company
370 Lexington Avenue, New York, NY 10017

Parts of this work have appeared before, in different form, in *Clive Staples Lewis: A Dramatic Voice* (San Francisco: Harper & Row, Publishers, 1986).

Printed in the United States of America

Library of Congress Cataloging-in-Publication Data

Griffin, William, 1935-
C. S. Lewis : spirituality for mere Christians / William Griffin.
p. cm. – (A spiritual legacy book)
Includes bibliographical references.
ISBN 0-8245-2506-X (pbk.)
1. Lewis, C. S. (Clive Staples), 1898-1963 – Biography.
2. Authors, English – 20th century – Biography. 3. Anglicans – England – Biography. 4. Christian biography – England. I. Title.
II. Series: Crossroad spiritual legacy series.
BX5199.L53G75 1998
230'.092–dc21
[B] 98-14901

1 2 3 4 5 6 7 8 9 10 02 01 00 99 98

for

WALTER HOOPER

Man, please thy Maker, and be merry,
And give not for this world a cherry.

–William Dunbar

Contents

Introduction

Clive Staples Lewis, professor of English language and literature at both Oxford and Cambridge universities from the 1920s to the 1960s, was a controversial Christian. He was an intellectual who believed in the brute force of syllogisms, but he also believed in the simple faith of credal formulations. These latter he had the gall to preach and write about and even to broadcast over BBC Radio. Of the seven deadly sins, he felt that sloth was his alone. Yet to others he appeared a furiously industrious man, a living reproach to sluggards everywhere. This too brought resentment to the slow of mind, the slow of heart. But no matter, to those who knew the real C. S. Lewis, he was a jolly fellow, a learned tutor, a loyal friend, a loving if reluctant husband, a faithful Christian.

When he was barely a boy, he abandoned Christianity, only to return to it as a young man. He rediscovered it, virtually reinvented it, as converts have a habit of doing, and by the time he was finished, he had bloomed where he was planted, in the Anglican Church. There was some irony in this and indeed some unhappiness; he felt he was surrounded with a bad crop of clergy. His Catholic friends commiserated; already they were worrying about their own *ordinati.*

By the end of his life, he'd propagated, not only in his own country but also in ours, "Mere Christianity," Christianity plain and simple, the sort of Christianity taught in the first few centuries of the Christian era. It wasn't necessary to propound further doctrines, he always felt when called upon to defend the faith, but only to reimagine the doctrines he already had. And it so happened that these were the ones that were already held in common by the major Christian denominations in the England of his day.

Admirers of his life and times haven't always been friends with each other. In fact, they have almost never been friends. From the time he was buried in the churchyard of Holy Trinity in Headington Quarry, they've engaged in an unfriendly free-for-all. And after decades of taking no hostages, no one, mercifully, has emerged the victor.

If all the combatants — American and British, believers and non-believers, High Christians and Low Christians — could be seated around one table, three points of contention would surely emerge:

Where is the real C. S. Lewis?

To whom does the real C. S. Lewis belong?

Who, finally, is the real C. S. Lewis?

Where Is the Real C. S. Lewis?

If someone wanted to hide in Oxford, T. S. Eliot once said, the best place would be the chapel. No university intellectual in his right mind would want to be found alive there. Nor would any British academic worth his Worcestershire want to be caught dead there.

But in Oxford, in the 1930s, Lewis could indeed be found in the chapel, the chapel of Magdalen College, every morning his schedule allowed. He entered the chapel at a gallop, leather heels clipping smartly down the marble floor, academic sleeves flying, and flopped in a wooden choir stall.

It was time for morning prayer — or Dean's Prayers, as they were called then. Sometimes the boys from Magdalen Choir School intoned the hymns of the day. Perhaps there was a creed; perhaps a litany. Obsecration such as this, in this and other college chapels, had been rising in curling wisps since the first monks invaded the swampy market town in the thirteenth century.

"That litany," said Lewis of a summer morning in 1933 as he emerged from Magdalen chapel, "makes one feel as if the royal family were not pulling their weight."

Why is that? asked the dean of divinity.

If they were, Lewis suggested, then we wouldn't have to

sandwich their welfare in between "holy church universal" and "all Christian rulers and magistrates!"

Over the years not many of Lewis's biographers have followed Eliot's advice. Although they've looked for him in a good many other places, they've shunned the chapels as though they were bedlams. But the modern biographer, or so I had been led to believe, had no such totems, no such taboos; he or she was supposed to look everywhere, leaving no stone unturned, no record unverified, no rumor unsubstantiated, no interested party uninterviewed.

May I use myself as an example?

When I set out to find the real C. S. Lewis, I wasn't happy about this unwritten principle, but wanting to be a writer of my own time and no other, I assented to it. I'd talk to everyone (both friend and foe), look at everything (between the sheets as well as behind the cupboards), and in every place (from the pulpit to the toilet).

First, I explored his sexuality, especially inquiring whether he was a homosexual. I asked dozens of people, male and female. In response, I got eyebrows raised, earlobes tugged, throats cleared... but not a lot of light shed. When I broached the question to one person — a university graduate and single lady of singular intellect, who'd never met him personally but knew his work intimately — she laughed out loud. *Heterosexual!* Emphasis hers. Dead end to that exploration!

Second, I explored his spirituality, especially the primrose pathway he took from Christianity to theism to apostasy to atheism, and back again along the same path to Christianity. As a younger man he traveled the roadway out of Jerusalem, to use a later figure of his own. But when it suited his intellect, he returned on the very same cobbled road back into Jerusalem — his pilgrimaging, of course, being up and down the macadamized motorway to and from Canterbury, seat of the Anglican Church. Here I found plenty of evidence of his spirituality, much of it epistolary, and hence, would-be modern biographer that I was, I had no hesitation about putting it in my biography.

Like intellectual converts before and after, Lewis had to think his way — and indeed imagine his way — through the conversion process. A red bus groaning up a steep hill. A solitary trudge around Addison's Walk. A green motorcycle with sidecar and a picnic at the zoo. A bottle of beer and Bultitude bolt upright. The Cherwell a-burble and fringed with osiers. Mythologizing near Mesopotamia. Midnight conversations, lapel to lapel. Rain in sheets and a rush of wind. A passage through a locked gate. More ratiocinations until the uncertain dawn. All to reach a conclusion that the Christian myth might just be the one true myth that had some basis in human history.

The whole process reminds me of Lewis's own description of *Hamlet*, as he read in a paper to the British Academy on April 22, 1942:

"Night, ghosts, a castle, a lobby where a man can walk four hours together, a willow-fringed brook and a sad lady drowned, a graveyard and a terrible cliff above the sea, and amidst all these a pale man in black clothes...with his stockings coming down, a disheveled man whose words make us at once think of loneliness and doubt and dread, of waste and dust and emptiness, and from whose hands, or from our own, we feel the richness of Heaven and earth and the comfort of human affection slipping away."

What Lewis drew from Shakespeare's play, we draw from his own descriptions of what took place when Christianity reentered his adult life. Only this time, "the richness of Heaven and earth and the comfort of human affection" weren't slipping away from Lewis—rather they were fluttering toward him.

Further exploring this religious strand, I wanted to see if theologizing his way out of mythology revealed a spirituality, an underground aquifer running though his conscious and unconscious and revivifying his spirit. This I did find — this I did dowse, did divine, if I may continue my aqueous figure of speech. There were telltale watermarks all through his personal correspondence, revealing a person of deep spirituality, fed by reading Scripture, nourished by Holy Communion, fortified by spiritual direction.

All of which is another way of saying that, as a modern biographer, I was duty-bound to report what I found. What I found was both an absence of sexual excess and a presence of what some biographers — certainly not I — would call spiritual excess. The *New York Times* reviewer of my Lewis biography thought that my conclusion was neurotic at best, psychotic at worst.

All of which is yet another way of saying, that both for biographers and readers of biography, it's not appropriate to look for the real Lewis in bedrooms and bordellos only; one has also to look in chapels and churches . . . and to report back exactly what one finds, neither more nor less.

And so it is when one comes to look for his spirituality.

To Whom Does the Real C. S. Lewis Belong?

Some intellectuals who feel affection for Lewis as a thinker have, since the time of his death, expressed the fear that a roving band of American Evangelicals has snatched his body; if not his body, then his soul; if not his soul, then his books; if not his books, then something else . . . anything else.

When I tried to beard Dame Helen Gardner in her book-lined den to interview her for my biography — she succeeded Lewis at Oxford and achieved a quiet notoriety of her own — I was rebuffed. Too many American Evangelicals already had sniffed around his religious writings, she felt, and one more would only drag his reputation down to the gutter. She didn't give me the opportunity to say that I wasn't an Evangelical; that I wasn't at all unhappy to be identified as one of that noble band of American Christians; that I was indeed a Catholic.

But her message — and the message of others like her — was quite clear. Some brands of Christianity ranked higher than others, and hence were better than others. To put it another way, Lewis was Anglican, and the Americans were Baptist; or worse yet, Roman Catholic. To put it yet another way, a way that Lewis himself would understand, there was hierarchy . . . and then there was lowerarchy. Clearly Gardner felt she and Lewis were in the former, where proper Anglicans ought to be. Clearly I and the rest of America were in the back pew — backbenchers, as it were — if inside the church at all.

Lewis's life as a whole seems to have made no one completely happy. American Evangelicals who liked what he believed didn't like the fact that he smoked and drank. British intellectuals who smoked and drank didn't like the fact that he believed and prayed. Some wags have even gone so far as to say that Lewis must be turning over in his grave for — you name the reason.

To which I'd reply, Where have these wagglers been for the last two thousand years? Theirs is — if I may coin a critical term — a *pathological fallacy* of the bizarrest sort, to think that Lewis, whatever state of immortality he may now be enjoying, cares a fig for what happens on earth.

No, Lewis's life and reputation are our property now, and we must treat, scientifically and circumspectly, all the facets of his life, not just the ones we happen to like.

Some, who have no church and hence no theology, fear that Lewis is being turned into a plastic saint. Others, who do have churches but no hagiology, fear far more: that Lewis is being turned into a plaster saint. The Roman Catholic Church, on the other hand, long a believer in purveying sanctity through statuary, has a rather merry attitude toward the saints; it doesn't discourage its faithful from praying either *with* the saints or *to* the saints, canonized or uncanonized, Catholic or otherwise — and Lewis among them.

To whom, then, does Lewis really belong?

He belongs to each and every one of us, of whatever denomination, of whatever education, who reads his books, of whatever genre, with a view to drawing whatever spiritual refreshment for the holy trudge ahead.

Who Is the Real C. S. Lewis?

Lewis's life is presented here, not as a proof of high personal sanctity, but simply as he lived it, warts and all. He was a good man, a talented man, and at the same time a flawed man trying to work out his salvation as best he could.

For us twentieth-century folk, he's something of an Everyman in that he was just a bloke. Some thought he looked like a farmer, and he certainly enjoyed a ploughman's lunch as much as the next fellow, especially with a pint of cider or a bottle of stout by the roaring cataract at The Trout, a public house near Oxford. But he was just one of the millions, trying to make his own spiritual way, and it was well known that he wasn't the best map-reader in his brigade. In a sense he was one of the people he described in his poem "In Praise of Solid People"; it was published in 1919 when he was twenty.

> Thank God that there are solid folk
> Who water flowers and roll the lawn,
> And sit and sew and talk and smoke,
> And snore all through the summer dawn.
>
> Who pass untroubled nights and days
> Full-fed and sleepily content,
> Rejoicing in each other's praise,
> Respectable and innocent.

But, let me hasten to say, Lewis wasn't Everyman or Everywoman. He was a bookish sort who found that the road out of Jerusalem and back into that holy city was, at least for him, paved not with cobbles but with books whose backs were rounded and hulled like cobbles. He couldn't take a step in the one direction or the other without its being supported by something he'd read. But what else could he expect of himself? From his earliest days books of all sorts were never far from his reach. "I had always the same certainty of finding a book that was new to me," he wrote in his autobiography, "as a man who walks into a field has of finding a new blade of grass."

These books he not only read but he also remembered, almost verbatim, being something of a savant in that regard. On occasion, he'd playfully ask an undergraduate to pull a book, any book, out of his book case.

"Give me a number from one to forty," he'd ask.

"Thirty."

"Right. Go to the thirtieth shelf," said Lewis, pouring some beer for them both. "Give me another number from one to twenty."

"Fourteen."

"Right. Get the fourteenth book off the shelf." Lewis dropped back into an armchair by the fireplace. "Now let's have a number from one to one hundred."

"Forty-six."

"Now turn to page 46. Pick a number from one to twenty-five for the line of the page."

"Six."

"So, read me the line."

From that one line Lewis recognized the title of the book and, to the undergraduate's further astonishment, was able to continue the quotation for lines.

Needless to say, there was a practical spiritual element in all of this. The professor was either putting the fear of God into the undergraduate, or scaring the bejesus out of him.

And so it is with us that, when we come to grips with an elephantine intellect like Lewis's, we feel like the dumbest undergraduates, and we too are properly humbled.

But Lewis himself could feel humbled too. Giving talks to RAF pilots in World War II, about to take off for raids over Germany from which they wouldn't return, he felt he was a complete failure. "One must take comfort," he wrote to his friend and confidante, Sister Penelope Lawson, CSMV, on May 15, 1941, "in remembering that God used an *ass* to convert the prophet; perhaps if we do our poor best, we shall be allowed a stall near it in the celestial stable—rather like this." He filled the rest of the piece of stationery with a poor drawing of an ass with a halo, flanked by stick figures of a nun and a professor, with the heavenly city in the background.

Lewis's literary taste was, if anything, catholic.

He read highbrow books, books characterized by adjectives like "literary," "classical," and "serious"; they were grave, weighty, and momentous; they offered artistic, esthetic, or spiritual satisfaction; and, presumably, they were good. Like *The Canterbury Tales* and the plays of Shakespeare, the *Faerie Queene* and *Paradise Lost*.

And he read lowbrow books, books characterized by adjectives like "popular," "common," "commercial"; they were cheap, trashy, and trivial; they provided escape, diversion, mere entertainment; and, presumably, they were bad. Like *She* and

King Solomon's Mines, exotic, fast-paced novels by H. Rider Haggard. And wasn't that "redskinnery" in the works of James Fenimore Cooper irresistible!

And so it is with us as we approach his life, which itself was something of an open book. In its pages we will find much that is highbrow and much that is lowbrow; that is to say, much to identify with. Much of that will amuse; much of that will edify; much of that will inspire imitation. And much of what we find will be the real C. S. Lewis.

What Is "Mere Christianity?"

The words "Mere Christianity" weren't original to Lewis. In the seventeenth century Richard Baxter, an Anglican divine with Puritan predilections, used the words "Mere Christianity" in *Church-History of the Government of Bishops* (1680). He is happily remembered for *The Saints' Everlasting Rest* (1650), which was something like the sixteenth-century Spaniard Ignatius Loyola's *Spiritual Exercises* in that it prepared the soul, through a series of measured steps, for its heavenly home. The first ten chapters described Heaven, who'll be there and who won't, and why one must pursue Heaven strenuously while on earth. The last six chapters prescribed the Anglican method, with Puritan overlay, of pursuing the heavenly, and indeed heavily contemplative, life.

Nor did the concept of "Mere Christianity" originate with Lewis. In the sixteenth century, Richard Hooker created a distinctive theology for a denomination that needed one, the new Anglican Church, and the prose he did it in was masterful. As Lewis said in *English Literature of the Sixteenth Century, Excluding Drama,* "The style is, for its purpose, perhaps the most perfect in English."

In his sermon "Of Justification," delivered in 1585, Hooker spoke of England's popish ancestors: "God, I doubt not, was merciful to save thousands of them." His parishioners weren't so generous, but he bade his hearers, "Beware lest we make too many ways of denying Christ."

As if this weren't scandal enough, Lewis noted, Hooker

went on to say that even a contemporary Papist, "yea, a cardinal or pope," truly penitent, and erroneous only on the doctrine of "merit," won't be rejected by "a merciful God ready to make the best of that little which we hold so well," no "captious sophister which gathereth the worst out of everything wherein we err."

"Those who find 'arrogance' in such a sermon, preached at such a date," commented Lewis, "hardly recognize that Hooker is going to the very limits of what his premises allowed him and far beyond the limits of personal or controversial prudence.

"Nor, I think, do they do justice to the humility and the almost agonized charity which vibrates in sentence after sentence.

" 'Woe worth the hour wherein we were born except we might persuade ourselves better things.'

" 'The hour may come when we shall think it a blessed thing to hear that if our sins were as the sins of the pope and cardinals, the bowels of the mercy of God are larger.'

"And finally 'if it be an error . . . my greatest comfort is my error; were it not for the love I bear unto this error, I would neither wish to speak nor to live.'

"If this be arrogance," Lewis concluded, "it might be wished that divines of all [three] camps [of the Reformation] had more often spoken arrogantly."

Of Hooker's masterwork, *Of the Laws of Ecclesiastical Polity*, a multi-volume work published in the 1590s, Lewis had this to say:

"Hooker had never heard of a religion called Anglicanism. He would never have dreamed of trying to 'convert' any foreigner to the Church of England. It was to him obvious that a German or Italian would not belong to the Church of England, just as an Ephesian or Galatian would not have belonged to the church of Corinth.

"Hooker is never seeking for 'the true Church,' never crying, like Donne, 'Show me, deare Christ, thy spouse.' For him no such problem existed. If by 'the Church' you mean the mystical Church (which is partly in Heaven), then of course, no man can identify her. But if you mean the visible Church, then we all know her. She is 'a sensibly known company' of all those throughout the world who profess one Lord, one Faith, and one Baptism (III.i.3)."

Sometime in 1943, Lewis began making the words "Mere Christianity" his own. It was in his Introduction to *St. Athanasius, On the Incarnation*, translated from the Greek by his friend Sister Penelope. "The only safety [against the theological errors in recently published books]," wrote Lewis, "is to have a standard of plain, central Christianity ('mere Christianity' as Baxter called it) which puts the controversies of the moment in their proper perspective."

In 1952 Lewis used the words again, this time in a book title. *Mere Christianity* was the overarching title for the BBC Radio talks, which had already been published in three books: *The Case for Christianity*, published in England under the title *Broadcast Talks* (1943), *Christian Behavior* (1943), and *Beyond Personality* (1945).

In the preface to this combined work, Lewis gave a descriptive definition of Mere Christianity. "Ever since I became a Christian, I have thought that the best, perhaps the only, service I could do for my unbelieving neighbors was to explain and defend the belief that has been common to nearly all Christians at all times."

Is Mere Christianity, then, a denomination?

Clearly, Mere Christianity isn't a denomination, but if it isn't, how may one describe it?

If one were to make a pie chart using a really good pie — the sort of pork pie or game pie readily available at most British pubs in Lewis's time and indeed in ours — the slices would stand for the denominations (Methodists, Anglicans, Presbyterians, etc.), and the size of the slices would indicate the membership, greater or lesser depending on the day the pie was sliced. Where is Mere Christianity on this chart? It's not any individual slice, but one may discover it if one describes a small circle with the focal point at the center of the pie.

This concentric circle, crossing as it does all the denominational lines, includes, constitutes, what may be called Mere Christianity. It's omni-denominational in one sense, and yet in another, it's nulli-denominational. It looks like a pork pie, tastes like a pork pie, and yet, centered around the center, it smacks of Heaven for all Christians. Now you taste it, now you don't. It's how you cut the pie. And Lewis cut it circularly.

"It is at her center," wrote Lewis in as generous a spirit as Hooker's, "where her truest children dwell, that each communion is really closest to every other in spirit, if not in doctrine. And this suggests that at the center of each there is something, or a Someone, who against all divergences of belief, all differences of temperament, all memories of mutual persecution, speaks with the same voice."

Who Is a "Mere Christian?"

If there's such a thing as Mere Christianity, but if Mere Christianity isn't a denomination, then can there be such a thing as a Mere Christian? I've yet to meet one. I presume there are many, but there's no way to count them or indeed no reason to hold them to account. There's no sacrament to mark them as MCs (if I may so abbreviate), no membership card, no sacred certificate declaring baptism or marriage, no profane piece of paper stating birth or death. Hence, the MC, if he or she exists, is an invisible, mysterious, perhaps even mystical being.

I suppose a case could be made that one who buys a copy of *Mere Christianity* is an MC, in potency if not already in act, but even here there's a fallacy. One is not what one reads. One may approach the cash register or cash point with a book plainly entitled *Homosexuality* and not be a homosexual, no matter what the snoops in the queue may think; and the same holds true for the homosexual waiting to purchase a copy of *Heterosexuality.* After all, Democrats buy books by Republicans, and Tories buy books by Labourites. The obese buy diet books, and the obtuse buy how-to books. Hence, it's not much of a hop, skip, and jump to Christians who buy copies of Bertrand Russell's *Why I Am Not a Christian* or A. N. Wilson's *Against Religion: Why We Should Try to Live without It.*

All readers buy books in order to know, not necessarily to follow. Which is another way of saying that buying a copy of *Mere Christianity* however ostentatiously, and reading it however surreptitiously, and stashing it under one's pillow however superstitiously doesn't make one an MC.

But if one takes the contents of *Mere Christianity* to heart and tries to put into practice some of its prescriptions, then one may be well on his or her way to becoming a bona fide MC. But who would know? Not many, if any. How, then, would one MC know another? There's no secret handshake, no variation in the Sign of the Cross. But Jesus Christ would know, and if that's the case, no one else need ever know.

What Is Spirituality?

After World War I, Noël Coward, a contemporary of Lewis's (he'll make a special guest appearance in chapter 2), redesigned much of public moral behavior in London and New York in the plots of his plays and musicals. Sadly, much of his audience redesigned their own lives along the Cowardy model. In the early 1930s he even entitled one play *A Design for Living;* in it three characters were plagued with sexual confusion; the best solution they could come up with, even with Coward's seemingly infinite moral boundaries, was a *ménage à trois.* "All the hormones in my blood are working overtime," Gilda tells Ernest. "They're rushing madly in and out of my organs like messenger boys."

For his own spiritual life, Lewis could have taken this model of morality-without-morals too, but he didn't. He could have developed a design from the spiritual masters who preceded him, but he didn't. He'd read Julian of Norwich (died after 1416) and John of the Cross (died 1591), and he'd perused Francis de Sales's *Introduction to the Devout Life* (1609) and William Law's *A Serious Call to a Devout and Holy Life* (1728). But these authors were members of the clergy and the religious orders, and Lewis wasn't. He was a layperson, and a layperson he wanted to remain. And so he took bits and bobs from these and other spiritual masters to design a spiritual life of his own. A sort of spirituality for — and, indeed, by and of — the MC.

Now, the first thing one notices about this new, this modern spirituality, especially as exemplified by Lewis, is that it was harried and hurried, heltered and skeltered, higgled and piggled. It wasn't at all the smooth, well-chrismed spirituality of the great religious orders — the Augustinians, Benedictines,

Dominicans, Franciscans, Jesuits. It wasn't driven by the Divine Office having to be recited or sung, at regular or irregular intervals, during the day or during the night, in whole or in part, in common or in private, inside or outside the monastery. Rather it was a patchwork of prayers and readings and exercises done as best as he could at a variety of times, most of them not at all convenient, and in a variety of places, most of them not at all conducive, to prayer or any other religious activity.

This isn't to say that Lewis never knew what was going to happen next.

"I love the monotonies of life — getting up and going to bed — looking out at the same view and meeting the same people at the same times every day," he once said to Anthony Sampson of the *Church of England Newspaper* in 1946; Sampson was beginning a series of word-portraits of lively and indeed living Anglicans.

"I never 'want things to happen.' They're always happening; and I'd rather they happened in the right order than in the wrong order. I don't like interferences in the normal order of events; and to me the most disagreeable experience would be one that suspended normality."

"But what about pleasant surprises?" asked Sampson. "They aren't in your catalogue of monotonies."

"No — and, of course, one is delighted at them; but there's a rich variety of surprises within the content of one's daily doings. For instance, when I walk across from these rooms to breakfast every morning, the view is precisely the same; but the sky is a different texture nearly every day. The trees vary from month to month; and even the angle of the sun makes a difference. I welcome changes."

Lewis welcomed the normality of the life of the layperson, if not the regularity of the life of the religious. But above and beyond the obligations of the cowled and coifed religious, he had his own life commitments. And, as well as any prior or prioress, any abbot or abbess, he knew that in an interruption — one of the many that continuously vex the normal life — there lay a potentially divine encounter.

"Things are pretty bad here," he wrote to a lifelong friend in Belfast in his Christmas letter for 1943. His adoptive mother's ulcer had gotten worse; domestic help was harder to come by; continued interruption to his daily round of activities caused him great unhappiness.

But what he was calling *interruption,* or so he came to learn from prayer and counsel, was very often "one's real life — the life God is sending one day by day; what one calls one's 'real life' is a phantom of one's own imagination. This at least," he concluded to his friend, "is what I see at moments of insight; but it's hard to remember all the time."

Lewis's spirituality, then, is the spirituality of the MC, man and woman, in the twentieth century. It's marked by interruption, distraction, coincidence. Its hallmark is encountering the divine in the oddest places.

This sort of reading of Lewis's life will reveal — not in all its pyrotechnics, but certainly in some of its pedantics — his spirituality, and just how he managed to pull it off.

Methodology

Spirituality is biography, whether written by oneself or someone else and, at least in Lewis's case, may be glimpsed on the hoof.

An example comes to mind.

As the winter of 1938 melted into spring, Lewis was enjoying an afternoon slosh around Addison's Walk, noticing that the white galanthus and yellow eranthis were bursting from the landscape.

"You look very pleased with yourself," said a university colleague approaching him on the muddy track.

"I believe," said Lewis, "I *believe* I have proved that the Renaissance never happened in England. Alternatively, that if it did, it had no importance!"

Lewis was jesting, of course, but A. N. Wilson, in his 1990 biography of Lewis, wasn't jesting at all when he said, albeit equivalently, that Lewis had no spiritual life; or if he did, that it had no importance.

Perhaps it had no importance to Wilson, but it does to me as a thoroughly modern biographer, and hence I think it's necessary, in each section of this book, to present biographical evidence first, and then to draw from it what spirituality, if any, may be found in it. Often the dividing line between the two will be a sentence like the following: *That's how it happened in Lewis's life — here's what it means.*

Another reason for the biographical approach is to keep Lewis's spirituality firmly grounded in place and time, thus preventing it from seeming to justify an already existing theory about what a good spirituality for Lewis ought to be and then cramming it down his throat.

Spiritualities are like clothes; they must fit; they mustn't be fubsy or flubsy, tripping us up at every turn. The day of "one size fits all" is over. Hence, the time has come for all good layfolk to speak up to the clerical and religious haberdashers of elderly if elegant spiritualities. If the sleeves are too long, we must tell them so. If the hems are too long, we must tell them so. "They'll ride up with wear" is no longer an acceptable response. In Lewis's case, his spirituality fitted him, but it won't necessarily fit us. We can only appraise it, perhaps admire it, perhaps even imitate one or another element in it... but no more.

Terminology

Before the invention of childhood in the second half of the nineteenth century, children were often considered nothing more than little adults, with their rights and privileges amounting only to their size. Now, for better or worse, they have more rights and privileges than they know what to do with.

In like manner, the terminology of spirituality, coined and refined over millennia, has been the handiwork of clerics and religious who were developing spiritualities for themselves; that is, for other clerics and religious. When they did do spirituality for layfolk, it still had about it the slap of the sandal and the itch of the burlap, the clap of the discipline and the clamp of the chain.

In other words, laypersons throughout the centuries have often been considered nothing more than little religious; that is to say, as though they were second- or third-order religious with dubious privileges like being buried in the habit of the affiliated order. Perhaps it's inevitable that it happened that way, and perhaps the trend is irreversible. I doubt if one can look forward with any confidence to the day when a Cistercian of the Strict Observance who's just breathed his last will be lowered into the hole wearing, not the soutane with cincture and scapular of the Order, but white tie and tails.

Hence, I hope the reader won't think it out of place for a layperson like myself, in describing the spirituality of another layperson and applying it to still other laypersons, to occasionally use a new term to describe a well-recognized spiritual phenomenon or classification.

I'd give examples here, but why would I want to ruin the surprise — the delight or the horror — of these terms as they will appear in appropriate places throughout the book? Which is another way of saying that when I err, I prefer it to be on the lay, rather than on the clerical or religious, side. *Pecca fortiter* is the only admonition Augustine would give in this regard.

Diction

From the first, the language of spirituality has been well-tempered. Refined, elegant, elevated. After all, that's the way God spoke to us in printed revelation. Highbrow dictation, Lewis might have called it.

An image comes to mind.

Madam Eglantyne was the bouncing prioress in Geoffrey Chaucer's *Canterbury Tales,* a work Lewis often mentioned in his lectures on medieval English literature. Her hips were wide, and her lips were consecrated. Her oaths were mild, and nary a naughty word saw the light of day. She sang through her nose, which was thought pleasing in the fourteenth century. Her English was particularly fastidious, and her French deliberately dainty. But that wasn't the way most people talked, read, indeed prayed even in the fourteenth century.

Then as well as now, most of the world's population have spoken to the Maker of the Universe in a less finicky, less persnickety way. Hence, when Lewis wrote for the layperson's eye and spoke to the layperson's ear, he used what he called in another instance a lowbrow style. But it communicated directly to the heart and mind.

Following Lewis, therefore, in preference to the highbrow word, I've often chosen the lowbrow word because it has street value; that is to say, it can be understood by the MC. And is it surprising that such words fairly leap from the pen?

In the chapters that follow, therefore, all words, highbrow or lowbrow, may be found in the *Oxford Dictionary of the English Language*, except for the odd, but obvious, neologism.

Caution

When I began nosing about Lewis's remains in preparation for the biography I'd write, I met Owen Barfield, a literary gent gone wrong. That is to say, he earned his living as a solicitor, and quite a successful one at that, but he'd rather have been reading Dante in a country cottage with Lewis than running Barfield & Barfield, the family law firm in London. An exact contemporary of Lewis's, he was in his eighties at the time I visited with him, some twenty years after Lewis's death. He told me much about his longtime friend and offered me some cautions. As I was leaving, he gave me the last one at the door.

"Lewis was a very funny man!"

I took that caution to heart and put into my biography all the jokes and japes I could find. In writing now about Lewis's spirituality, I've observed the Barfield caution once again. Hence, don't be surprised when you come upon some humor in the sober pages that follow. If I may quote the Professor. . . .

"A little comic relief in a discussion does no harm, however serious the topic may be," he wrote in *Reflections on the Psalms*. "(In my own experience the funniest things have occurred in the gravest and most sincere conversations.)"

Sentences

In *Studies in Words* (1960), Lewis discusses the word "sense," and its derivatives "sensibility," "sensible," and "sentence." He quotes the Roman playwright Terence's oft-quoted phrase, *quot homines, tot sententiae* ("there are about as many opinions as there are people who hold them)." And so it is with this book.

Toward the end of each chapter, after "What It Means" and before "Scriptures," there will appear some of Lewis's opinions about one or another of the topics covered in that chapter.

In this sort of usage, Lewis's sentences are not unlike those in *The Four Books of Sentences* by Peter Lombard (1100–1160), the theologian whose work was considered the standard theological text of the Middle Ages; he ended his career as bishop of Paris. His sentences consisted of texts and opinions of the fathers of the church; these he analyzed, compared, criticized, and drew conclusions from.

Scriptures

Each chapter of the book will conclude with some Scriptures suitable for prayerful reading. The New Testament translation, really a paraphrase, is that of J. B. Phillips, a contemporary of Lewis's and a friend. The Psalms rendering is that of Miles Coverdale, as found in the Book of Common Prayer; it was Lewis's favorite.

The following is the classical spiritual text about spirituality; that is to say, it includes the essential elements one may prayerfully expect to find in a true Christian spirituality:

"God, in his foreknowledge," begins Phillips's rendering of Romans 8:29–30, "chose [those who love God] to bear the family likeness of his Son, so that he might be the eldest of a family of many brothers. He chose them long ago; when the time came he called them, he made them righteous in his sight, and then lifted them to the splendor of life as his own sons."

Readings

At the end of each chapter, the reader will find some suggested readings that will further illustrate and develop the themes of the chapter.

Here, at the end of the Introduction, may I bring to the reader's attention the major biographies of Lewis, arranged chronologically.

- Roger Lancelyn Green and Walter Hooper's *C. S. Lewis, A Biography* (1974).
- Margaret Patterson Hannay's *C. S. Lewis* (1981).
- My own *C. S. Lewis, A Dramatic Life* (1986); in England, *C. S. Lewis: The Authentic Voice* (1987).
- George Sayer's *Jack, C. S. Lewis & His Times* (1988).
- A. N. Wilson's *C. S. Lewis, A Biography* (1990).
- Walter Hooper's *C. S. Lewis, A Companion & Guide* (1996).

All but Wilson's acknowledge the validity of Lewis's religious experience.

All including Wilson's have much to enrich the reader's knowledge of the complexities of Lewis's life and times.

Chapter 1

Diversion

When Lewis was ten years old — that was in 1908 — he lost his mother to cancer, and from that moment on he began to lose his faith. He was literate and articulate as a child and young adult and hence could frame his feelings and thoughts about both these losses as they were taking place and indeed as he was looking back some decades later.

At one moment of introspection, the young Lewis realized that he was an apostate, but he wasn't much of one, certainly not on the scale of the great Julian the Apostate in the fourth century of the Christian era. That rogue was a nephew of Constantine, the emperor who at the urging of his mother became a Christian, and with her help unearthed the true cross, or so it was reported at the time; together they helped Christianize the Roman Empire in the East and the West. Julian had the good fortune of being baptized and brought up as a Christian, but, nostalgic for the red beef and strong beer of the pagan gods of his parents' generation, he fought — and with some success — to reintroduce paganism throughout the Greco-Roman Empire.

If not much of an apostate, Lewis thought he was an atheist, but he certainly wasn't on the grand scale of, say, Karl Marx, whose influence during his lifetime wasn't all that great, but after whose death was the inspiration, with Friedrich Engels, of the Communism that spread like a caul over Russia and a pall over Europe.

No, Lewis's apostasy and atheism were mild-mannered enough, if sharply worded at times, but he never proselytized either position. He merely entertained them intellectually, moving honestly from one position to another until, one day, looking back, he found himself on a new hill with a commanding view. Pausing for a moment, he looked back and saw that his journey, such as it was, had three distinct stages, each one marked by an exotic conveyance.

The Long Serpent

First of these conveyances was a Norse craft with a curved, and indeed carved, prow....

Lewis was born into the Church of Ireland in 1898. Living in Belfast, his mother and father, Florence and Albert, he a lawyer, she a graduate of Queens College, Belfast, with First Class Honours in Logic and Second Class Honours in Mathematics, labored to bring him up in the faith, as it was taught in that denomination. But at the age of ten, that faith was dealt a staggering blow.

At that time the Lewis family was living in a new house that was a horror of residential architecture, but for two young boys with hyperactive imaginations, Lewis and his older brother, Warren, its irregularities were a delight.

"I am a product," Lewis would write in *Surprised by Joy*, the autobiography of his early years, "of long corridors, empty sunlit rooms, upstair indoor silences, attics explored in solitude, distant noises of gurgling cisterns and pipes, and the noise of wind under the tiles."

One of the attics he converted into his own private study and decorated its walls with pages cut from magazines. This was where he wrote stories of his own and drew the illustrations for them. Chief among his literary creations were chivalric tales about honest mice and upright rabbits dressed in chain mail who set off to destroy dishonest and disgusting cats, who were clothed as rapacious ogres.

Little Lea, as the house was called, was full of people. Besides his mother and father and his older brother, Warren, there were his grandfather (his father's father), Maude the housemaid and Martha the cook, a dog called Tim, a black-and-white mouse named Tommy, and Peter, a twittering canary. A happy household, it certainly seemed.

One night he woke up with a headache and a toothache. He called for his mother, but she didn't come. She was in her bedroom, sick for some time with cancer, but this very night, as he came to learn, a team of doctors was operating on her cancer in that very bedroom. For hours, worried voices, and the rude sound of doors opening and shutting in rapid succession, reverberated throughout the house. It took several months before Flora Lewis succumbed.

Her death profoundly unsettled her husband; he couldn't control his grief or his temper, nor could he channel the grief and fear in his two sons; he sent them away to school in England. There the younger Lewis began to lose his faith. Forced prayer of all sorts produced no relief for his soul. Oddly, he thought at the time, he felt no sense of loss; rather it was some kind of relief.

His reading didn't help. Studying the pagan classics of ancient Greece and Rome improved his mind, but did his soul no good. Nor did his teachers place the ancient literature in any sort of perspective; that is to say, no one mentioned that perhaps, just perhaps, paganism prefigured Christianity and in some senses Christianity fulfilled it. Add to all these uncertainties puberty and sexual temptation, and the public schools' laissez-faire attitude toward sexual expression and experimentation, and it was no wonder that the young Lewis withdrew, slowly but surely "from Divine protection" and began to labor very hard to make himself into, among other things, "a fop, a cad, and a snob."

His reading list during these impressionable years was impressive, titles often being chosen at whimsy, and comparatively unguided by a knowledgeable and concerned adult.

When he was nine years old, he picked up *Tales of a Wayside Inn* by Henry Wadsworth Longfellow and read "The Saga of King Olaf":

> These, and many more like these,
> With King Olaf sailed the seas,
>   Till the waters vast
> Filled them with a vague devotion,
> With the freedom and the motion,
> With the roll and roar of ocean,
>   And the sounding blast.

This and other ballad-like stanzas gave the boy a fit of motion sickness, but he boarded the *Long Serpent* in his imagination and sailed northward toward the ice-blue seas of Icelandic mythology.

In that same volume he found "Tegner's Drapa," a poem commemorating the death of Esaias Tegner, a Swedish contemporary of Longfellow's, whom the American poet considered was prefigured in Icelandic mythology.

> I heard a voice, that cried,
> "Balder the Beautiful
> Is dead, is dead!"
> And through the misty air
> Passed like the mournful cry
> Of sunward sailing cranes.

The body of Balder the Beautiful, "God of the summer sun, Fairest of all the Gods" was loaded onto his ship, decorated funerarily, put to the torch, and shoved off. It "floated far away Over the misty sea." As the flaming pyre slipped beneath the waves, the young Lewis was incinerated in the spirit.

When he was thirteen and a student at Cherbourg, a small preparatory school at Malvern, about fifty miles from Oxford, he came across, in the Christmas 1911 number of *The Bookman*, a supplement reproducing some passages from *Siegfried and the Twilight of the Gods,* translated by Margaret Armour and illustrated in color by Arthur Rackham.

"I had never heard of Wagner nor Siegfried" he wrote in *Surprised by Joy*. "I thought the twilight of the gods meant the twilight in which the gods lived. How did I know, at once and beyond question, that this was no Celtic or silvan or terrestrial twilight?"

The following summer, as he was perusing record catalogs, he came across, in a magazine entitled *Soundbox*, synopses of the *Ring of the Nibelungen*, the four Germanic operas derived by Richard Wagner from the Scandinavian myths. "I read in rapture and discovered who Siegfried was and what was the 'twilight' of the gods."

When he was fourteen, he was in a record shop in Belfast,

where he heard, quite by accident, the *Ride of the Valkyries.* "To a boy already crazed with 'the northernness,' whose highest music experience had been [Sir Arthur] Sullivan, the *Ride* came like a thunderbolt." From that moment on, Wagnerian records became the chief drain on his pocket money and the presents he invariably asked for.

When he was fifteen, while visiting a cousin who lived near Dublin, he found on the drawing room table a copy of the very book itself, *Siegfried and the Twilight of the Gods*. Rackham's pictures seemed "to be the very music made visible" and plunged him "a few fathoms deeper" into delight. He seldom coveted anything as he coveted that book; and when he heard that there was a cheaper edition, he knew he could never rest until it was his.

When he was sixteen and studying Latin and Greek with an aged tutor in Surrey, William F. Kirkpatrick, he composed a tragedy in the Greek mode — with prologos and exodos and three epeisodia in between — but with materials from the mythology of the north. Already he was the best translator of Greek plays the Great Knock, as the former schoolmaster was called behind his back, had ever seen. He patterned his work after Aeschylus's *Prometheus Bound*. He named it *Loki Bound.*

The play is set in Asgard, the center of the universe inhabited by the gods. Loki, the spirit of evil and mischief who had done Balder in with a spearpoint of mistletoe, challenged Odin for supreme authority. Aided for a time by Fasold, a giant lovesick for Freya, goddess of love, Loki found himself at tragedy's end, like Prometheus before him, bound to a rock and blaspheming the supreme god and creator.

In a letter dated October 6, 1914, he told Arthur Greeves, who became his best friend, about the play, which ran thirty-two pages in his notebook. He encouraged Greeves to turn it into an opera; Greeves, who was artistically inclined, demurred, but said he'd draw the illustrations for the book.

Lewis had known Greeves no longer than six months. They lived across the street from each other in Strandtown, on the eastern perimeter of Belfast. One day Mrs. Greeves telephoned the Lewis household to say that her son was sick in bed and would enjoy a visit from either of the Lewis boys. Jack, as Lewis had been nicknamed by his older brother, went across the road none too enthusiastically, but when he saw a copy of *Myths of the Norsemen* at Greeves's bedside, he perked up. "Do you like that?" they asked each other at the same time. Not only did they like the work as a whole — pointing at passages and talking excitedly — but also they liked the same parts and in the same way.

As a result of reading all this poetry, all this mythology, the clear line between religion and mythology had, slowly but surely, disappeared from Lewis's perception.

"All religions, that is all mythologies, to give them their proper name, are merely man's own invention — Christ as much as Loki," he wrote to Greeves on October 12, 1916. On December 6 of that year, to please his father and to avoid useless argument, he allowed himself — hypocrisy of hypocrisies! — to be confirmed in the Church of Ireland.

Entrance into Oxford University in 1917, fighting in the trenches in France, enduring a wound in the rear from friendly fire, getting a "blighty leave" back to England, suffering the battlefield death of his friend Paddy Moore, inheriting the care of Paddy's mother for life, being graduated from the university with degrees in philosophy and English, and eventually getting a job at Magdalen College, Oxford — none of these altered his view that religion and mythology were really one, and that any distinction between the two was intellectually unacceptable.

The Doubledecker

Second of the conveyances was a red bus....

On the night of April 27, 1926, Lewis, now a full-time member of the Magdalen College faculty, had a fire going in his rooms in New Buildings (a single edifice built in the eighteenth century, the first of what Magdalen College hoped would become one of a complex of structures — but only the first was built, and the plural name remained carved in stone) and was sitting down to a book — Walter William Skeats on English language — when there was a knock on the door. It was Weldon. Without invitation he walked in and plumped down, wanting to talk. Thomas Dewar were his first two names, but he was called Harry. He was Lewis's age; he taught philosophy at Magdalen; in the late war he rose to captain; his conspicuous behavior under fire brought him mention in dispatches and, ultimately, a decoration on his tunic.

Whiskey was splashed; it enkindled some light banter and not a little bawdy, Weldon laughing the louder and the longer. Whiskey was splashed again, and the talk turned to *The Golden Bough*, James Frazer's study of comparative folklore, magic, and religion. According to Frazer, there were many parallels between the rites and beliefs of early cultures and those of early Christians. There were chapters entitled "Incarnate Human Gods" and "The Killing of the Divine King" and "Sacrifice of the King's Son." Magic seemed to have preceded religion everywhere was Frazer's thesis; Weldon would surely agree, or so Lewis thought, that man turned toward religion only after magic had failed.

"Rum thing, all that stuff of Frazer's about the dying god," said Weldon, mixing musings with whiskeys. "It almost looks as if it really had happened once."

After admitting that the gospels were more or less true, Weldon went on to reveal that he believed in the Trinity, at least as presented by G. W. Hegel, the nineteenth-century German philosopher. The kingdom of the Father was expressed in logic. The kingdom of the Son was expressed in philosophy of nature. The kingdom of the Spirit was expressed in philosophy of spirit, which appeared in the union of God and the faithful in the church. The Triune God, said Weldon, attempting to quote Hegel from memory, was the Father and the Son, and this differentiation in the unity was the Spirit. The whole thing seemed to fit in. It was well past midnight, but not long after a final splash, when Weldon stopped talking about the extraordinariness of mistletoe and the absoluteness of spirit and tottered off to his rooms. Lewis was tottering too, not so much from the wonderfulness of fermented grain as from the fresh realization that Weldon, this cynical, tough-minded secularist, was a Christian, even if of a vague and philosophical sort.

Lewis at the age of thirty-one, even in a state of unreligion, found religion attractive in books. He read G. B. Shaw and H. G. Wells, Edward Gibbon and John Stuart Mill, writers who weren't in the theistic tradition; he found them mildly entertaining and at the same time mildly soporific. Christian writers, on the other hand, with whom he was bound to disagree — Donne and Browne, Spenser and Milton, Johnson and Chesterton — he read again and again. The Christians might be wrong, but at least they weren't boring, he thought as he boarded a red bus outside Magdalen for the run up Headington Hill.

If books had the power to move men's minds, perhaps also they had the power to move men's souls. In 1929, during Hilary term, named after the fourteenth-century saint whose feast was celebrated on January 13, he reread Euripides' *Hippolytus*, which made chastity into a martyr, and Alexander's *Space, Time, and Deity*, which distinguished "enjoyment" from "contemplation." He reconsidered Hegel's philosophy of the absolute and festooned it with Berkeley's notion of the spirit. What resulted was a philosophical construct he called God. He couldn't know this God any more than Hamlet could know Shakespeare, but with this sort of concept, he felt comfortable. In fact, he felt free to accept it or reject it. When his stop came at the top of Headington Hill, he got off the bus believing what he hadn't believed when he got on, that an Absolute Spirit or God did indeed exist.

But how could he commune with Absolute Spirit? That was the question. He looked inside himself and was appalled by what he saw, "a zoo of lusts, a bedlam of ambitions, a nursery of fears, a harem of fondled hatreds." The immediate result of the introspection was that he no longer wanted to speculate about a philosophical construct; he wanted to pray. But to whom? He'd gone about as far as a philosopher could go.

"I think the trouble with me," he wrote on Christmas eve to Greeves, "is *lack of faith*. I have no *rational* ground for going back on the arguments that convinced me of God's existence . . . and often when I pray, I wonder if I am not posting letters to a non-existent address."

The Daudel

The third conveyance was a green motorcycle.....

On July 28, 1931, Lewis invited his friend Nevill Coghill to dinner at Magdalen as well as Coghill's friend, Henry Victor Dyson Dyson [*sic*], a lecturer and tutor in English at Reading University who happened to be on a visit to Oxford.

During the dinner and for many hours thereafter, serious conversation was interspersed with laughter. "How we roared and fooled at times in the silence of the night," he wrote of the occasion to Greeves, "but always in a few minutes buckled to with renewed seriousness."

Magdalen's gates were locked by the porter every night at midnight. When 3:00 a.m. came and went, Lewis had to escort his friends through pitch black cloisters to let them out by the little gate near Magdalen Bridge, where the street lamps illumined the bell tower.

By ten o'clock the following morning, he was awake and "feeling rather morning-after-ish," but there lingered pleasantly the memory of Dyson as "a man who really loves the truth, a philosopher and a religious man, who makes his critical and literary activities depend on the former — none of your damned dilettanti."

Having met Dyson for the first time in July and seeing the verbose and vivacious little man four or five times since then, Lewis was beginning to rank him as a friend of the second class, first class still being reserved for Greeves and Owen Barfield, whom he met as an undergraduate at Oxford in 1919. Saturday, September 19, was one of those times. Dyson was invited to Magdalen to dine; Tolkien was also invited.

After dinner they set out for a stroll on Addison's Walk, a woodsy pathway along the Cherwell, a river that flanked Magdalen's property and flowed into the Thames; it had gotten its name from Joseph Addison, a fellow of Magdalen's in the late seventeenth century. It was a warm, still night. The conversation turned toward myth and metaphor.

Myths were enjoyable in themselves, argued Lewis; he had certainly enjoyed them more than most, but they were believed only by children. Adults knew better; myths were lies; although the better ones had been breathed through silver, or so Tolkien proposed, they were none the more believable for that.

Tolkien and Dyson were quick to disagree. However untrue they might seem to be, they contained elements of the truth. Created as he was by God, the myth-maker was himself a creator, albeit a subcreator, when he undertook to spin a tale or develop a plot, and when he did so, shafts of truth were bound to dot the forest floor.

The argument was interrupted by a rush of wind. It began to rain, or so the strolling arguers thought at first. Leaves pattered down on their shoulders, not raindrops, but they decided to head back to New Buildings anyway, where the conversation turned toward Christianity and its doctrines.

He was having difficulty, Lewis said, not so much in believing a doctrine as in knowing what a doctrine meant. When asked for an example, he gave the doctrine of redemption. Drunkenness could lead a person down the primrose path where only a redemptive act could save him. He could see that, but what he couldn't see was how the life and death of someone else (whoever he was) two thousand years ago could help them there and then — except insofar as his *example* helped them. He'd read the gospels, but nowhere did he find this *example* business; instead he found "propitiation" and "sacrifice" and "blood of the lamb," expressions that he could interpret only in the sense that seemed to him "either silly or shocking."

What was wrong with sacrifice? asked Tolkien, who was Church of Rome, and Dyson, who was Church of England.

There was nothing wrong with the idea of sacrifice, Lewis had to concede. He'd always liked the idea of sacrifice in a pagan story, the idea of a god sacrificing himself to himself, the idea of a dying and reviving God. But the idea of such notions of sacrifice was entirely out of place when it came to interpreting the gospels. If pagan stories were God expressing himself through minds of poets, using such images as he found there, then Christianity might very well be construed as God expressing himself through what they called "real things."

Why couldn't the story of Christ be construed as a myth, argued Tolkien and Dyson with vigor, but a myth that was true?

"A myth working on [them] in the same way as on the others, but with this tremendous difference, that it *really happened*"?

What about the doctrines derived from the one true myth? asked Lewis. Were they in any sense truths? Whatever else they were, they were "translations into our *concepts* and *ideas* of that which God has already expressed in a language more adequate, namely the actual incarnation, crucifixion, and resurrection."

As the evening wore on, Lewis grew more certain that the Christian story had to be approached in the same way he approached the other myths and that it was "the most important and full of meaning." By three in the morning he was almost certain that it had really happened. He and Dyson made haste to let Tolkien out "by the little postern on Magdalen Bridge"; Tolkien was a married man with children and had a fair walk ahead of him and a tired wife to explain to. Then Lewis and Dyson returned to New Buildings, where they paced the colonnade until four.

"I have just passed on from believing in God to definitely believing in Christ—in Christianity," wrote Lewis twelve days later to Greeves. "My long talk with Dyson and Tolkien had a good deal to do with it."

At this particular time, Lewis was reading the text of *Hamlet* with great care; he found he could no longer reproach the Prince of Denmark for being slow to decide.

As Monday, September 28, 1931, began in Headington Quarry, where he now lived with his brother, Warren, and Paddy Moore's mother, Janie, and sister, the ground was carpeted with fog. During breakfast young Maureen rehearsed the reasons for and against their planned excursion to the Whipsnade Zoo. At 11:15 Warren started his motorcycle, by make a Daudel. Lewis hopped into the sidecar, and the brothers roared off on a *Daudelspiel;* the others followed in the family car, a Singer. Halfway there, the fog broke and the sun shone through. Having stopped for beer and fuel on the way, they still arrived at the village of Whipsnade before one.

There they spread the Daudel's waterproof on a slope of short turf, opened the bottles of beer, and recovered from the vibrations of the forty-mile run. At 2:20 the Singer arrived. Mr. Papworth, a lovable old fleabag, bounded from the window of the car; Maureen emerged from behind the wheel, followed by her mother and her mother's friend Vera Henry. Sandwiches were passed around; the Brothers Lewis were ravenous.

At 3:00 they entered the zoo; all, that is, except Lewis, who had to mind the dog. He felt pleasantly relaxed, emotionally refreshed, somewhere between sleeping and waking. Lounging on the waterproof, he became aware that, sometime during the last few hours, he'd come to a conclusion without the intervention of ratiocination. When he set out from Headington, he hadn't fully believed — and when he arrived in Whipsnade he did believe — that Jesus Christ was the son of God.

At four Warren emerged from the gates and took over the watch. He suggested his brother pay special attention to the kangaroos hopping about in Wallaby Wood, to the American timberwolves and the bears, one of whom stood up and saluted for buns.

When Lewis emerged about 5:30, he found Warren eating Whipsnade Rock, sugar candy that was on sale at the zoo's gate. He said he too liked the brown bear the best. It was the sort of creature they wished they'd included among the menagerie they created for Boxen, an imaginary land they created when they were children; in a series of tales, the great Boxonians were, in descending order, Lord Big (a frog), King Benjamin VII (a rabbit), King Hawki V (a man), and naval officer James Bar (a bear).

The brothers cycled off; the others drove off. When Lewis stepped from the sidecar back at the Kilns, he was a bit stiff, but the belief that Jesus Christ was definitely the son of God was still very limber indeed.

So thorough was his conversion that Lewis continued the journey for the rest of his life. He went to church regularly, read Scripture, prayed, confessed (a devotional practice in the Anglican Church), and acquired a spiritual director.

That's how it happened in Lewis's life....

What It Means

There are three quick observations to make about Lewis's decades of trekking over rough intellectual and imaginative terrains.

First of these has to do with conveyances. If the atheist, as Lewis once noted, wanted to protect his atheism, then he shouldn't read books about theism. So if Lewis valued his unbelief, then he should have avoided exotic modes of transportation. But of course, he didn't, and therein lies the tale.

Second, each conveyance carried Lewis only part way on his journey. The Long Serpent freighted him only as far as the conclusion that all religions were mythologies. The Doubledecker bus ferried him uphill to the conclusion that the Absolute Spirit, so often found fluttering around the pinnacle of mythologies and philosophies, might just be what people commonly called God. The green Daudel smarted and farted him to the conclusion that Jesus Christ was not only the son of God but also the one true myth.

Third, the three-stage journey in the three colorful conveyances inevitably encountered a *diversion;* or as Americans would call it, a *detour;* not just one such diversion but a succession of them. How did Lewis handle them? On board a Singer or a Jowett, Lewis wasn't exactly a speedist; he generally handled the wheel of an automobile—and then only as a young adult—as though it were the helm of a Cunarder. No, Lewis chose to disembark from his machine and treat each road obstacle in turn. So much for the automotive metaphor, which, be it noted, is mine, not Lewis's.

About the young Lewis's random, and occasionally randy, reading list. If he'd wanted to remain an atheist and to that end read books only by atheists, he'd have had to avoid most of the literature of the West, highbrow as well as lowbrow. That, for an omnivorous reader like Lewis, would have been pretty small beer. He read, and let the ideas fall where they might. But soon he found out that one pile of ideas was higher than the others and ultimately better than all the rest.

The Diversion Process

In the diversion process, Lewis went through several steps, stages that people before him and after him have trod. In truth many of us have had to tread them over and over again in our lifetimes. In order to keep our sanity, it's well from time to time to reflect on just what these steps were in Lewis's life.

Thrum from Afar

First of these is *desire....*

In the very early days of Lewis's life, his older brother brought into the nursery of their Belfast home a miniature woodland scene; he'd created it on the inside lid of a biscuit tin by lining it with lichens, sprigs, and petals.

This proved to be a moment of illumination for the young boy. The garden opened up a world not only of toydom but also of beauty suggested by the paltry material objects gathered and clumsily arranged by his older brother. And in his autobiography written some five decades later, Lewis was able to say that the toy garden, or the indelible print of that garden in his imagination, had to be a premonition of Paradise.

That and the view of "the Green Hills" from the windows of his house, the low line of the Castlereagh Hills he and his brother saw from the nursery windows in the detached villa in which they lived. "They were not very far off but they were, to children, quite unattainable. They taught me longing — *Sehnsucht;* made me for good or ill, and before I was six years old, a votary of the Blue Flower."

If I knew where the Blue Flower were greenhoused, I and thousands of others before me would have hastened to that cerulean place and enlisted as votaries too. But, thankfully, it's a lost place, perhaps hidden in Maurice Maeterlinck's *The Blue Bird* (1909), an allegorical fantasy in dramatic form for children that denies the reality of death, perhaps holding court in the Royal Britannic Gardens at Kew, but certainly implanted in Lewis's boyhood imagination.

This wasn't the only illuminating experience; Lewis described another such epiphany standing by a currant bush; it too was a blinding revelation, but the young fellow wasn't sure just what it was an illumination of.

The epiphany was a sight, but it was also a sound.

Perhaps a whip from an arrow shot, as from the longbow at Agincourt, launched into the air at a target unseen.

Perhaps a twang, a sympathetic vibration from a string plucked somewhere in the Universe.

Perhaps a thrum plected by the Master Lutenist of the Universe.

Perhaps a royal blast from a metal tube with a flared bell; a tantivy; a tantara.

Perhaps a mournful blow from a dented horn somewhere deep in elfland.

Whatever it was, sight or sound, it created in the boy Lewis a desire for the beyond, an aching desire for the person and place from which all these phenomena had to come.

It was, as some Athenian philosophers and Parisian theologians had already described it, an appetite, a natural appetite for the good, a sort of natural revelation.

This every normal person may expect to experience in his or her lifetime. Certainly every normal convertend does today when he or she experiences first or second or even third conversion.

Chin-Wag

Second stage is *dialectic*. . . .

The convertend must argue, or submit to argumentation of whatever sort, all of the propositions — some of them quite sublime, some of them quite ridiculous, at least at first blush — that genuine belief generates. He or she must submit them to the deductive logic of the ages, product of the ancient peripatetics in Athens and the medieval scholastics in Paris, all that in the syllogisms and sorites of syllogisms in his or her own mind.

But man or woman, the convertend must also commit them to a contemporary chin-wag with friends. In Lewis's case, his friends were intellectuals, albeit of a bright and imaginative sort — Tolkien and Dyson among them — but with the aid of their logic and, finally, a little common sense, he was able to arrive at some sort of consensus that they'd already accepted and that he could now bring himself to accept.

This the modern convert must also do if he or she expects to achieve some sort of closure of the conversion process: weigh the Christian arguments against the best logic contemporary life can offer.

Spot of Bother

Third stage is *struggle*. . . .

The convertend is never what may whimsically be called a sweatless wonder, a plaster saint. Rather it's someone who's met with a spot of spiritual bother in his or her time and has the scars to prove it. . . .

Beginning sometime around the *Long Serpent*, Lewis began filling his mind with mythologies of all sorts, Norse and Icelandic, Grecian and Roman, and his inner ear began to think that it heard sounds, the sounds of a song, perhaps the Sirens' songs he'd encountered in the *Odyssey?* Depicted as sea nymphs with the bodies of birds and the heads of women and the voices of gods, they lured sailors to shipwrecks on the very rocks on which they roosted.

Odysseus, at least as Homer told it, was on a ten-year voyage home after the Trojan War, and everywhere he encountered almost unendurable delay. In order to survive the sweetness of the Sirens' songs, he stuffed his ears with fabric, according to one report, and according to another, he lashed the rudder in place and himself to the mast in order to sail past yet another isle of delay, another island of destruction.

Lewis himself had to do much the same thing to avoid coming a cropper on the irrational deadweight of his old skeptical habits, the spirit of the age, the cares of the day, all of which stole away his lively feeling of the truth. The sweetness of *Sehnsucht,* as he called it in his autobiography, far sweeter than the Sirens' song, was leading him to his soul's true home, or so he hoped.

And so the modern convert hopes. He or she hears the *Sehnsucht;* its sound is sweeter than the Sirens', but being farther away, it's intermittent, teasing, beckoning. Being nearer, the Sirens' sound is louder, never seems to stop, luring and alluring. Contemporary culture roosts on that jagged coastline wrecking one conversion after another, one tender craft after another trying to find its own true port.

White Flag

Fourth and last stage is *surrender*, unconditional surrender symbolized by the white flag. . . .

In 1929, somewhere between the red bus and the green motorcycle, Lewis noticed that the "philosophical theorem, cerebrally entertained, began to stir and heave and throw off its gravecloths, and stood upright and became a living presence."

It was, he could hardly wait to tell a friend with whom he'd once wanted to collaborate on a shocker play in 1919. As Lewis recalled, the two of them, undergraduates then, created the characters. A Scientist with "a bright red beard, Mephistophelian in shape but reaching to the waist, very thick lips, and one leg shorter than the other." A Corpse whose body lay in a coffin packed with ice, but whose brain and nerves were kept alive by injections. A Hero and a Heroine who found "a poor fellow whose face was badly smashed in the war" huddling by the fire, complaining of the cold and how the Scientist was always chasing him about. Of course, the Heroine would be the Scientist's next victim. . . .

The narrative, such as it was, continued in a dream sometime later. The Corpse escaped and ran amok, pursuing Lewis about the streets of London and down into the Underground. He managed to reach the lift; the Liftman was terrified. As the Corpse was about to strike, Lewis screamed, "There's going to be an accidennnnnt!"

That was in 1919, but what was happening to Lewis in 1929 was a sort of *theological shocker*. Shades of Mary Shelley's *Frankenstein*, but with a remarkable difference. Lewis's figure in the gravecloths could speak, not only could speak in a gravelly basso profundo but also could mouth the Authorized Version.

"I am the Lord."

"I am that I am."

"I am."

Lewis heard the words, heard them clearly, and was aghast!

Now Lewis was a private person; he called his soul his own; he didn't pursue pleasure as a matter of course; most of his time he spent avoiding suffering. But the presence, the person, who had talked to him was unwelcome, discomforting, unreasonable; he was also unrelenting. Into New Buildings, up staircase 3, sporting the oak of room 3, was the person Lewis dreaded most. He grabbed the shroud, as it were, and waved it like a flag.

"I gave in, and admitted that God was God, and knelt and prayed: perhaps, that night, the most dejected and reluctant convert in all England."

And so it is with the modern convert, especially the one who comes into Christianity kicking and screaming. Unconditional surrender, never an admirable choice for one who's lost the fray, is demanded by the unforgiving victor. How like a bad opera! Worse, how like a good opera! But what other recourse does the convert have? None. Lewis found that out. Dejected and reluctant he might have felt at the time, but the Victor turned out to be generous in victory, and the vanquished was able to rise, seemingly unscathed, already the richer for the loss. And the modern convert will find the same.

Chipped Cup

To this four-stage diversion process, which must traverse potholes, detours, loose chippings, and all the other detritus of suburban British roadways, I would add a fifth: *wreckage*. Not all of one's china, no matter how well the dishes are packed or how securely the boxes are stacked, can survive intact the jouncing and jousting of the moving van, even when the trip is no more than a mile or two.

So it was with Mrs. Moore when, on October 10, 1930, she and the Lewis brothers moved from Hillsboro, a house in Oxford proper, to the Kilns in Headington Quarry. Lewis was at the wheel, one of the few times in his life that he was at the helm of a motorized vehicle, and he negotiated the van rather poorly along the rutted road leading up to the Kilns. Upon unpacking, Mrs. Moore found chipped cups and cracked saucers; half of her "unmatchable tea-things" hadn't survived the stress.

And so it was with the diversions in Lewis's life — the unlikely and indeed unwelcome detours that eventually returned him to religious belief and practice. They didn't endear him to the university establishment; eventually, it cost him promotion and advancement. His Christianity did get him some notoriety as an evangelist of sorts, but at the same time it generated beams and motes in the jealous eyes of his peers.

But wreck though he was after the diversion — or perhaps I should say *conversion* — process, covered with muck and mire, he survived and moved on at a surprisingly brisk pace. Psychiatrists would call it anything but normal; confessors would call it nothing but normal.

And so it is with us — thrum from afar, chin-wag, spot of bother, white flag, chipped cup. We all go through the conversion process once, perhaps twice, perhaps even thrice. Sometimes it's a rite of passage as one grows up inside a denomination. Sometimes it's from one denomination to another. But for the MC it's often from a tepid to a fervent observance within one's own denomination.

That distinction having been made, why is conversion so hard? It's the almost universal experience of converts that however much spiritual ground one gains the one day, that much is lost the next day, or seems to be lost, and one must forever contend with the maddening thrum, the interminable chin-wag, a botheration of bothers, the tattered white shirt tied to a stick, the tea cup with the brownish vein. The perpetual conversion, if it may be so called, Lewis grew accustomed to, and in like manner the modern MC will soon discover that the never-ending conversion process is normal, part and parcel of the MC's daily life.

Sentences

"All right," wrote Lewis in an essay entitled "Man or Rabbit?" a pamphlet published in 1946 or thereabout, by the Student Christian Movement in Schools. "Christianity will do you good — a great deal more good than you ever wanted or expected. And the first bit of good it will do is to hammer into your head (you won't enjoy *that!*) the fact that what you have hitherto called 'good' — all that about 'leading a decent life' and 'being kind' — isn't quite the magnificent and all-important affair you supposed.

"It will teach you that in fact you can't be 'good' (not for twenty-four hours) on your own moral efforts. And then it will teach you that even if you were, you still wouldn't have achieved the purpose for which you were created. Mere *morality* is not the end of life. You were made for something quite different from that....

"The people who keep on asking if they can't lead a decent life without Christ, don't know what life is about; if they did, they would know that 'a decent life' is mere machinery compared with the thing we men are really made for. Morality is indispensable; but the Divine Life, which gives itself to us and which calls us to be gods, intends for us something in which morality will be swallowed up.

"We are to be re-made. All the rabbit in us is to disappear — the worried, conscientious, ethical rabbit as well as the cowardly and sensual rabbit. We shall bleed and squeal as the handfuls of fur come out; and then, surprisingly, we shall find underneath it all a thing we have never yet imagined: a real Man, an ageless god, a son of God, strong, radiant, wise, beautiful, and drenched in joy."

Scriptures

Lewis's call was like Abraham's (Genesis 12:1–4), more like Samuel's (1 Samuel 3:1–19), but most like Moses' (Exodus 3:1–14), as recounted in the Authorized Version.

"Now Moses kept the flock of Jethro his father-in-law, the priest of Midian: and he led the flock to the backside of the desert, and came to the mountain of God, even to Horeb.

"And the angel of the Lord appeared unto him in a flame of fire out of the midst of a bush: and he looked, and, behold, the bush burned with fire, and the bush was not consumed.

"And Moses said, I will now turn aside, and see this great sight, why the bush is not burnt.

"And when the Lord saw that he turned aside to see, God called unto him out of the midst of the bush, and said, Moses, Moses. And he said, Here am I.

"And he said, Draw not nigh hither: put off thy shoes from off thy feet, for the place whereon thou standest is holy ground.

"Moreover he said, I am the God of thy father, the God of Abraham, the God of Isaac, and the God of Jacob. And Moses hid his face; for he was afraid to look upon God. . . .

"Come now therefore, and I will send thee unto Pharaoh, and that I should bring forth the children of Israel out of Egypt.

"And Moses said unto God, Who am I, that I should go unto Pharaoh, and I should bring forth the children of Israel out of Egypt? . . .

"Behold, when I come unto the children of Israel, and shall say unto them, The God of your fathers hath sent me unto you; and they shall say to me, What is his name? what shall I say unto them.

"And God said unto Moses I AM THAT I AM: and he said, Thus shalt thou say unto the children of Israel, I AM hath sent me unto you."

Readings

The myriad of details in Lewis's conversion, and many passages for meditation, may be found in such autobiographical works as *Surprised by Joy: The Shape of My Early Life* (1955); *They Stand Together: The Letters of C. S. Lewis to Arthur Greeves, 1914–1963* (1979; paperback edition has the subtitle as title, 1986); and *Letters of C. S. Lewis, edited with a Memoir* by W. H. Lewis (1966), revised and enlarged edition edited by Walter Hooper (1988); and *All My Road before Me: The Diary of C. S. Lewis, 1922–1927,* edited by Walter Hooper (1991).

Chapter 2

Blues

Lewis's religious conversion was slowed down a good deal by "the Spirit of the Age," or so he said. No doubt that was true, but exactly what he meant isn't immediately obvious to us poor readers some seventy years later.

Things weren't much better for the early Christians in the third and fourth centuries of the Christian era. The desert fathers were excoriating the Spirit of the Age even then, without adequately telling what it was or how an individual was affected by it. But for them at least two things were sure.

First, there were harlots in those deserts, real and imagined; and some of the real ones even made it to repentance: Mary of Egypt, "that hot whore" who hopped a ship to the Holy Land and while at sea seduced a fair number of the holy throng; Pelagia, the actress of Antioch, who paraded her beauty in public, even stunning a bishop into seeing not just her body but her immortal soul; Thaïs of Alexandria, a professional prostitute, wealthy and beautiful, who counted among her dalliances Alexander the Great and his general Ptolemy First. But have no fear: all of these women were converted from their meretricious ways and died meritorious deaths.

Second, there were devils in those deserts. Reportedly, to the international port city of Alexandria, there was assigned only one devil; it was a cushy job; the city was thought to be so morally corrupt that not more than one was needed to do the dirty deeds, and even he had time left over for leisurely pursuits. The rest of the devils, uncountable legions of them, brandishing the baubles of contemporary culture as temptations, chased the fathers and mothers of the desert up and down the dunes in pursuit of their immortal souls.

The Spirit of the Age, as it has come to be called, is something like "a London particular," as once Dickens put into the mouth of a character; that is to say, a fog, the famous British fog. Difficult to describe, impossible to contain, but very real nonetheless. Appearing harmless, soft enough to caress the skin, it can be lethal on the motorways. One has to live with it, but one never knows when he or she will be swallowed up in it.

And so it was with Lewis. World War I had been horrid, especially to young men with poetic natures, turning topsy-turvy all their notions of morality, revealed and unrevealed. Lewis himself wasn't especially predisposed to deviate much from the decalogue; nonetheless the Spirit of his Age proclaimed that he could, if he wanted to, flout the rules of public and private conduct without having to wear a helmet; that is to say, without fear of divine, and if one was extremely fortunate, civil retribution. Immorality seemed to reign, and the artistic community provided the jesters; they added gaiety to the inevitable grayness of life without morals. And lubricant to this new freedom was sexual intercourse of all types.

To better gauge how Lewis reacted to his time, then, it would seem appropriate to compare him with people that we, on looking back, would consider his peers. Perhaps with G. K. Chesterton (the moralist who was twenty-four years his senior), or with Fulton J. Sheen (the archbishop who was only three years his senior but lived in another country), or J. R. R. Tolkien (the mythmaker who was six years his senior and a professor of philology at Oxford).

But comparisons with these well-upholstered gentlemen in their later years, who were like Lewis in so many ways in his own later years, yield little insight about what Lewis was up to and indeed up against as a young man. For a sharper focus we need to contrast him with a contemporary who wasn't like him, but someone whose subsequent reputation rivaled his, at least in numbers. Noël Pierce Coward would seem to be a good choice.

A word of caution.

Any contrast between the two from a religious perspective is likely to be unflattering, if not devastating, to Coward, and hence I must make a declaration here. My purpose isn't to bash Coward but to illumine Lewis. The actions and words of Jesus about who are the just and who the unjust are enough to shake the righteous in their boots; between the righteous and the self-righteous there would seem to be only a hair-breadth's difference, if that . . . and Jesus is the only one who can see it.

Hence, for the purposes of this contrast, may I respectfully suggest three things? That Coward, whatever his spiritual shortcomings on this earth, is in Heaven today; that his presence there is by virtue of celestial mathematics; that my contrast here is the result of some hasty terrestrial mathematics, showing considerable moral discrepancies during his life on this earth. Coward had his gifts, but it's not the gifts I'm talking about here.

Born in 1899, Coward was a year younger than Lewis. Both had youths aggravated by poverty and the threat of poverty. Coward sought salvation in the theater, playing in a wide variety of parts suitable for children; Lewis, on the other hand, devoured life as it was presented in books and operas. Lewis was educated at public schools and university; Coward learned his on the streets of London, where he became something of an Artful Dodger, but in shoplifting instead of pickpocketing.

As young adults during the Great War, both served in the army with no joy. Coward was drafted and found himself, after what he felt were humiliating medical examinations, in a labor corps. With some finagling, he was able to attach himself to the Artists' Rifles, where he proved not to be fodder for the Officers Training program. A succession of medical crises followed, some self-provoked, but all were welcomed by him anyway. After a few months of inspired malingering, he was released from military duties "with his pension, a suit, and overcoat, and a medal to commemorate his discharge."

At eighteen years of age, Lewis was completing his first year at Oxford when the call to Officers Training came. After a summer of digging trenches and marching routes, he was made a second lieutenant. On November 17, 1917, he crossed over to France and reached the front on November 29. On arriving in the trenches, he barely escaped death. When the enemy fire began, he stuck his head up; someone yanked him down before it got shot off, but not before he had the happy if unholy thought, *This was what Homer was writing about*.

Not much else is known of his military career. At one moment, in some battle area, he saw field-gray figures, perhaps as many as sixty, moving toward him, wearing military uniforms — Germans all right — but with no weapons, their hands in the air; they wanted to surrender. Lewis acquiesced and ushered them in. Later, he remembered, he either forgot to point his gun at them, or remembered that he should have pointed it, but didn't think it appropriate at the time. On April 15, 1918, he was felled by friendly fire from the rear, hospitalized, and eventually invalided out of the army.

Both lost friends in the war. Coward lost two handsome young men to tuberculosis, which was deadly as the noxious gases released by the Jerries. Lewis lost Paddy Moore. "He was last seen," wrote the adjutant in his brigade, "on the morning of [March 24, 1918] with a few men defending a position on a river bank against infinitely superior numbers of the enemy. All the other officers and most of the men of his company have become casualties, and I fear it is impossible to obtain more definite information."

Later Paddy's mother, Mrs. Moore, was able to learn that her son was taken prisoner, overthrew his guards, and got back to British lines only to be sent over the top again. He was hit in the leg, and as he lay in a field, his batman trying to scotch the blood, a bullet tore through his head, killing him instantly.

The Great War, whether experienced personally as with Lewis or vicariously as with Coward, was indeed hell. But both young men managed to carry on. Coward continued to audition and get parts; to write song lyrics, tunes, sketches; and to produce a nosegay of dramatic compositions that vaulted him, first to solvency, then to stardom.

In 1922, his play *The Young Idea* encapsulated the wants and needs of the generation who came to their majority during the war; that included Sholto and Gerda, characters in the play.

"Sharp, smart, elegant and witty, *mondaine* beyond their years," as Coward biographer Philip Hoare put it, "they [Sholto and Gerda] are perfect Coward youths, exemplars of an entire generation. Boy-child and girl-child and yet sexually knowing, they are the anarchic antithesis of the pompous county set ('They're all against us just because we're not narrow and horsey like them'). Sholto and Gerda are the acid drops in this bag of marshmallows.

"Jennifer Brent, 'chic, golden-haired . . . dressed in a scarlet overall,' is another pristine Coward creation: 'I have never been able to take anything seriously after eleven o'clock in the morning.' Of her maid, she observes, 'Isn't Maria attractive? She has no morals and many more children than are usual for a single woman. . . .' "

According to Hoare, Sholto and Gerda attempt to bring their parents, long separated, back together again, and with some success; they'd parted, it seemed, because "they were too temperamental." In one scene the father accuses the mother "of reveling in the tease of argument"; as the father continues, 'You've wanted me all these years as much as I have wanted you. The sight of you has completely annihilated the time we've been parted. The only thing that matters in the world is Youth. And I've got it back. . . .' It was the cry for immortality which pervaded Coward's work — an image as gilded and artificial as Sholto and Gerda, prototypes to populate his places for the next two decades."

Sex came early and easily to Coward, who, at least according to his biographer, seemed never to have enjoyed heterosexuality. He loved men in uniform, "close-fitting scarlet tunic, highly polished brass and silver, patent leather straps and belt." His love for at least one Coldstream Guard went unrequited, but for at least one prince it was reportedly very much requited indeed. He enjoyed himself with virtually everybody he met; yes, it was *eros* with the males, but with the females it was only *philia.*

Bathing and sunbathing and partying seemed to be the chief industries of the idle young in the pop-culture set. A fancy-dress party at the Tower of London. A nursery party where guests dressed as babies and were wheeled about in prams. A "come-as-the-person-you'd-most-like-to-sleep-with" party. With his clothes on he was something of a Puck, a master of revels. With his clothes off he was, reportedly, proud as a puffin.

Sex came early to Lewis too, but clumsily; that is to say, in the British public schools to which he'd been sent by his father. Even without the aid of *eros*, he managed to acquire a family; he and Paddy Moore had promised each other that they'd take care of the surviving parent if one of them should die. And so it came to pass that he "adopted" Mrs. Janie Askins King Moore and her young daughter, Maureen Daisy Helen; without benefit of divorce, she'd left her husband Courtenay Edward Moore in 1907.

As for the opposite sex he seems to have met his fair share. For example, in 1926 he rashly promised the president of Magdalen College that he'd teach philosophy to "a troupe of performing bagbirds" if he had to; he had to; the president had already promised his services to Lady Margaret Hall for a term.

When Lewis arrived for the first class, he was relieved to find six girls waiting for him. In numbers there was safety; one pupil, having a tutor to herself for a whole term, could play disciple so charmingly that tutelage would turn into marriage. None of them had read Plato. With a little help from Lewis, however, they were soon chattering away.

Colbourne, as he wrote in his diary that first night, was "dignified and fairly sensible." Scoones was "lanky, dark." Grant was "a very massive, lumpish person who never opened her mouth." Thring was "the most talkative." House was "nervy, a trifle soulful, and worried." Johnson was "perhaps the best." A seventh girl, Carter, arrived well after the discussion had started; something about searching for a lost tortoise, she said; she was "the prettiest and perhaps rather a bitch."

They met once a week during Trinity term; for each session Lewis was paid £1. Plato having been dispatched, eighteenth-century philosophers like George Berkeley and David Hume were exposed and discussed. Papers were read on causation ("What happened when one billiard ball hit another?"), and skepticism ("They kissed, silly, but nothing really happened!"). "It is as if, not content with seeing your eyes," said one of the girls during a discussion of how one comes to know her self, "you want to take them out and look at them — and then they wouldn't be eyes."

"The pretty ones are stupid," wrote Lewis to his father, his bachelorhood intact at end of term, "and the interesting ones are ugly."

So much for the young Lewis and the young women he met; far from alluring creatures who'd tempt him from the straight and narrow, they must have appeared to him as a sure cure for concupiscence.

Neither Coward nor Lewis had much taste for religion in their early twenties. Even as Coward was being prepared for confirmation at Holy Trinity Church at Clapham Common, he was groped by a clergyman. "There's a time and place for everything," Coward reportedly remarked, removing the invasive hand; "and if I ever want a bit of fun, I'll let you know." It was downhill from there, at least so far as church and worship were concerned.

By the time Coward was thirty-three, he'd become spokesman of his age, which was, according to his biographer, "nearly amoral, reputedly modern, always smart"; female liberation was "a compromise between pederasty and normal sex" and the post-war boy; "it was a time of emancipation: birth control and sexual liberation; drink, drugs, and dance-crazy clubs; divorce and adultery."

So much for contrasting the young manhood of Lewis and Coward.

Let me say again that both of them had tremendous gifts, and each in his own way exploited them. And no doubt, even as I write, they're enjoying the heavenly banquet and whiffing the heavenly bouquet. But I'm not talking about their gifts; I'm talking about how during their young lives they came to grips with the Spirit of their Age. The one helped create it; the other found himself fighting against it. The one was in the performance arts; the other, in the literary arts; both attempted to draw some attention from the influential audiences of their time.

It was 1932. Just as Coward had justified his immoral ways in play and song, so Lewis wanted to memorialize his religious conversion from atheism to Christianity in some literary way. Lewis's passage had indeed been a pilgrimage, albeit an interior one, and pilgrimage literature was no stranger to him.

There was *Everyman*, a fifteenth-century Dutch play, which had been Englished early in the sixteenth century. The central character was, not one individual, but all individuals. Summoned by Death and hence facing the final pilgrimage, Everyman looked among his friends for a companion....

There was "The Dream of the Rood," an old English poem in which the anonymous poet, in vision, talked with the cross that Christ was crucified on, and the cross talked back....

There was *The Vision of William concerning Piers the Plowman*, a sprawling allegorical poem written by William Langland in the second half of the fourteenth century....

There was also *The Pilgrim's Progress, from This World to That Which Is to Come, Delivered under the Similitude of a Dream*, a prose allegory published by John Bunyan in 1678....

The dream-vision would be a far better model than a drama; it would allow for the many uses of allegory. Lewis could move backward and forward in time without respect to causality. He could fabricate the incidents of the allegory in such a way that they had one meaning for the characters and an additional meaning, perhaps several meanings, for the reader. What was philosophically complex in his own pilgrimage, therefore, Lewis felt he could make ridiculously simple and not a little interesting.

Dreams were no strangers to Lewis. When he was a child, ghosts visited him frequently at night, and insects — "their angular limbs, their jerky movements, their dry metallic noises" — terrorized him as they lumbered forward with the inexorability of French locomotives.

In 1930 he had dreamed — and woke to remember — that he went to the kitchen to get something to eat. As he opened the cupboard door, a package rolled off the shelf and hit the floor with a thunk. Thinking it a cabbage, he picked it up and, unwrapping the brown paper, he found, looking up at him with baleful eye, a woman's head, Mrs. Lovell's, the woman who'd done odd jobs for Mrs. Moore but in recent weeks had disappeared without a trace.

Then there was the dream about his father. "I was in the dining room at Little Lea, with all the gases lit, and talking to my father," was the way he described it to Greeves. "I knew perfectly well that he had died, and presently put out my hand and touched him. He felt warm and solid. I said, 'But of course, this must be only an appearance. You can't really have a body now.' He explained that it was only an appearance, and our conversation, which was cheerful and friendly, but not solemn or emotional, drifted on to other topics."

With much of this on his mind, Lewis left Oxford on the night of Monday, August 15, 1932, for Liverpool, where he boarded the overnight ferry for Belfast.

Personified and prancing about allegories like *Piers the Plowman* and *The Pilgrim's Progress,* he recalled as he leaned against the railing of the boat, were characters like Death and Good Deeds, abstractions of a sort he was sure he could use in his own work. In Langland there was a trio of Do-ables (Do Well, Do Better, Do Best), the Seven Deadly Sins, and Tom-true-tongue-tell-me-no-tales-nor-lying-stories-to-laugh-at-for-I-loved-them-never. In Bunyan there were Evangelist, Worldly-wiseman, Faithful and Hopeful, Passion and Patience, Obstinate and Pliable, and virgins named Prudence, Piety, and Charity.

If Langland could invent Lady Holychurch to stand for Christianity, then Lewis felt that he could create Mother Kirk. Mr. Enlightenment could represent the intellect triumphing over religion; his son Sigismund could stand for psychology tromping on rationality; Mr. Sensible could stand for reasonableness in search of happiness. And there could be three young men — Mr. Neo-Classical, Mr. Neo-Angular, Mr. Humanist — who'd found a community based on Classicism, Catholicism, and Humanism.

As allegories created characters out of abstractions, so also they created out of nothing places that had no geographical reality. Langland placed, on already existing topography, the Tower of Truth, in which dwelled God the Father, and the Castle of Care, in which lived the Father of Falseness, and the earth itself he called "a fair field full of folk." Bunyan exnihilized Vanity Fair, the Slough of Despond, the Valley of the Shadow of Death, Doubting Castle and Palace Beautiful and the Delectable Mountains.

In his own work, for which he'd eventually draw a map, Lewis—and he was writing rapidly now at a table in his friend

Greeves's house — dotted the landscape with places like Thrill, Claptrap, and Puritania. He laid down the Isthmus Sadisticus and the Isthmus Mazochisticus. There was a North, where people were pale, austere, taciturn; there was a South, where people were dark, indulgent, loquacious. Slashing across the landscape that had once been paradise but was now crevassed with a fault of spiritual origin was the Grand Canyon, an exotic name from the American West. If he weren't in Shanghai, his brother, Warren, would surely insist on a military railway, one that'd link such major population centers as Zeitgeistheim, Occultica, and Orgiastica; after all, he'd devised the principal steamship routes on the map of Boxen.

The central character of an allegory was usually the author himself and, as that author fervently hoped, a multitude of readers would identify themselves with that character. Langland was Long Will; many a medieval prelate and clerk would recognize himself in Will. Bunyan was Christian as he set out on the sort of journey all Puritans could understand. And Lewis was John, the twentieth-century pilgrim who would be drawn inexorably toward the island and mountain of his desires.

In a sense, Lewis began his work where Bunyan's left off. Christian had to face every temptation the seventeenth century had to offer. John, setting out from Puritania, met, first of all, the eighteenth century in the character of Mr. Enlightenment; in the next seventy-two chapters he would meet personifications of just about every philosophical, literary, and political movement from that time right down to the 1930s.

To root the allegory somewhere in the theological firmament, there had to be a creation story, and Lewis decided to have Mother Kirk tell it to John about halfway through. There was this Landlord who had a farm. He "decided to let the country to tenants, and his first tenant was a young married man." Under the influence of the Enemy, who was one of the Landlord's children, the farmer's wife ate "a nice mountain apple," something she'd been told not to do. "And then — you know how it is with husbands — she made the farmer come round to her mind." *Peccatum Adae* it was called by Mother Kirk in her own peculiar language, "the sin of Adam." At this blatant act the Landlord's gorge rose; there was an earthquake, and the paradisal park became a gorge.

Having traversed half the world in search of the Landlord, having been beguiled by a variety of temptations and interpretations of existence, but seemingly no closer to the island or mountain of his desires, John uttered a cry for help. He prayed, and "a Man came to him in the darkness" and spoke.

"Your life has been saved all this day by crying out to something which you call by many names, and you have said to yourself that you used metaphors."

"Was I wrong, sir?"

"Perhaps not. But you must play fair. If its help is not a metaphor, neither are its commands. If it can answer when you call, then it can speak without your asking. If you can go to it, it can come to you.

"I think I see it, sir. You mean that I am not my own man; in some sense I have a Landlord after all?"

Like a common criminal to a police sergeant, John turned himself in. He accepted the veracity of the myth and the credibility of Christianity. Equanimity restored, he found himself retracing his former steps. The temptations and interpretations that had so tormented him before, he now saw with clearer eyes.

Like the yachtsman in Chesterton's *Orthodoxy,* who'd sailed around the world only to discover that what he sought was on the coast of England, John arrived back in Puritania. The pilgrimage was within, he concluded; the philosophical battles were fought quite independent of geography; and the many temptations had to be wrestled with on the topsoil of one's own soul.

As a guest in the Greeves's household, Lewis wrote furiously, and by the end of his two-week stay he'd completed a first draft. *The Pilgrim's Regress, or Pseudo-Bunyan's Periplus* wouldn't be an inappropriate title, he thought; for a subtitle he considered "An Allegorical Apology for Christianity, Reason, and Romanticism."

An allegory it certainly was. A defense of Christianity it was without doubt, John having taken a header into the pool of belief at the foot of Mother Kirk. Reason as man's primary philosophical tool had been argued at length, reason being more than a knight cloaked in blue, a virgin who triumphed with naked sword or confounding riddle. But was it romantic enough?

It was romantic, thought Lewis after lunch one day with Tolkien. What drew John from the serenity and security of Puritania and set him on the road was "a sweetness and pang so piercing" that he could scarcely resist. Such a ringing desire sustained him throughout the pilgrimage, and as he neared the end, he came to the realization that "the wanting, though it is pain too, is more precious than anything else we experience."

One thing both Lewis and Tolkien agreed on as they rose from their tables at the Eastgate Hotel. For a truly successful work, for a truly romantic work, it should give one an entrance into another, perhaps a better, world. One should "hear the horns of elfland."

Sometime after Christmas 1932, Lewis sent the manuscript of *The Pilgrim's Regress* to J. M. Dent and Sons in London. By the beginning of February 1933, Dent's replied that they'd publish the work if he met certain conditions. He'd have to simplify the title, shorten the manuscript, and submit to illustrations. If these conditions were acceptable, they'd have galley proof by mid-April and bound books by the end of May.

If Dent's left *An Allegorical Apology for Christianity, Reason, and Romanticism* intact, Lewis replied, he'd drop the last three words from the title. If they forewent illustrations, he'd provide a *mappa mundi* of the various places mentioned in the text. And he'd look through the manuscript again for passages that might possibly be cut. Dent's was agreeable. A contract was struck.

Lewis had already sent the manuscript to several of his friends, asking them to read it for "confusion, bad taste, unsuccessful jokes, contradictions."

Greeves replied at length. He pointed out "passages where one word less would make the difference." Many of the words Lewis did use he found too "idiomatic and racy," not classical enough.

Lewis replied to the effect that he preferred the colloquial to the literary and was only following Bunyan's example in this respect.

The characters in the allegory quoted too often from previously published works and in languages other than English, one of his friendly critics said.

They were almost always from the mouth of Mr. Sensible, countered Lewis, and almost always this character was misquoting. Besides, "one of the contentions of the book is that the decay of our old classical learning is a contributory cause of atheism."

Regress was divided into ten books, and each one was preceded by as many as four epigraphs. Too many, said Greeves, and too confusing.

Most readers, said Lewis, never look at epigraphs anyway, and why, if he was pleased by them, should he remove them?

The argument of the allegory Greeves found too complex, even though he already knew the sinuous and tortuous path of his friend's conversion.

"The *intellectual* side of my conversion was not simple," complained Lewis, "and I can describe only what I know."

When Dent's offered Lewis an agreeably phrased contract, however, and as he set about preparing the manuscript for composition, he made many of the changes indicated by Greeves, and he rewrote those passages in which he couldn't accept his friend's suggestions.

"I suppose you have no objection to my dedicating the book to you?" he asked rhetorically of Greeves in a letter dated March 25. "It is yours by right — written in your house, read to you as it was written, and celebrating (at least in the most important parts) an experience which I have more in common with you than anyone else."

On August 17, 1933, the brothers went to see *Cavalcade,* a film of Coward's musical pageant presented the year before in London's West End. It chronicled British history, as experienced by the members of two families, from New Year's eve 1899 to New Year's eve 1930. As play and film began so they ended, with champagne glasses raised, the families having survived the Boer War, the death of Queen Victoria, the Great War, and the shimmering if disillusioning twenties.

A light sign spelled out the news. Newsboys shouted the headlines. Steam rivets, loudspeakers, jazz bands, airplane propellers — the noise grew in decibels until, as Coward intended, the general effect was one of "complete chaos." As if to bring order out of chaos, coming into focus on the screen was the Union Jack, and the discord changed to "God Save the King."

"I thought it would be historically interesting, and so I suppose it was; and certainly very clever," wrote Lewis to Greeves. "But there is not an idea in the whole thing from beginning to end; it is a mere brutal assault on one's emotions, using material which one can't help feeling intensely. It appeals entirely to that part of you which lives in the throat and chest, leaving the spirit untouched. I have come away feeling as if I had been at a debauch."

Just after the final toast in the movie, but just before the Union Jack, there was a brief scene in a night club. Fanny was seated on a piano. The set was, as Coward intended, "angular and strange"; the song she sang, which Coward had written, was "oddly discordant."

Verse:
Why is it that civilized humanity
Must make the world so wrong?
In this hurly burly of insanity
Your dreams cannot last long.
We've reached a headline —
The Press headline — every sorrow,
Blues value is News value tomorrow.

Refrain:
Blues, Twentieth Century Blues, are getting me down.
Who's escaped those weary Twentieth Century Blues?
Why, if there's a God in the sky, why shouldn't he grin?
High above this dreary Twentieth Century din,
In this strange illusion, Chaos and confusion,
People seem to lose their way.
What is there to strive for,
Love or keep alive for? Say —
Hey, hey, call it a day.

Blues, nothing to win or lose.
It's getting me down.
Blues, I've got those weary Twentieth Century Blues.

If England suffered from anything on New Year's eve 1930, it was twentieth-century blues. At least that was Coward's diagnosis; from close and continuing contact he too seemed to have contracted it. Lewis identified the same virus, but would rather have called it artistic and spiritual bankruptcy. As such he treated it, he thought, with devastating effect in *The Pilgrim's Regress.* Into the mouth of Guide, who was helping John the Pilgrim pass through Ignorantia, he put a song: it appears under the title "Deception" in *Poems* and *Collected Poems:*

Iron will eat the world's old beauty up.
Girder and grid and gantry will arise,
Iron forest of engines will arise,
Criss-cross of iron crotchet. For your eyes
No green or growth. Over all, the skies
Scribbled from end to end with boasts and lies.
(When Adam ate the irrevocable apple, Thou
Sawst beyond death the resurrection of the dead.)

Clamor shall clean put out the voice of wisdom,
The printing-presses with their clapping wings,
Fouling your nourishment. Harpy wings,
Filling your minds all day with foolish things,
Will tame the eagle Thought: till she sings
Parrot-like in her cage to please dark kings.
(When Israel descended into Egypt, Thou
Didst purpose both the bondage and the coming out.)

The new age, the new art, the new ethic and thought,
And fools crying, Because it has begun
It will continue as it has begun!
The wheel runs fast, therefore the wheel will run
Faster for ever. The old age is done,
We have the new lights and see without the sun.
(Though they lay flat the mountains and dry up the sea,
Wilt thou yet change, as though God were a god?)

For Coward, God was something of an ant-watcher, ogling from on high the antics of the populace who had less notion than the insects about order in the physical as well as the moral universe.

For Lewis, the skyscrapery world was eroding the natural world, the invention of all kinds of rolling stock was overtaking the walker, natural light was being replaced by artificial light, but still the God of Scripture held his place in the universe and in the hearts of humankind.

Without perhaps knowing Coward's work firsthand, Lewis satirized his satyrical view of the world, reducing it to its logical absurdity by creating a New Year's Eve party in *Pilgrim's Regress*. It was held in "a big room rather like a bathroom; it was full of steel and glass, and the walls were nearly all window." "Drinking what looked like medicine and talking at the tops of their voices" were the Clevers. "They were all either young, or dressed up to look as if they were young. The girls had short hair and flat breasts and flat buttocks so that they looked like boys; but the boys had pale, egg-shaped faces and slender waists and big hips so that they looked like girls — except for a few of them who had long hair and beards."

In what followed at the party, Lewis laid low the proponents of "the poetry of the silly twenties," "the swamp literature of the dirty twenties," and "the gibberish literature of the lunatic twenties." Victoriana sang a song that wasn't appreciated and had the temerity to accompany herself on a toy harp. A bearded man wearing "a red shirt and a codpiece made of the skins of crocodiles" "began to beat on an African tom-tom and to croon with his voice, swaying his lean, halfclad body to and fro and staring at them all, out of eyes which were like burning coals." And then there was Glugly, "very tall and as lean as a post; and her mouth was not quite straight in her face." "Globol obol oogle ogle globol gloogle gloo." It was unclear whether she was attempting to sing or to recite, but she "ended by pursing up her lips and making a vulgar noise such as children make in their nurseries."

So much for Lewis's driving a satirical stake right through the heart of Coward's work.

✣

Cavalcade brought Coward bags of mail, raves from reviewers, crowds at the box offices, and there were those who said that the patriotic pageant would eventually result in a peerage from the grateful monarch. But what, Lewis thought to himself, would the publication of *Regress* bring him? It brought him into direct contact with the Spirit of the Age, and he was victorious, albeit in a mysterious sort of way.

Both Coward and Lewis eventually ended up on their monarch's Honours List. George VI offered Lewis Commander of the British Empire in 1951; he declined politely. Elizabeth II offered Coward a knighthood in 1970; he accepted gratefully.

But in 1933, when Lewis's *Pilgrim's Regress* was published, there was hardly a ripple of critical comment, pro or con; and at that time Coward was the most highly paid creative writer in the known world.

So much for following the thrum from afar, the aching desire, that was supposed to be draw all humankind to the Godhead! Lewis heard it and followed it, but to no public acclaim; he valued it as a record of his trek through the spiritual wilderness of life. Coward, so far as we know, didn't hear the thrum over the din of his crowded life; or if he did hear it, he didn't act on it. Lewis, in the person of John in *Pilgrim's Regress,* passed through Ignorantia, but Coward preferred to stop there and enjoy a really good cream tea.

At age six Lewis wanted to be a votary of the Blue Flower. At age thirty-five he was surrounded — but not outnumbered — by the votaries of twentieth-century blues. God's in Coward's Heaven, but he's grinning; back on earth, the lesser gods — Chaos and Confusion — are jangling the keyboards.

That's how it happened in Lewis's life. . . .

What It Means

What moral is there in this for us MCs?

We all confront the Spirit of the Age when trying to make spiritual sense of the world. When we're young, it often appears attractive, but quickly becomes seductive, swallowing us up like the Vacuum Machine Creature in *The Yellow Submarine*, who when there's nothing left to swallow up, swallows himself. And for those of us who don't flee the confrontation, the Spirit of the Age, which specializes in short-term gains, continues to attract us even as we grow older; which is another way of saying, we're never too old to make the wrong choice.

All the commentators on the spiritual life note that one's own life experiences invariably lead to an early crossroad. One may choose to veer to the left or veer to the right. But there's always a third choice. One may turn around and retrace one's tracks to the cloister of the womb.

The fathers and mothers of spiritual direction did just that; from the earliest centuries of the Christian era, they were loners, eremites and stylites. They retreated from the city to the desert, there to await the Second Coming, which, if the Scriptures were worth the parchment they were written on, was sure to come on the morrow; if not on the morrow, then on the morrow thereafter.

When that sacred event didn't come, these loners became cenobites; that is to say, they gathered together in a city of their own: a community, a convent, a monastery. Their bond was, among other things, their hatred of the city and everything in it. When not praying, they wove mats one day and unwove them the next. It was the praying that counted.

When Jesus refused to come on the short schedule, the cenobites extended their frame of reference still further. They no longer undid the mats they wove; they collected them until they had enough to visit the city, where they sold them for as much as the market would bear. Humanism, yes, but with an eschatological tinge.

This return to the marketplace, which they'd left in such a huff some decades before, marked the beginning of incarnational humanism, the sort that Jesus personified in his recorded life. He too participated in the city life of his time. He too approached the crossroad early in his public life. He too was tempted, three times, to accept the apples of this earth for little or no cost, and three times he refused.

So too with Lewis. When he came to the early crossroad, he

chose not to retreat from the confrontation. Rather he considered the two options in front of him and, hearing the thrum of spiritual desire, he chose the harder but surer way. No doubt he drew some consolation from a writer whose epics he admired, John Milton. "I cannot praise a fugitive and cloistered virtue, unexercised and unbreathed," wrote Milton in a combative prose work entitled *Areopagitica* (1644), "that never sallies out and sees her adversary, but slinks out of the race where that immortal garland is to be run for, not without dust and heat."

Lewis chose the incarnational way, and the result of this choice would hold for him many surprises.

Coward, on the other hand, had a different concept of God. When a young woman friend of his was attracted to Christian Science, he immediately labeled the group as the "new policemen . . . overzealous in obstructing traffic." That is to say, he'd gotten around all the old policemen, and here now was a new group; yet another group he'd have to buy off before he could receive some sort of moral respectability.

This isn't to say that Coward did no virtuous acts during his life; I have personal knowledge of many acts of kindness done by him to a now-deceased friend of mine. But it must be said that his virtue was centrifugal. What he was fleeing, however, was his own misguided notion of just who God was.

Coward favored certain dwarfish notions of God, which Lewis's friend J. B. Phillips described in his book *Your God Is Too Small* (1953). Parental Hangover. Grand Old Man. Meek-and-mild. Absolute Perfection. Heavenly Bosom. God-in-a-box. Managing Director. Second-hand God. Perennial Grievance. Pale Galilean. And so on. Sad to say, if Coward had a half-way decent image of God in his own mind, he might have found God in his soul.

A final and indeed contradictory word about the Spirit of an Age.

Coward wasn't the Spirit of his Age any more than Lewis was, but the print and broadcast media made him appear to be so. "Spirit of the Age" is really a product manufactured by the communications industry about a comparatively small but noisy, even flashy, person or group of persons. Sometimes, as a result of appearances on or in the media, these persons or these groups of persons come to have influence over others not of their group.

Which is another way of saying that as often as Coward didn't go to church of a Sunday, there were tens, perhaps hundreds, of thousands in England who did go to church, synagogue, mosque on their holy day; and so on, with other traits and practices.

Journalists, and the historians who traipse after them, and even the contemplatives who write about the Spirit of the Age, all often mistake notoriety like Coward's as indicative of a nation as a whole. In reality, Lewis was more the Spirit of his Age because he did believe in God and godliness; and so on with other acts and aspects of morality. But the journalists and historians didn't do their homework; they didn't get the quantity or quality right. Like Sam, the cheap tailor in a bawdy song, they made the pants too short! And so it is, on into our own age.

This isn't to say that the Spirit of an Age doesn't exist. It's just that it's one thing today, something quite different tomorrow. Its chief characteristic is worldliness; the blues, as Coward called it; a blowziness that doesn't give a fig about God and neighbor, revelation and salvation, or any of the other great issues of human existence.

What oftentimes makes this worldliness seem so attractive is that it's like the stout British fog, which tosses everything into a soft focus, rounding off angles and distorting distances, making even the most menacing objects look warm and cuddly. About the best one can do in a situation like this is grab hold of the nearest lamppost and hang on for dear life; or at least until the fog lifts. The fog always lifts. Like a fat cat it eventually pads off to its morning saucer.

Sentences

"In the New Testament," wrote Lewis in an essay entitled "Christianity and Literature," which appeared in the March 1940 issue of *Theology*, "the art of life itself is an art of imitation: can we, believing this, believe that literature, which must derive from real life, is to aim at being 'creative,' 'original,' and 'spontaneous'? 'Originality' in the New Testament is quite plainly the prerogative of God alone; even within the triune being of God it seems to be confined to the Father. The duty and happiness of every other being is placed in being derivative, in reflecting like a mirror. Nothing could be more foreign to the tone of Scripture than the language of those who describe a saint as a 'moral genius' or a 'spiritual genius' thus insinuating that his virtue or spirituality is 'creative' or 'original.'

"If I have read the New Testament aright, it leaves no room for 'creativeness' even in a modified or metaphorical sense. Our whole destiny seems to lie in the opposite direction, in being as little as possible ourselves, in acquiring a fragrance that is not our own but borrowed, in becoming clean mirrors filled with an image of a face that is not ours. I am not here supporting the doctrine of total depravity, and I do not say that the New Testament supports it; I am saying only that the highest good of a creature must be creaturely — that is, derivative or reflective — good. In other words, as St. Augustine makes plain . . . pride does not only go before a fall but is a fall — a fall of the creature's attention from what is better, God, to what is worse, itself. . . .

"The unbeliever may take his own temperament and experience just as they happen to stand, and consider them worth communicating simply because they are facts or, worse still, because they are his. To the Christian his own temperament and experience, as mere fact, and as merely his, are of no value or importance whatsoever: he will deal with them, if at all, only because they are the medium through which, or the position from which, something universally profitable appeared to him.

"We can imagine two men seated in different parts of a church or theater. Both, when they come out, may tell us their experiences, and both may use the first person. But the one is interested in his seat only because it was his — 'I was most uncomfortable,' he will say. 'You would hardly believe what a draft comes in from the door in that corner. And the people! I had to speak pretty sharply to the woman in front of me.' The other will tell us what could be seen from his seat, choosing to describe this because this is what he knows, and because every seat must give the best view of something. 'Do you know,' he will begin, 'the molding on these pillars goes on round the back. It looks, too, as if the design on the back were the older of the two.' Here we have the expressionist and the Christian attitudes toward the self or temperament."

Scriptures

"My kingdom is not founded in this world," wrote the Evangelist John, when he had Jesus responding to Pilate; "if it were, my servants would have fought to prevent my being handed over to the Jews. But in fact my kingdom is not founded on all this!" (John 18:36)

"Don't let the world around you squeeze you into its own mold," wrote the Apostle Paul to the Romans, "but let God re-mold your minds from within, so that you may prove in practice that the plan of God for you is good, meets all his demands and moves towards the goal of true maturity." (Romans 12:2)

"If any man among you thinks himself one of the world's clever ones," wrote Paul to the Corinthians, "let him discard his cleverness that he may learn to be truly wise. For this world's cleverness is stupidity to God." (1 Corinthians 3:18–19)

"The spirit of this world has blinded the minds of those who do not believe, and prevents the light of the glorious gospel of Christ, the image of God, from shining on them," wrote Paul in his second letter to the Corinthians. "For it is Christ Jesus as Lord whom we preach, not ourselves; we are you servants for his sake." (2 Corinthians 4:4–5)

Readings

Lewis's imaginative account of his conversion is contained in *The Pilgrim's Regress*. It's more interesting to read, at least for a modern intellectual, than John Bunyan's *The Pilgrim's Progress*, which was written in the seventeenth century. In it the reader will find more points at which Lewis's view of life intersects, perhaps vivisects, Coward's. It was originally published in the

United States by Sheed & Ward in 1935 and quickly went out of print; it's now available from Eerdmans and Bantam.

For the particulars of Coward's plentiful life, I refer you to Philip Hoare's *Noël Coward: A Biography* (1995) as well as Coward's autobiographies *Present Indicative* (1937) and *Future Indicative* (1954).

About chastity and its relevance to a young man's life, may I point to Charles Williams, a publishing executive who was invited by Lewis to lecture on Milton's *Comus* in wartime Oxford. *Comus,* by the way, was a masque, that is to say, a dramatic work written in poetic form; its subject matter was chastity. The general expectation was that the Oxford students who liked to sleep around would only be put to sleep by a lecture on a work about not sleeping around. Instead, Williams made a spellbinding presentation, in the Divinity School of all places. Indeed, Williams's own preface to Milton's *Collected Works,* published two years before, corrected Miltonic criticism for the previous hundred years. "Apparently," wrote Lewis, "the door of the prison was really unlocked all the time; but it was only you who thought of trying the handle. Now we can all come out."

After the lecture, Dyson, ever a wag, went about Oxford referring to Williams as "a common chastitute." No one, I think, ever called Coward that.

Chapter 3

Broadcasts

In Lewis's and Coward's time there were more churches in England than theaters, and more people went to those churches than to the playhouses. The churches upheld the other-worldliness urged by the evangelists and epistolarists of the New Testament. But the theaters held a this-worldliness which, as Coward expressed it, was a bluesy, blowzy attitude toward the moral world.

As gravity would have it, the one seeped into the other.

Attendance, especially in Anglican churches, dropped off. A vicar might count twenty-five thousand living within the boundaries of his parish, but of a Sunday as few as twenty-five might show up at the early service. Perhaps it was a remnant of the reformational rebellion against mandatory Sunday attendance. More likely, it was the Hatch-Match-Dispatch attitude that had grown up among many Anglicans; the only three times in life that one might conveniently be seen in the church were birth, marriage, and death. Whatever the trouble was, it came to a point in 1941 when Lewis received a most unexpected letter.

"I write to ask whether you would be willing to help us in our work of religious broadcasting. . . ."

British Broadcasting Corporation

It was Monday, February 10. Lewis had just opened a letter from the Rev. J. W. Welch, director of the BBC's religious broadcasting department.

"The microphone is a limiting and often irritating instrument, but the quality of thinking and depth of conviction which

I find in your book [*The Problem of Pain*, published in 1940] ought surely to be shared with a great many other people; and for any talk we can be sure of a fairly intelligent audience of more than a million."

Lewis was amazed. He hardly listened to the radio and couldn't remember ever having heard a religious program.

Welch suggested two possible topics. The first was "the Christian, or lack of Christian, assumptions underlying modern literature." The second subject was "a positive restatement of Christian doctrines in lay language."

"Even if you feel you cannot help us in our work," said Welch at the end of the letter, "may I take the opportunity of thanking you for *The Problem of Pain?*"

As for the first topic, Lewis felt he could talk about that. But it was the second topic that caught his fancy. He took up his pen and responded that he would indeed give some talks. They'd have to be during the long summer vacation, though. In university terms, that meant somewhere between the middle of July to the end of September.

The law of nature, or objective right or wrong, Lewis wrote, would be just right for him. New Testament writers assumed that the Hebrews knew this law even when they disobeyed it. But in modern England Lewis, later encouraged by Welch, felt he couldn't assume this. Christianity, if it were mentioned at all in the talks, would have to come at the end. Some general title like "The Art of Being Shocked" or "These Humans" would be suitable.

Early in May Lewis showed up at the BBC building in London for a dry run. The Rev. Eric Fenn, assistant head of the religious broadcasting department, a Presbyterian, whose job it was to supervise the preparation and delivery of the talks, gave him some printed material and pointed to a microphone. Lewis read. A recording was made. When it was played back, Lewis was flabbergasted.

Fenn was impressed, though. Lewis read smoothly enough, but he paused for rhetorical effect. That he couldn't do, said Fenn. In such interstices Lord Haw Haw, William Joyce, the British traitor to the Nazis, broadcasting on BBC frequencies from German-occupied territory, was known to insert false, misleading, even insulting remarks, all in the nature of propaganda.

Would the four Wednesdays in August be acceptable as broadcasting dates? Fenn asked.

When Lewis said yes, Fenn asked when the scripts would be ready.

He'd begun them, but why would Fenn need them so soon?

Because they'd have to be read by the censor. Besides, changes were requested in most scripts; the changes themselves would have to go through the censorship process.

Remember, said Fenn to Lewis as they parted, be as colloquial as you possibly can.

Eventually there were four series of talks. They found their way into print, and they've been in print in a variety of forms ever since. Under the title *Mere Christianity*, they've been a perennial paperback bestseller — and something of a cult classic — in the United States.

For the MC and the would-be MC there are at least two benefits in rehearsing here some of the points he made. First, they countered the Spirit of the Age he lived in with the doctrines of the ages. Second, they provided the solid building blocks with which one may safely begin to design and construct a spirituality.

For easy reference, the highlights are grouped under the titles of the individual series of talks and the books that followed. As for Lewis's arguments, some of them have been condensed; some, paraphrased. In each instance his clarity shines through, and in any case a quick reading of the originals will provide the necessary correctives.

Right and Wrong

On Wednesday afternoon, August 6, 1941, Lewis boarded the train at Oxford and headed southeast toward London. As the carriage rattled down the line, he looked over the typescript sent back to him by the BBC. "Right and Wrong as a Clue to the Meaning of the Universe" was now the overall title of the four talks.

When he arrived at Broadcasting House, he was met by Fenn, who conducted him to a studio. They rehearsed the talk. As 7:45 approached, the studio door was closed. Lewis sat poised at the microphone. "On the air" was flashed, Fenn gestured, Lewis began to read.

"Everyone has heard people quarreling. Sometimes it sounds funny, and sometimes it sounds merely unpleasant; but however it sounds, I believe we can learn something very important from listening to the kinds of things they say. . . . "

Law of Human Nature

For amateur boxing championships in 1897, the Marquess of Queensberry wrote down some rules. Among them it was permissible to knock an opponent's block off, but impermissible to hit him below the belt. When the rule was broken, someone cried foul, the rule was appealed to, and some redress was immediately made.

In the less combative confrontations of everyday life, where the assault and the subsequent defense were carried on with words rather than blows, both parties seemed to recognize some similar rules of engagement. That was to say, there was a right way of going about it, and there was a wrong way. In other words, a natural Law of Right and Wrong.

From there, Lewis proceeded to such physical aspects of the natural law as gravitation, heredity, and chemistry. But try as hard as human beings might, they couldn't violate these particular laws simply by doing their opposites. It was the Law of Human Nature that Lewis was headed for; a law generally recognized by nearly all the countries of the world nearly all the time. Accordingly, a citizen must do to others what one expects them to do to oneself; a man may have as many wives as he wants, but he may not have every woman he desires.

Any student, then, whether of the history of the world or just the history of one's own neighborhood (Agatha Christie's Miss Marple came to know that all the perfidy of the Western world lurked inside the inhabitants of her tiny village, St. Mary Mead), knows these Laws of Human Nature well, many of them as yet unwritten, but virtually all of them known by the human heart.

Reality of the Law

Since we insisted that there was a Law of Human Nature, Lewis argued, then we must conclude that it wasn't made up just for the fun of it. People used it, knew it, expected its observance by others. Odd thing, though. The people found this law pressing hard upon them. Even when they didn't do good, and that might be often, they knew they should. They knew that with regard to themselves; they expected it of their spouses; they taught it to their children. And they just hoped and prayed that the families living on either side of them were doing the same thing. And so, Lewis concluded, it seemed that human behavior was shadowed by another sort of behavior, a silhouette larger and more perfect than our own, and when we stood against it, we just didn't measure up.

What Lies Behind the Law

If there was such a law, Lewis pointed out, then there was someone or something out there in the universe that made the law. Probably more on the order of a mind than a moon. A lawmaker. A lawgiver. Someone like that. "A controlling power." "A Power behind the facts, a Director, a Guide." Lewis didn't want to come right out and say God; at least not yet. What seemed clear was that the Lawmaker made the law especially for us. He, she, or it designed the Law of Human Nature especially for humankind.

We Have Cause to Be Uneasy

As to the identity or identification of the Somebody or Something behind the Law of Human Nature, the Moral Law, there appeared to be two clues.

First, that Whoever or Whatever that shadowy presence was, He, She, It made the universe, which was, at one and the same time, a beautiful and a fearful place.

Second, the Maker of the Universe installed the Law of Right and Wrong in each and every one of us in the full expectation that we'd obey it. Right off, our ancestors seemed to have put that law to the test by disobeying it, and it has been to our peril ever since. There wasn't one of us — babes and brigands excepted — who hadn't disobeyed the moral law and regretted it almost instantly.

If our good behavior amounted to anything at all, and if our bad behavior had any meaning at all, the first thing we wanted to do was mend our manners and get back into the good graces of the Power of the Universe. Then, and only then, did religion come into play. If we repented of the bad behavior, religion, especially Christianity, promised us forgiveness.

In September the British public felt they were being manipulated. What the press and radio were telling them to think was quite different from what they were really thinking about such topics as Churchill's secret meeting in the Atlantic with Roosevelt, Russia's chances against Germany, even food rationing and the rationing of clothes....

Of the audience who listened to Lewis's "Right and Wrong" broadcasts in August, a goodly number took exception to some of the extraordinary claims he made about the natural law; they made their complaints known by writing to the BBC. Lewis answered them all by hand, except the one that began, "Dear Mr. Lewis, I was married at the age of 20 to a man I didn't love," and the one that was signed "Jehovah."

What Christians Believe

Overhead at night in the spring of 1942, there was the roar of bombers, British now, hundreds of them, heading for German cities. A year before, the roar was from German planes, sometimes as many as four hundred, ready to unload bombs, incendiary devices, parachute mines, leveling historic as well as commercial and residential architecture.

Now no more than twenty planes with the black and white cross on the wings made it across the British Channel each night. They still carried bombs; wherever they dropped them, there were destruction and death. For one of the fatalities, Lewis wrote an epitaph, which appeared in the June 6 issue of *Time and Tide*. The child was killed by a bomb, he noted; both of them were "beautifully, delicately made."

Rival Conceptions of God

Most of humankind believe in God, but is God good or bad? So much had gone right in the world, but so much had gone wrong. One could become an atheist, or one could be a pantheist. But somehow, just to have the notions of right and wrong was a clue, not just to the meaning of the universe, but to why Christians believed as they did. Theism made sense, atheism didn't, for it didn't take into account the moral virtues and vices, truths and untruths, etc.

Invasion

Lewis proposed two philosophical explanations.

Monism had it that there was one God and that God has created one world that had in it good and bad both in memory and in fact. Dualism, on the other hand, was the theory that there were two equal powers in the universe, a Good Power and a Bad Power, in a constant and almost comic battle for control of the universe. It was a sort of Punch-and-Judy show, hand-puppets of a husband and wife who shrilled at each other, thumping and thwacking it out with paddles; so evenly matched were they that neither of them ever won, but their paddling each other was always good for a laugh.

Philosophies had their place, but Lewis looked to the real world. "Enemy-occupied territory — that is what the world is. Christianity is the story of how the rightful king has landed, you might say in disguise, and is calling us all to take part in a great campaign of sabotage."

Shocking Alternative

Yes, there was another power in the world, but a power not equal to God — the Devil — and his chief task was to mess about with humankind's freedom. On any given day, half of humankind did good, and the other half mucked up. The Devil tried to engineer what small gains he could. But the gains were mainly in infiltrating the hearts and minds and souls of humankind, ultimately to sabotage the idea that they could find happiness with God.

The trouble with God, the Dark Power would have us think, was that there were rules, rules that reined in the rebellious spirit. And the question quickly arose, Who was going to be boss, God or man and woman? But through it all came a man who claimed to be God, Jesus of Nazareth, who claimed to forgive sins. He was either God or a lunatic; and if he were a lunatic, he'd be, according to Lewis, either a poached egg or the Devil in Hell.

Perfect Penitent

Jesus has suffered and died for us, and various Christian denominations have developed theories to explain precisely how that happened. But the theories were merely word-pictures of a mystery whose full meaning was known only to God. In this regard Lewis cited the efforts of James Jeans, the physicist and mathematician, and Arthur Stanley Eddington, the astrophysicist, who in the 1930s and '40s attempted to explain the invisible world of atoms with word-pictures. But these scientists were the first to say that these pictures were merely attempts to illustrate mathematical formulas known only to a few. And so it was with the atonement. Sadly and yet happily, the reality was that Jesus was killed and that his death wiped away our sins.

Gratitude was the right emotion on our part, and we expressed our gratitude by repenting of our sins. Lewis used the war metaphor again. Repentance was "this process of surrender — this movement full speed astern." The bad person could repent. The good person could repent, but only God, sinless by definition, could repent perfectly. That having been done, mercy, as Portia said in Shakespeare's *Merchant of Venice*, "droppeth as the gentle rain from heaven."

Practical Conclusion

In an increasingly Darwinian world, evolution was gaining sway as a workable theory. But to Lewis, it wasn't so much that organisms were related by common *descent* but that humankind might be related by common *ascent*. The Christian act of Calvary, with all its intentions and purposes and effects, seemed to have already happened. Jesus was the new kind of man. And insomuch as we became like Jesus, we too would become the new kind of men.

Lewis went on to suggest three ways this might just happen: "baptism, belief, and that mysterious action which different Christians call by different names — Holy Communion, the Mass, the Lord's Supper."

As for the invasion, it would come. God would come, but he was waiting for us to join his side freely. "I do not suppose you and I would have thought much of a Frenchman who waited till the Allies were marching into Germany and then announced that he was on our side." When God invades, the war will be over, the world will be over. But, Lewis said, it was important to take sides now.

Christian Behavior

Lewis originally wrote eight fifteen-minute talks for a series to be broadcast on Sunday afternoons from September to November. But what the BBC had asked for was for ten-minute, not fifteen-minute, talks. Lewis hastened to condense, and when the series was published, he restored the cuts and added four "fifteen-minute" chapters: "Cardinal Virtues," "Christian Marriage," "Hope," and "Charity." They were published in book form in April 1943.

Three Parts of Morality

According to Lewis, people noted three things about morality. First, it had to do with fair play and harmony between individuals. Second, it had to do with tidying up or harmonizing the things inside each individual. Third, it had to do with the general purpose of human life as a whole: "what man was made for; what course the whole fleet ought to be on; what tune the conductor of the band wants it to play."

Most people agreed with the first, but became slack about the other two. But, as Lewis said, if one were going to live only as long as the actuary predicted, then it probably didn't make much difference. But if, as Christianity suggested, one was going to live forever, then the second and third points made a great deal of difference indeed.

From this point on in his talks — and in the books that followed — Lewis began to propose the Christian point of view.

Cardinal Virtues

First of all, there were such things as *virtues;* that was to say, there were habits of acting in one manner rather than another. And there were, sadly, bad habits as well as good ones. Serial murderers would tell you that the first stabbing was the hardest, but it became easier with repetition. And so it was with the good habits. The first act of virtue might require gargantuan effort; but the next would require ever-decreasing foot-pounds of spiritual, psychological, and intellectual energy.

Some virtues were said to be *cardinal,* but not in the sense that they dressed up in red silk soutanes and swanned about the Vatican in fat, flat prelate hats with cords and tassels flying. Rather they were pivotal virtues, *hinge* virtues as the Latin root of "cardinal" suggested. Another name for them was the moral virtues; perhaps even the humane virtues. All of which was a way of saying that one needed nothing more than reason to identify them, and that there was no rational excuse for not putting them into practice.

Traditionally, four cardinal virtues were mentioned.

Prudence meant common sense, a little planning ahead so that the mistakes of the past wouldn't have to be repeated. *Temperance* had to do with pleasure; one should enjoy the things of this earth but not to excess. *Justice* meant the product manufactured by the legal system, but it also included individual acts of justice between individuals that might not be required by law, but seemed fair at the time. *Fortitude* had to do with holding fast, clinging, to a course once begun; it had nothing to do with being knocked down; it had everything to do with getting up and hewing to the line.

All of these were the virtues, one might fairly suppose, that reason revealed to the laurel-wreathed, curly-haired Roman emperors (as some have identified them) whose busts adorned the iron fence between the Sheldonian and the Clarendon buildings on the Broad — a patch of Oxford that Lewis could call Heaven, situated as it was between two great libraries (the Old Bodleian and the New Bodleian) and two public houses (the King's Arms and the White Horse).

Social Morality

Lewis made two points.

First, Christ didn't come to preach a new morality, although he had impressive enough credentials to do so. No, he reinforced the Golden Rule, a rule that even human reason could arrive at. At the western end of the Roman Empire, the Roman poet Horace clung to the *aurea mediocritas,* "the golden mean"; that was in the generation before Christ was born in the eastern part of the empire.

Second, the church, however defined, should have no political program for putting the Golden Rule into every civil and legal action. That was the duty of the well-informed Christians within the church.

Sexual Morality

Chastity was the most unpopular of all the Christian virtues invited to the party. In a way, she was reminiscent of Mary, one of the Bennett girls in Jane Austen's *Pride and Prejudice,* a favorite novel of Lewis's. She was, as Austen described her, "the only plain one in the family, worked hard for knowledge and accomplishments, was always impatient for display.... [But she] had neither genius nor taste; and though vanity had given her application, it had given her likewise a pedantic air and conceited manner."

For better or for worse, at least in Christianity, chastity was the belle of the ball. Which was another way of saying that, for the Christian at least, it was either marriage or abstinence. That was hard to do, Lewis conceded, given "our warped natures, the devils who tempt us, and all the contemporary propaganda for lust."

Christian Marriage

Marriage joined two persons into one organism. And the married couple functioning as one tended to reproduce images of themselves and aimed to remain faithful to the end. Lewis was to argue, as he will later in this book in another context, that the cross came before the crown. But in marriage, the crown came before the cross. Romantic love came before the drudge of everyday life and the trudge of everyday spirituality.

Sexual love outside of marriage Lewis called a "monstrosity." The participators stripped the sexual act from the rest of the marital pact, much as one would strip a tenderloin from a living cow. It was an inhumane, not to say ungodly, act.

Great Sin

The great canker, the great cancer, of the spiritual life was pride. It was the sin of Satan, the sin of Adam and Eve, and indeed the sin of the rest of humankind. But it wasn't the child's pride at being praised by a teacher. It wasn't a husband's being proud of his wife's accomplishments. It was really something quite different. It was a person's being consumed with the wonderfulness of his or her own self. First ones to know it were the person's family and business associates; last one to know was the prideful person himself or herself.

The really humble person has often been portrayed as a wheezy, queasy clerk in a Dickensian office, suffering from osteoporosis of body and soul. In reality, he or she was a rather affable person whom you'd either like or dislike. You'd like the person because he or she had some of the qualities you lacked. Or you'd dislike the person because he or she had all the qualities you lacked, and quickly you got the clammy feeling that he or she was crowding you, reproaching you, for the wretch that you truly were.

Theological Virtues

Unlike the moral or cardinal virtues, which are concerned with a person's duties as arrived at through reason and which are related only indirectly to God, the supernatural or theological virtues are gifts from God and have God as their object.

Faith. Faith generally meant accepting or regarding as true what one couldn't prove by reason or logic; in this case, the doctrines of Christianity. It sounded simple enough until the day came when, for one good reason or another, one felt one's faith becoming kind of wobbly. Here Lewis added a nuance. Faith was the grasping of a belief and a not-letting-go no matter what the ebb and flow of moods, the dawn and dusk of doubts. That sounded like fortitude, but it was rather more. Fortitude had to do with clinging to a course of action; faith had to do with holding one's focus on the object of one's belief; that was to say, God.

Knowing that the answer to the following question was "for a lifetime," one still had to ask, How long did one have to hold this focus? For a day would seem to be long enough. For a week would seem to be more than we can bear. For a month would seem to be far too long, for we've begun to feel that we're worse off than when we first began to believe in a serious fashion. What kind of a deal was this? A pretty good deal actually; before our conversion we didn't really know how bad off we were, how subject to temptation we were, how like a penguin we were when we paraded our humility.

Hope. Hope had several faces. To some it seemed to be escapism from the present and wishful thinking about the future; to others, it's a peering into the darkness toward the sound of the distant buoy. Which direction should the Christian turn?

Lewis discerned three possibilities.

First was the way of the fool. What one wanted was obtainable, but it was always just over the horizon — another wife, another job, another hobby — and once that was obtained, it too failed to satisfy. Once again it was over the horizon for, if not the rainbow, then for another pot of gold. The result was a daisy chain of frustrated desires.

Second was the way of the sensible disillusioned man. He was satisfied with what he'd got. He soldiered his way through the status quo until death dropped him in his tracks. Here Lewis pointed out for the umpteenth time that we didn't die at death; we lived on forever. The stiff upper lip just wasn't enough.

Third was the Christian Way. It suggested that we have desires whose satisfaction would come only in the next world. The slow-witted Christian replied that he didn't expect to spend the next world playing a harp or lyre; he'd rather be drinking a Harp lager in the local pub. The fast-witted Christian knew that all the symbols festooning Heaven in Scripture were just that, images, of ecstasy, infinity, power, joy. But the slow-witted Christian was still likely to think that "when Christ told us to be like doves, He meant that we were to lay eggs." Too many Harps, not enough harps!

Charity. When it came to charity Lewis focused on forgiveness by sketching out a parable of his own about the Two Neighbors. It was easy to love the Lovable Neighbor next door because she was a lovely person. But the person on the other side of your house might well be the Unlovable Neighbor. He'd thrown his garbage over the fence separating your property from his; he'd put razor blades inside the candy he offered your children; he'd tracked down your dogs and cats as though he were last of the big-game hunters.

But the Golden Rule, and indeed the Lord's Prayer, encouraged us to forgive the sins of the Unlovable Neighbor as we'd wish him to do ours. We didn't have to like our neighbor, but we did have to forgive him.

Jesus gave us some splendid examples of what he meant. At the same time as he was excoriating a sin, he was forgiving the sinner. Which might not be so hard as it looks. It was the sort of thing we did every day — and sometimes many times during a day — when we forgave ourselves for having made such a sinful botch of our lives.

Beyond Personality

After all the natural theology contained in his preceding talks, and all of the biblical references, Lewis felt the need to theologize. To him theology was a little like cartography. One could make a map of the terrain across which Christians had to travel to get from this world to the next. The features on that map were, of course, the doctrines, and over the centuries they've proven to be quite helpful to Christians on the holy trudge.

Making and Begetting

In particular, theologizing gave Lewis a somewhat clearer picture of the incarnation. God begat God, not in the way that two human beings came together to make a third, but in a way mysterious to humankind. Something like the way a sculptor, say, made a statue, but not quite the same. Greek myth had the sculptor Pygmalion fashion out of ivory such an idealistic, yet realistic, woman that he fell in love with it. He prayed to Venus; the goddess of love brought the statue to life; sculptor and sculpted lived happily ever after. "And that is precisely what Christianity is about. This world is a great sculptor's shop. We are the statues, and there is a rumor going round the shop that some of us are some day going to come to life."

Obstinate Toy Soldiers

Displayed at Blenheim Palace in Woodstock, a town some five miles from Oxford, is Winston Churchill's childhood collection of tin soldiers, regiments of them arranged in a glass case. There's no indication that Lewis ever saw this collection, but when he and his brother, Warren, were young, they had a brigade of their own.

What Lewis asked was, What would happen if those toy soldiers came to life? And suppose they didn't want to be turned into another substance, human flesh? Suppose they thought that the bloodshot eyes glaring down at them on the table had declared war on them, and they had to defend themselves. Suppose they expressed their displeasure at the transmogrification by shooting at the large creatures around them and sticking them with their — now real — bayonets?

On coming to life, in a minute's time the company of riflemen, meticulously painted in regimental colors, would move from a column into a hollow square. Swiftly, calmly, and without impediment, having practiced the maneuver so often that they could do it in their sleep. Three deep, the outermost prone, the middle on one knee, the innermost standing, all with rifles pointing outward toward the enemy, awaiting the order to fire. Giving that deadly order were the field officers, with drums and colors in the center of the enclosure.

Without answering the question, Lewis proposed that Jesus did indeed become man, no matter how great the descent, and instead of complaining about it, did the job he was sent for, suffering and dying for our sins. That was to say, Jesus became a tin soldier if only to urge the tin soldiers to become more like him. In theological terms, he became a son of man, and he urged us to becomes sons of God.

Let's Pretend

That Lewis had an active imagination, everyone would agree, but when he applied it to the incarnation, he came up with an extraordinary comparison based on two stories.

In *Beauty and the Beast* a raving young beauty was repelled by the looks of her companion; he had a sweet-sounding voice, but he looked like a boar or a grizzly. But such was the human voice sweetly sounding that she eventually gave his hairy hide a kiss. That did it; his animality dropped to the floor, revealing a young man as handsome as she was beautiful.

The other story, which Lewis didn't identify but smacks of *Phantom of the Opera,* was about a man who was ashamed of the hideous features he saw in the mirror. He bought the face mask of a handsome young man and wore it for many years. When he finally took it off, he saw in the mirror that the mask had refashioned his face into that of a handsome young man.

Both of these stories Lewis applied to the incarnation. He urged us to dress up like Christ, to do what He asked in the gospels, and eventually we'd become like Jesus.

Is Christianity Hard or Easy?

To be a Christian, according to Lewis, was both harder and easier than trying to be a decent chap. In the gospels Jesus said to take up the cross; after all, he took his up, and he carried it. At the same time he advised us to take up the yoke, to carry the burden, he promised that the yoke was easy and the burden light.

From his experience as a teacher, Lewis gave a homely example. The laziest boy in the class was also the one who'd work hardest in the end, having to cram round the clock for the exam to achieve only a passing understanding of the subject matter. The industrious boy, on the other hand, had studied all along and mastered the material with comparative ease.

Master the subject, that was what the Christian was supposed to do. Take all of Christianity, not just the attractive bits. Take on the Lord Jesus Christ, wear his garb, tramp in his steps, and he'd be with you, and you'd become like him, sons of God.

What It Means

Lewis didn't think much of the Spirit of the Age, at least as he found it expressed in the public's mind during his youth. When given a chance to express the perfect antidote to that Spirit, he chose to present the doctrines of the ages. In the radio talks he talked about what reason, the promulgator of natural revelation, told the honest person to think about values and behaviors. With only reason as their guide, some embraced the moral virtues and tried to put them into practice in their lives. But others, claiming that they were just nice, decent, ordinary chaps who wanted to be left alone — they sound a bit like Henry Higgins in George Bernard Shaw's *Pygmalion* — they never answered the door of their humble cottage for fear that morality was the knocker.

For this kind of chap Lewis didn't have much use. Nor did his friend J. B. Phillips, who in a series of radio talks for the Australian Broadcasting Commission in 1953 (which later appeared in book form under the title *Plain Christianity*,) had some discerning words to say about "the nice, kind, decent, honest people you know who make no religious pretensions of any kind."

"Of course I know quite a lot of such people too. But I really do think that there are three things which ought to be said quite kindly but firmly about good men without faith.

"The first is this, that I think you will find, as I have found, that in the life history of these nice good people there has usually been genuine Christian influence....

"The second difference that I must point out between 'nice people' and Christians is that the nice people have not really in practice *enough* 'niceness....'

"The third weakness of nice people without faith is that they have literally nothing to offer to those who are *not* nice people....

"You may think that I have been a bit hard about the nice, good, decent, kindly people who have no religious faith," Phillips concluded. "I certainly don't mean to be hard on them; indeed, I am extremely grateful that there are so many such people about. But for the reasons I have given, they don't really provide much hope for a wrongheaded and sinful world. Plain Christianity, on the other hand, does hold out hope for every man who is prepared to believe in Christ."

When Lewis finished with reason, he turned to the Scriptures, the promulgator of supernatural revelation, and began to unfurl the reigning doctrines of Christianity, centering all the time on Jesus Christ.

"What are we to make of Jesus Christ?"

A compiler-editor once asked Lewis to write some paragraphs on this subject for a book entitled *Asking Them Questions,* which was published by Oxford University Press in 1950.

There was a comic aspect to the question, Lewis thought. It was like asking a fly to comment on the elephant it was buzzing. But he went about trying to develop just such a commentary.

The one recurring answer to the question, and the favorite one of non-Christians, was that Jesus was a moral teacher par excellence.

The other, rather alarming, answer was that Jesus made claims no moral teacher had ever made. Not Buddha, not Socrates, not Allah, not Confucius.

If you went to Buddha and asked, "Are you the son of Bramah?" he'd say, "My son, you are still in the vale of illusion."

If you went to Socrates and asked, "Are you Zeus?" he'd laugh at you.

If you went to Mohammed and asked, "Are you Allah?" he'd rend his clothes and then cut your head off.

If you asked Confucius, "Are you Heaven?" he'd probably reply, "Remarks that are not in accordance with nature are in bad taste."

The idea of a great moral teacher saying what Christ said was out of the question. His were the claims either of a megalomaniac like Hitler or of the son of God himself.

"The only person who can say that sort of thing is either God or a complete lunatic suffering from that form of delusion which undermines the whole mind of man."

So much for what Lewis made of Jesus Christ. That much MCs should make of him also.

Sentences

"I think all Christians would agree with me," wrote Lewis in *Mere Christianity*, "if I said that though Christianity seems at first to be all about morality, all about duties and rules and guilt and virtue, yet it leads you on, out of all that, into something beyond. One has a glimpse of a country where they do not talk of those things, except perhaps as a joke. Everyone there is filled full with what we should call goodness as a mirror is filled with light. But they do not call it goodness. They do not call it anything. They are not thinking of it. They are too busy looking at the source from which it comes. But this is near the stage where the road passes over the rim of our world. No one's eyes can see very far beyond that: lots of people's eyes can see further than mine."

Scriptures

"Treat other people exactly as you would like to be treated by them," wrote the evangelist Matthew in 7:12; "this is the essence of all true religion."

"Treat men exactly as you would like them to treat you," echoed Luke in 6:31–35. "If you love only those who love you, what credit is that to you? Even sinners love those who love them! And if you do good only to those who do good to you, what credit is that to you? Even sinners do that. And if you lend only to those from whom you hope to get your money back, what credit is that to you? Even sinners lend to sinners and expect to get their money back. No, you are to love your *enemies* and do good and lend without hope of return. Your reward will be wonderful, and you will be sons of the most high. For he is kind to the ungrateful and the wicked!"

About Christian behavior in general, Paul had a great deal to say to the Romans (12:9–19). "Let us have no imitation Christian love. Let us have a genuine break with evil and a real devotion to good. Let us have real warm affection for one another as between brothers, and a willingness to let the other man have the credit. Let us not allow slackness to spoil our work and let us keep the fires of the spirit burning, as we do our work for the Lord. Base your happiness on your hope in Christ. When trials come, endure them patiently; steadfastly maintain the habit of prayer. Give freely to fellow-Christians in want, never grudging a meal or a bed to those who need them. And as for those who try to make your life a misery, bless them. Don't curse, bless. Share the happiness of those who are happy, and the sorrow of those who are sad. Live in harmony with each other. Don't become snobbish but take a real interest in ordinary people. Don't become set in your own opinions. Don't pay back a bad turn by a bad turn, to *anyone.* See that your public behavior is above criticism. As far as your responsibility goes, live at peace with everyone. Never take vengeance into your own hands, my dear friends; stand back and let God punish if he will."

In the language of the section about the toy soldiers, the Apostle Paul encouraged the Romans to put on the armor of the Lord Jesus Christ, the way that the Roman soldiery strapped on greaves and breastplates, swords and scutums, to swagger down the Via Flaminia as if they owned it. Lewis's friend J. B. Phillips put it this way when Englishing Romans 13:12–14:

"The night is nearly over, the day has almost dawned. Let us therefore fling away the things that men do in the dark, let us arm ourselves for the fight of the day! Let us live cleanly, as in the daylight, not in the 'delights' of getting drunk or playing with sex, nor yet in quarreling or jealousies. Let us be Christ's men from head to foot, and give no chances to the flesh to have its fling."

Readings

In presenting the arguments of Mere Christianity, I've had to paraphrase and festoon, condense and abridge, some of Lewis's wording. A close, and indeed a prayerful, reading of his text as it appears in *Mere Christianity* will correct the errors I may have made. Such a reading will also help firm up one's knowledge of what one must believe to become a Christian and what one must to do to remain a Christian.

Another way to approach the material in this chapter is to read it twice. Once through the eyes of Noël Coward; you'll see how often he chose the easier road, the road more traveled. And once through the eyes of Jack Lewis; you'll see how he chose the harder road, the road less traveled. Both men may be in Heaven, but the journey was the longer, the more perilous, for one of them.

A companion work to *Mere Christianity* (1952) may well be Phillips's *Plain Christianity* (1953) and is well worth a leisurely read. In it he gave three characteristics of the Plain Christian: "A kind of inward tranquillity." "An unquenchable gaiety of spirit." "A quality for which we can only use the word 'love.'" The MC would be pleased if these very same characteristics could be used to describe him or her.

Chapter 4

Buffoon

In the preceding chapter, Lewis talked about that shocking alternative to Jesus Christ: the Devil.

But did Lewis, whose adult life saw much of Protestant scholarship demythologizing the New Testament, really believe in the Devil?

That was a question asked of him many times. It presupposed, he'd say in reply, that there was "a power opposite to God and, like God, self-existent from all eternity." Put that way, the question was a false one.

He went on to point out that when one talked of the Devil, all too often he or she was talking about just such a separate but equal being. He was quick to remind us, as Charles Williams was to remind him, that Satan was at war, not with God, but with Michael; one archangel against another.

Did Lewis believe, then, in the Devils, and in their ability to do mischief to mortals?

He did believe, he said in the preface to the paperback edition of *The Screwtape Letters*, which he dated May 18, 1960.

"I believe in angels, and I believe that some of these, by the abuse of their free will, have become enemies to God and, as a corollary, to us."

His reason for believing in angels, bad ones as well as good, wasn't that they were found in the various Christian creeds.

"It agrees with the plain sense of Scripture, the tradition of Christendom, and the beliefs of most men at most times."

Writing about Angels

Lewis wrote much about angels, both good and bad, in the 1940s. *The Screwtape Letters, A Preface to "Paradise Lost,"* and *The Great Divorce* all saw the light of day during that decade. The question then arises, How did he describe Satan?

He did have precedents. . . .

Dante and Milton

Lewis could have described the Devil as the epic poets did. . . .

In fourteenth-century Italy, Dante Alighieri described Satan in the *Inferno*, thirty-four Cantos, one of the three parts of his *La divina commedia,* as emperor of the dolorous realm, frozen from the waist down in ice. On his shoulders was a head with three faces. Under each face was a pair of mighty wings the size of sea sails. His six eyes wept tears that ran down his countenance like rivulets down a glacier. Each mouth had a sinner in it, and each set of teeth ground the sinner to mastication.

In seventeenth-century England, John Milton described Satan in several grandiose ways in *Paradise Lost,* an epic poem in twelve books, which together with *Paradise Regained,* an epic poem in four books, comprised a poet's-eye view of salvation history. Here, under the nom de plume "Lucifer," the archfiend was limned as a reptilian chained to a burning lake. At moments, with Heaven's permission, he could slip his bonds to insinuate himself into the world at large where he bagged, with all too much frequency, a human lunch, and returned to the lake to enjoy it. Not that he enjoyed his catch. "Treble confusion, wrath and vengeance pour'd about his head." Apparently, he never got much beyond the condiments.

Rubens and Flandes

Or Lewis could have described Satan the way that Renaissance painters, engravers, and woodcutters did in works depicting the temptation of Christ.

One good example is a woodcut by Christoffel Jegher (1596–1653), a Fleming who often popularized designs by Peter Paul Rubens. Scene is the Mount of Temptation, a rise somewhere in the Judean wilderness. Our point of view is below two figures, close enough to eavesdrop on the conversation. A surprised Jesus turns toward an old man with lively beard and wiry eyebrows; his muscular arms thrust stout loaves toward the starving man. The two are locked in eye contact, and if we didn't know the outcome of the confrontation from the New Testament, we might fairly assume that Jesus had met his match.

Another good example is *The Temptation of Christ,* a canvas by another Fleming, Juan de Flandes (*floruit* 1496–1510). Approaching the peaceful Christ is a Devil cleverly disguised as a pious monk, perhaps more a friar, in a hairy habit cinctured with a rough rope. But Jesus needn't have been the Second Person of the Blessed Trinity to realize that something was wrong here. The holy man was sprouting a goatee on his chin and sporting goat horns in his tonsure; and as if these weren't enough, the bare-footed mendicant's toes were webbed: all painterly symbols of a devilish presence.

Luther and Loyola

Or Lewis could have described Satan the way that Reformation writers had in the sixteenth century....

Luther and Loyola were on opposing sides of that dreadful doctrinal conflict, but one thing they continued to agree upon, that there were Devils who weren't afraid to exercise their works and pomps....

Martin Luther was brought to his knees by a thunderstorm so severe that he propositioned St. Anne! For his life he'd give his life to the clergy. As happens with storms, it passed, but Luther followed his call. He took the Roman Church to task, and when the Roman Church wasn't properly responsive, he took some of the membership with him. Christendom was divided yet again, but Satan could take little consolation in that. Perpetual enmity toward him and his works and pomps remained in place in all of the divided parts.

In *Sermons on the Catechism* Luther preached on the Our Father. When he came to the sixth and seventh petitions — "And lead us not into temptation, but deliver us from evil" — he didn't treat the temptation of Christ, but the temptation of the ordinary Christian. "He tempts you by causing you to disregard God's word: Oh, I have to look after the beer and the malt, I can't go to hear a sermon; or if you do come to a church to hear the sermon, you go to sleep, you don't take it in, you have no delight, no love, no reverence for the Word. . . .

"Then, too, it is Satan's temptation when you are assailed by unbelief, diffidence, by fanatics, superstition, witchcraft, and the like. When you feel such temptations, go running to the Lord's Prayer!"

Ignatius Loyola, of minor Basque nobility and a military officer who'd taken a ball in the shin, underwent a conversion during his convalescence that deepened his spiritual life and resulted, eventually, in his attending the University of Paris and founding the Society of Jesus. In his masterwork, the *Spiritual Exercises*, now an ascetical classic, he laid out a meditation, entitled "The Two Standards," as though he were coordinator of a theological reenactment; in it he gave a classic description of Lucifer and his strategy; it has the ring of authenticity about it even today, as though it might just be another volume in the Osprey Military Campaign series.

"Imagine you see the chief of all the enemy in the vast plain about Babylon, seated on a great throne of fire and smoke, his appearance inspiring horror and terror.

"Consider how he summons innumerable demons, and scatters them, some to one city and some to another, throughout the whole world, so that no province, no place, no state of life, no individual is overlooked."

"Consider the address he makes to them, how he goads them on to lay snares for men and bind them with chains. First, they are to covet riches (as Satan himself is accustomed to do in most cases) that they may the more easily attain the empty honors of this world, and then come to overweening pride.

"The first step, then, will be riches, the second honor, third pride. From these three steps the evil one leads to all other vices."

Marlborough and Mephistopheles

Or Lewis could have written about Satan in military or dramatic metaphors.....

He could have combined something like Loyola's description with depictions found within five miles of Oxford, in the town of Woodstock. There, in Blenheim Palace, were the artistic records of the Duke of Marlborough's military successes at the beginning of the eighteenth century.

Parenthetically, they're on display to the public now, if not in Lewis's time; but Lewis could have seen similar ones in the Tate Gallery in London.

The medium was tapestry, floor-to-ceiling, and running sometimes the length of a wall, sometimes longer. Marlborough himself commissioned them; de Hondt designed them; de Vos was the weaver in Brussels.

In the Green Writing-Room, for example, the tapestry traveled down one wall, then turned at the corner to run to the fireplace. As the commemorative booklet describes it, "Marlborough in his hour of triumph as he accepts Marshall Tallard's surrender at the Battle of Blenheim (1705)." In his countenance, Marlborough reminds the MC of "the sovereign and true commander, Christ Our Lord," as Loyola described him, ready to face Satan/Lucifer in battle.

The visage may be princely, even Christlike, but Marlborough was no more generous in victory than Jesus. "Behind the grenadier with the captured French standard are burning watermills and a field dressing station; behind them the village of Blindheim (Blenheim) packed with French troops; and beyond that, in the far distance, the Danube, into which the allies are driving thousands of the enemy."

No, Lewis chose not to cast his Devil in the military mold. If there was to be a literary predecessor for his Devil, it would have to be Mephistopheles; he pursued the soul of Faust, only to lose it in the end. But in Goethe's hands the satanic figure has begun to mellow.

"It is Faust, not [Mephistopheles], who really exhibits the ruthless, sleepless, unsmiling concentration upon self which is the mark of Hell," wrote Lewis. "The humorous, civilized, sensible, adaptable Mephistopheles has helped to strengthen the illusion that evil is liberating."

Lewis thought this an error, at least an error he wasn't going to perpetuate when he came to write *Screwtape*.

Screwtape Proposes Test

It was July 14, 1940, a Sunday....

Detesting the liturgical music that he'd have to encounter at the sung Eucharist at 10:30 a.m., Lewis regularly kept holy the Sabbath by attending Communion at 8:00 a.m. at Holy Trinity, Headington. Perhaps during, but certainly after, the service, he got the image of a poor soul's making his life's pilgrimage escorted by a guardian angel on the one hand and on the other by a fallen angel.

As Lewis walked up the hill from Holy Trinity to the Kilns, the image developed into a story with characters. The soul would probably be as much like himself as John in *The Pilgrim's Regress*. The narrative would begin with the man still young. He'd be either an atheist or an agnostic, but theism would be fast approaching, followed not long after by conversion and commitment to a church. He'd have an overbearing mother not unlike Mrs. Moore, but unlike Lewis he'd eventually marry a nice Christian girl.

Back from the blood feast, as Mrs. Moore liked to call the Communion service, he went to his library and looked for his copy of *Confessions of a Well-meaning Woman* by Stephen McKenna. An epistolary novel published in 1922, it contained twelve letters from the heroine to a "friend of proved discretion." The letter-writer was humorless, but the work itself managed to be quite humorous; there seemed to be a moral chiaroscuro, the virtues seeming like vices and vice versa. Perhaps this was the sort of format that'd be appropriate for his story.

War, of course, would be raging, the story being set in the present. Germany had invaded Poland on September 1, 1939, and Hitler's forces were advancing quite nicely in other directions, England included. Lewis's young man would have to entertain such possibilities as patriotism and pacifism. Bombs would fall, death would be imminent, choices would have to be made. But the real battle would be taking place, not on British or European soil, but on spiritual firmament. Bad Angel was provoking battle with Good Angel. Instead of trying to create a melee of Miltonic proportions, Lewis decided to pitch the battle at a somewhat lower level.

"The idea," he wrote to his brother on July 20, "would be to give all the psychology of temptation from the other point of view." That not only would make the story more interesting but also would enable him to say something about the nature of Hell. Hell would have to be "something like the bureaucracy of a police state or the offices of a thoroughly nasty business concern" with "clean, carpeted, warm, and well-lighted offices" run "by quiet men in white collars and cut fingernails and smooth-shaven cheeks who do not need to raise their voice."

He then created a lowerarchy, which no doubt enjoyed the "miserific vision," and assigned specific tasks. Triptweeze, Toadpipe, and Scabtree were names that had a devilish ring about them. Tempters there would be: Glubose would harangue the young man's mother; Slumtrimpet would harass his wife. Slubgob — Dr. Slubgob, if you please — would head the Tempters' Training College, a polytechnic institution somewhat lower in scale and style than Oxford and Cambridge universities.

Wormwood, newly graduated from that ignoble institution, would be assigned to the nameless young man. For advice the stripling tempter would correspond with his uncle, a tempter of no small reputation, now elderly and retired, but able still to sign himself *His Abysmal Under Secretary, Screwtape, T.E., B.S., etc.* No special guest appearance by the Devil of Devils in this work, but Screwtape does make a pious reference or two to "Our Father Below."

No bombastic blitzkrieg here. No black chutes silkily descending; no boot-blackened faces laboriously crawling. Although spiritual warfare was always in effect whenever Satan and his minions rose to invade Flatland, and though a real-life Satan was already rocketing southern England nightly, Lewis meant his Screwtape and Wormwood to be non-combatants, rather dapper fellows albeit in a dull way, whose weaponry was less the fixed bayonet than the rolled bumbershoot. By the time he got through with them, they were also non-competents, just as transparent as Dante and Milton's Satan, Luther and Loyola's Lucifer.

Lewis took some notepaper, sat down at his desk, dipped his nib into the ink.

My dear Wormwood. . . .

It was as though he were writing to one of his friends. His pen fairly flew across the page.

The result was thirty-one letters, many of which were read to the Inklings, a group of academic friends, for their amusement and amendment. They were serialized in *The Guardian*, an Anglican weekly, from May 2 to November 28, 1941; published by Geoffrey Bles, London, in 1942 and by Macmillan, New York, in 1943; and they've been in print ever since.

The work brought him to the cover of *Time* magazine on the September 8, 1947, issue; probably working from photographs, cover artist Boris Artzybasheff did him up as an intense, even a handsome young man. To achieve an angelic effect, Artzybasheff swagged a massive seraph wing over his head, and on his shoulder he placed a Devil; yes, with goat whiskers and goat horns; as if these weren't enough, he added a satiny tail and a steely trident. The Devil's enormous nose I don't think was meant to be the artist's symbol of a diabolic presence; rather it was the Englishing of the Devil, what with the prodigious beak being a recognizable replica of the Duke of Wellington's proboscis; the field marshal who humbled Napoleon twice was called by the cartoonists of his time, invariably yet affectionately, "Nosey."

And there was a movie deal. In September 1948, acting as agent for Lewis, Bles entered into an option agreement with Twentieth Century-Fox Film Company. Signed to adapt "the novel about Hell" to the screen was playwright, scenarist, wife of the *Time* magazine founder and publisher, and recent convert to Catholicism Clare Boothe Luce.

"Clara Boot Lace?" asked Lewis when he heard.

She began in November, but in a month or two she had to

give up. By March 1949 Christopher Morley was inquiring if his screenplay, done in 1943, might not be acceptable.

In the meantime, and indeed since that time, the book has been bought not only by the pious few who've wanted to know what was happening within, but also by the impious many who had no idea what it was about but enjoyed it anyway.

And then there was the stage version in 1959. . . .

What are you going to call it? asked Lewis.

"Dear Wormwood," responded James Forsyth.

He and his wife had arrived at the Kilns, having been invited to tea. They apologized for being late, having miscalculated the time it would take them to drive from Sussex to Oxford. Lewis's wife Joy poured and passed the cakes.

Forsyth hastened to explain that his play *Heloise* had just closed in New York; the reason he was imposing on Lewis at this time was that the Dramatic Publishing Company in Chicago had asked him to dramatize *The Screwtape Letters*. He'd already approached Bles and Curtis Brown, both of whom said that Lewis was less than keen on dramatization.

That was correct, said Lewis, remembering how he had to reject radio dramatization of *Lion, Witch, Wardrobe* the year before; but he promised to listen with an open mind to what the playwright had to say.

After tea, Joy picked up her target rifle and invited Mrs. Forsyth to follow her out into the garden while the men talked. Mrs. Forsyth followed somewhat reluctantly, Mrs. Lewis having severely admonished her on the telephone not to be late for tea.

Picking up the cups and saucers, and urging Forsyth to collect the plates and silver, Lewis led the way to the kitchen.

"All right, treat the story in your own way," said Lewis, mopping the dishes with steaming water. "But why not use another name, another title?"

Forsyth wouldn't agree to that, nor could he; there was copyright to respect and royalty to be paid.

"But you will have trouble," said Lewis as they left the kitchen. "Doing anything with the Devil, you are sure to have trouble."

The wives returned from the garden, Joy leaning the rifle, unfired, much to Mrs. Forsyth's relief, against a bookcase.

"One thing the Devil can't stand," said Lewis, ushering the Forsyths to the door, "is humor."

The Devil as Buffoon

Inevitably, Lewis created a comic character. Indeed *The Screwtape Letters* is a comic work; "a comic novel" or "a comic epistolary novel" his fellow Inklings could easily have labeled it.

Adorning the front matter of *The Screwtape Letters* were two epigraphs — one from each side of the Reformation — telling that Lewis's comedy is very serious comedy indeed, serious in that it deals with the life-and-death issues in spirituality.

The first is from Martin Luther: "The best way to drive out the Devil, if he will not yield to texts of Scripture, is to jeer and flout him, for he cannot bear scorn."

The second, from Thomas More: "The Devil . . . the prowde spirite . . . cannot endure to be mocked."

This is the sort of comedy often found in medieval European drama. In the mystery, miracle, and morality plays, the Devil, if still a cosmic character, was becoming a comic character in baggy pants, who after a multitude of jokes and japes, all of which backfired, was sent scurrying off the scaffold with a good, swift kick in the arse.

And therein lies an incidental connection between Lewis's *Screwtape Letters* and Milton's *Paradise Lost*.

In a letter dated March 11, 1941, Lewis received an invitation from the principal of University College of North Wales to deliver the Ballard Matthews lectures that fall. Three lectures. Any subject. Three consecutive evenings. Lewis accepted and by October 30, 1941, Lewis had completed a book-length treatment on Milton's epic, running some sixty to seventy thousand words. From this manuscript he extracted the lectures, which he delivered on December 1–3, 1941.

Among the many points of interest on the Miltonic landscape, Lewis felt, was the character of Satan, who was, like his own Screwtape, something of a buffoon. Even in so magisterial a portrayal as *Paradise Lost,* Satan's predicament was a comic one. In Book V he attempted to maintain that he wasn't, as other Devils were, a dependent creature. He was independent, "self-dependent" as Lewis described him in the subsequent publication *A Preface to "Paradise Lost."* He too was an uncreated being.

"The quality of a created being is that it just finds itself existing, it knows not how or why. Yet at the same time, if a creature is silly enough to try to prove that it was not created, what is more natural than for it to say, 'Well, I wasn't there to see it being done'? Yet what more futile, since in thus admitting ignorance of its own beginnings, it proves that those beginnings lay outside itself? Satan falls instantly into this trap — as indeed he cannot help doing — and produces as proof of his self-existence what is really its disproof.

"But even this is not Nonsense enough. Uneasily shifting on the bed of Nonsense which he has made for himself, he then throws out the happy idea that 'fatal course' reproduced him, and finally, with a triumphant air, the theory that he sprouted from the soil like a vegetable. Thus, in twenty lines, the being too proud to admit derivation from God had come to rejoice in believing that he 'just grew' like Topsy or a turnip."

Incidentally, and perhaps even coincidentally, as good comic characters will, Satan and Screwtape stole the show. Milton's snookered the epic away from the central character, God Above, even though He-Must-Be-Obeyed had a fair number of pentameters devoted to his own works and pomps. And Lewis's burgled the novel away from its central character, "Our Father Below," who had the good sense not to appear in the work; and of course, Wormwood, whose own correspondence didn't survive, remains a shadowy, spidery figure on the fringe of the temptational process.

Screwtape to Wormwood

Perhaps it's appropriate here to give some samples of the sort of advice given by Uncle to Nephew.

On War

Consider . . . what undesirable deaths occur in wartime. Men are killed in places where they knew they might be killed and to which they go, if they are at all the Enemy's party, prepared. How much better for us if all *humans died in costly nursing homes amid doctors who lie, nurses who lie, as we have trained them, promising life to the dying, encouraging the belief that sickness excuses every indulgence, and even, if our workers know their job, withholding all suggestions of a priest lest it should betray to the sick man his true condition!*

On Anxiety

There is nothing like suspense and anxiety for barricading a human's mind against the Enemy. He wants me to be concerned with what they do; our business is to keep them thinking about what will happen to them.

On Lust

Never forget that when we are dealing with any pleasure in its healthy and satisfying form, we are, in a sense, on the Enemy's grounds. I know we have won many a soul through pleasure. All the same, it is His invention, not ours. He made the pleasures: all our research so far has not enabled us to produce one. All we can do is to encourage the humans to take the pleasures which our Enemy has produced, at times, or in ways, or in degrees, which He has forbidden.

On Worldly Companions

No doubt he must very soon realize that his own faith is in direct opposition to the assumptions on which all the conversation of his new friends is based. I don't think that matters much, provided that you can persuade him to postpone any open acknowledgment of the fact, and this, with the aid of shame, pride, modesty, and vanity will be easy to do."

On Humility

Your patient has become humble; have you drawn his attention to the fact? All virtues are less formidable to us once the man is aware that he has them, but this is specially true of humility. Catch him at the moment when he is really poor in spirit and smuggle into his mind the gratifying reflection, "By jove! I'm being humble," and almost immediately pride—pride at his own humility—will appear. If he awakes to the danger and tries to smother this new form of pride, make him proud of his attempt — and so on, through as many stages as you please. But don't try too long, for fear you awake his sense of humor and proportion, in which case he will merely laugh at you and go to bed.

On Gluttony

One of the great achievements of the last hundred years has been to deaden the human conscience on [Gluttony] so that by now you will hardly find a sermon preached or a conscience troubled about it in the whole length and breadth of Europe. This has largely been effected by concentrating our efforts on Gluttony of Delicacy, not Gluttony of Excess.

On Reinterpreting Jesus

A good many Christian-political writers think that Christianity began going wrong, and departing from the doctrine of its founder, at a very early stage. Now this idea must be used by us to encourage once again the conception of a "historical Jesus" to be found by clearing away later "accretions and perversions" and then to be contrasted with the whole Christian tradition.

In the last generation we promoted the construction of such a "historical Jesus" on liberal and humanitarian lines; we are now putting forward a new "historical" Jesus" on Marxian, catastrophic, and revolutionary lines. The advantages of these constructions, which we intend to change every thirty years or so, are manifold.

In the first place, they all tend to direct men's devotion to something which does not exist, for each "historical" Jesus is unhistorical. . . .

In the second place, all such constructions place the importance of their "historical Jesus" in some peculiar theory He is supposed to have promulgated. . . .

Our third aim is, by these constructions, to destroy the devotional life. . . .

And fourthly, beside being unhistorical in the Jesus it depicts, religion of this kind is false to history in another sense. No nation, and few individuals, are really brought into the Enemy's camp by the historical study of the biography of Jesus, simply as biography. . . .

So much for the subtlety of the temptational life as propounded by a master. Perhaps Lewis was a trifle too subtle, for the letters, while entertaining, can confound. Each statement needs decoding. One must first understand the literal meaning, then translate to the figurative meaning; the longer the context, the harder the translation.

But before we depart from the world of unwisdom, we should consider Screwtape's last appearance, in 1959, some twenty years after his creation. Lewis was asked to revive Screwtape in order that the *diabolus emeritus* might speak to the world on the eve of the 1960s.

Screwtape Proposes a Toast

"Mr. Principal, your Imminence, your Disgrace, my Thorns, Shadies, and Gentledevils. . . ."

Lewis couldn't bring himself to write another letter, but he could have Screwtape address the annual dinner of the Tempters' Training College for Young Devils. Dr. Slubgob, principal, would propose a toast to the guests; Screwtape, guest of honor, would rise to reply.

The banquet was a gastronomic disaster, said Screwtape, feasting as they were on "Anguish of Poor Souls." "Municipal Authority with Graft Sauce" was flavorless. "Casserole of Adulterers" was lukewarm. "Trade Unionist Stuffed with Sedition" was palatable, but barely so.

There were no great dishes such as the ones served at the banquets when he was a pupil; there was no "Farinata," no "Henry VIII," no "Adolf Hitler." "There was real crackling there; something to crunch; a rage, an egotism, a cruelty only just less robust than our own. It put up a delicious resistance to being devoured. It warmed your inwards when you'd got it down."

But, Screwtape was very quick to point out, "Is the dullness of your present fare not a very small price to pay for the delicious knowledge that His whole great experiment is petering out?"

As Lewis was writing, a longtime friend and university colleague dropped by for a visit and asked what he was doing.

Writing an article for the *Saturday Evening Post.*

How did he know what to write about or what to say?

"Oh, they have somehow got the idea that I am an unaccountably paradoxical dog, and they name the subject on which they want me to write; and they pay generously."

"And so you set to work and invent a few paradoxes?"

"Not a bit of it. What I do is to recall, as well as I can, what my mother used to say on the subject, eke it out with a few similar thoughts of my own, and so produce what would have been strict orthodoxy in about 1900. And this seems to them outrageously paradoxical, avant-garde stuff."

When they stopped laughing and his friend left, Lewis returned to the toast. He had Screwtape rehearse human history from the second half of the nineteenth century down to 1960, first distinguishing and then attacking varieties of liberty and democracy and such manifestations of social and educational theory as togetherness, being-like-folks, and I'm-as-good-as-you....

"Your Imminence, your Disgrace, my Thorns, Shadies, and Gentledevils: I give you the toast of — Principal Slubgob and the College!"

The "Toast" appeared in the December 19, 1959, issue of the *Saturday Evening Post*. The magazine paid handsomely, in American dollars; and Lewis put the money to good use, paying the mounting medical expenses at the Kilns.

Lewis might have joked with his friend about the sort of stuff he was writing — "discernment of spirits," Loyola might have called it — but he'd come by his knowledge of the inner workings of the soul honestly.

"Some have paid me an undeserved compliment," he wrote in 1960, "by supposing that my *Letters* were the ripe fruit of many years' study in moral and ascetic theology. They forgot that there is an equally reliable, though less creditable, way of learning how temptation works. 'My heart' — I need no other's — 'showeth me the wickedness of the ungodly.' "

What It Means

In Letter XI of the infernal correspondence, Screwtape instructs his errant nephew on the uses of human laughter in the tempter's trade. He doesn't speculate on how many Devils can trip the light fantastic (a Miltonic metaphor) on the point of a pin (a Thomistic metaphor), but he does distinguish four causes of laughter: *Joy, Fun, Joke Proper*, and *Flippancy.* But herein lies a philosophical error, that literary Devils are philosophical Devils.

Expecting the answer yes, I once asked American philosopher Mortimer Adler if there was humor in Heaven. Heavens no! he replied. Angels intuit; they don't have to think things through. No syllogisms for them; no enthymemes or epicheiremes; no sorites. Major premise, minor premise, conclusion, all are one. With regard to a joke, Adler explained, a philosophical angel would intuit the punch line before the shaggy joke got much beyond the first word. And the same would apply to a theological angel, I should think, a cherub or seraph, a principality or domination. Hence, Screwtape needn't have specified "human" laughter in his letter to Wormwood since all laughter is, by its very nature, human; that is to say, only humans can be joyful, funny, jocular, and flippant.

This philosophical error having been accounted for, I'll allow Screwtape to define his terms.

Joy

You will see [*Joy*] *among friends and lovers reunited on the eve of a holiday. Among adults some pretext in the way of Jokes is usually provided, but the facility with which the smallest witticisms produce laughter at such a time shows that they are not the real cause. What that real cause is we do not know. . . . Laughter of this kind does us no good and should always be discouraged. Besides, the phenomenon is of itself disgusting and a direct insult to the realism, dignity, and austerity of Hell.*

Fun

Fun is closely related to Joy — a sort of emotional froth arising from the play instinct. It is very little use to us. It can sometimes be used, of course, to divert humans from something else which the Enemy would like them to be feeling or doing: but in itself it has wholly undesirable tendencies; it promotes charity, courage, contentment, and many other evils.

Joke Proper

A thousand bawdy, or even blasphemous, jokes do not help toward a man's damnation so much as his discovery that almost anything he wants to do can be done, not only without the disapproval but with the admiration of his fellows, if only he can get itself treated as a Joke. And this temptation can be almost entirely hidden from your patient by that English seriousness about Humor. Any suggestion that there might be too much of it can be represented to him as "Puritanical" or as betraying a "lack of humor."

Flippancy

Flippancy is the best of all. In the first place it is very economical. Only a clever human being can make a real Joke about virtue, or indeed about anything else; any of them can be trained to talk as if virtue were funny. Among flippant people the Joke is always assumed to have been made. No one actually makes it; but every serious subject is discussed in a manner which implies that they have already found a ridiculous side to it.

If prolonged, the habit of Flippancy builds up around a man the finest armor plating against the Enemy that I know, and it is quite free from the danger inherent in the other sources of laughter. It is a thousand miles away from Joy; it deadens, instead of [sharpens], the intellect; and it excites no affection between those who practice it.

These four definitions, because they're descriptive, seem easy to understand. They're certainly amusing, entertaining, and in places hilarious, but are they the definitions of a bad angel? They sound like those of a very good angel indeed describing just how a very good "bad angel" works.

What Screwtape is talking about here, at least philosophically, is not causes (Joy, Fun, Joke Proper, Flippancy) or effects (laughter is but one of many possible effects) but comedy itself, of which Lewis was both critic and practitioner. Sad to say, nowhere, in any of his works, does he — or indeed any other spiritual writer in the history of the Western world — define comedy in relation to the spiritual life. In Lewis's life and works, however, such an application is supremely possible.

Before making the grand attempt, I think I must make several distinctions based on my own reading of Lewis and my own personal experience with comedy in a variety of forms, dramatic as well as literary.

First, comedy is always conservative in nature. It scourges the assumed inanity of the present by contrasting it with the presumed sanity of the past.

Second, comedy is always in bad taste. The comedian can't peek under a lady's hem or tweak a gentleman's hairpiece, then make a caustic if correct observation, and still expect to remain in good taste or good odor. The result on the one hand is disgust; on the other, laughter.

Third, comedy is always cruel. We laugh at the caustic comment because it's all too true, but there'll always be someone else within earshot to whom it's almost too true. It's like a feathery shaft to the heart. There's a whoosh, a thunk, and a slump to the floor, the glassy eyes having that "But-why-me? I-wasn't-doing-anything-to-hurt-you" sort of stare.

Fourth, comedy is always a mirror, not of our perfections, but of our imperfections. We live in an age of comedy, what with more comic novels and plays and films and television series than we know what to do with. We're constantly being bombarded by comic images of humankind on the hoof. We laugh outwardly, sometimes loudly, when the images are of other people, but we cry inwardly, uncontrollably, when the images are of ourselves.

Now to the application of comedy to the spiritual life.

In Letter XI and indeed in the entire correspondence, Lewis

seems to be saying, look to the comic, for therein one will see oneself. It's instantaneous recognition, a Polaroidal caught-in-the-act portrait of oneself. First thing we notice, however, is that the image in the polished mirror with the wavy surface is distorted. That's the imperfection. That's what needs improvement in one's spiritual life. "Vanity of vanities," saith Ecclesiastes in the Authorized Version, "all is vanity," and nowhere is this vanity better shown than in comedy.

Madam Eglantyne, the prioress in *The Canterbury Tales,* is vain about her table manners, ever applying the napkin to her upper lip. Malvolio, the gangly steward in *Twelfth Night,* is vain about his yellow stockings and crossed garters. The Rev. Mr. Collins in *Pride and Prejudice* is vain about his marriageability, believing that a young woman's public refusal is really a mask for her private acceptance.

Laugh at others, then. That's what Lewis would have us do not only in *Screwtape* but also in *Preface,* for it's to laugh at oneself.

Poet as Devil

In the 1940s the reigning literary critic and sometime poet was T. S. Eliot. He had no like for the Miltonic epic, but then this was only one of a long line of disagreements Lewis had with him.

In 1925 Lewis and his friends wrote parodies of the sort of poems that the young free-verse mongers like Eliot and his friend Ezra Pound were achieving some success with. Meter and rhyme and nature as a reliable source of imagery were going right down the drain. He tried to get the work published but failed to raise the money.

From time to time after that, Lewis submitted, but without success, poems of his own to *The Criterion,* a literary quarterly launched and edited by Eliot in 1922; it reigned until 1939 when, in Eliot's words, it expired in "a depression of spirits" induced by "the present state of public affairs."

Back to 1941. . . .

"If Mr. Eliot," wrote Lewis in *Preface,* "disdains the eagles and trumpets of epic poetry because the fashion of this world passes away, I honor him. But if he goes on to draw the conclusion that all poetry should have the penitential qualities of his own best work, I believe he is mistaken. . . ."

As far as Lewis was concerned, Eliot had taken Poetry against her will, laid her upon a table, anesthetized and hysterectomized her, then amputated her lovely limbs.

"Mr. Eliot may succeed in persuading the reading youth of England to have done with robes of purple and pavements of marble. But he will not therefore find them walking in sackcloth on floors of mud—he will only find them in smart, ugly suits, walking on rubberoid. . . ."

Wasn't this the garb that Wormwood and his fellow tempters wore as they padded about London seeking whom they might trip up?

Was Lewis insinuating here that such was the appropriate attire for a morbid free-versifier?

"It has all been tried before," Lewis concluded. "The older Puritans took away the maypoles and the mince pies; but they did not bring in the millennium, they only brought in the Restoration."

No Puritan, Lewis! Bring back the maypoles and mince pies, he seems to be saying.

Bring back the joy, the fun, the joke proper, the flippancy.

Bring back the baggy-pants Beelzebub, and let us toss the rancid vegetables at him and shout HOORAY when the other characters kick him in the arse.

Bring back the comedy that we may see ourselves and find our faults.

Only then can we truly see to the repenting.

Such laughter can also be found in a third work of Lewis's written in the 1940s.

Sentences

The Great Divorce

If William Blake could write about the marriage of Heaven and Hell, asked Lewis of Tolkien one spring morning in a pub, why couldn't he write about the divorce that would be sure to follow? The basis for the fictional work he had in mind was the *refrigerium*, a pleasant doctrine emanating from Prudentius in the fourth century to Jeremy Taylor in the seventeenth to the effect that the damned in Hell had holidays of sorts — one day a year — and could take excursions.

Where would the ghostly parolees go and what would they do? That depended on their imaginations. A few would queue up at a bus stop and take the omnibus up to the other place. Once there, some would haunt houses, spy on their children, play tricks on poor daft women who called themselves mediums. Others, literary ghosts, would hang about public libraries to see if anyone was still reading their books.

A perfect Hell, thought the Inklings to a man.

The beginning of the work was good, said Tolkien, but he wasn't so sure about the ending. What was Lewis going to call it?

Who Goes Home?

These were the words traditionally hollered in the House of Commons to clear the corridors before the building was locked for the night.

In chapter 10 there's a perfect example of how comedy in general — and in particular this comedy about some Lost Souls in Hell — can mirror human imperfections.

I should not dream of staying if I'm expected to meet Robert. I am ready to forgive him, of course. But anything more is quite impossible. How he comes to be here . . . but that is your affair. . . .

It was Thursday night in Trinity term, 1944. Lewis was reading a new chapter of his work-in-progress to the Inklings. A female ghost who'd made the excursion from Hell was talking about her late husband to one of the Bright Women, Hilda by name, on the plains of Heaven.

You always thought Robert could do no wrong. I know. Please don't interrupt for one moment. You haven't the faintest conception of what I went through with your dear Robert! The ingratitude! It was I who made a man of him! Sacrificed my whole life to him! And what was my reward? Absolute, utter selfishness. . . .

Lewis's brother, Warren, was acting as host, passing the liquid refreshment. Tolkien and Williams were there as well as

David Cecil and Dyson. Each was hoping that it wasn't their wife Lewis was characterizing, but each had contributed morsels from his own domestic situation to the wife's monologue.

No, but listen. He was pottering along on about six hundred a year when I married him. And mark my words, Hilda, he'd have been in that position to the day of his death if it hadn't been for me! It was I who had to drive him every step of the way. He hadn't a spark of ambition. It was like trying to lift a sack of coal. I had to positively nag him to take on that extra work in the other department, though it was really the beginning of everything for him. The laziness of men! He said, if you please, he couldn't work more than thirteen hours a day. . . .

"The Useless Quack," as Robert Havard, the Lewises's doctor, was often called, had rejoined the Inklings. The UQ was in naval uniform and sported a red beard. He'd been summoned back from the Far East to Oxford to do research on malaria. There were tears of laughter in his eyes as Lewis continued.

I used to spend simply hours arranging flowers to make that poky little house nice, and instead of thanking me, what do you think he said? Said he wished I wouldn't fill up the writing desk with them when he wanted to use it; and there was a perfectly frightful fuss one evening because I'd spilled one of the vases over some papers of his. It was all nonsense really because they weren't anything to do with his work. He had some silly idea of writing a book in those days . . . as if he could. I cured him of that in the end. . . .

Of all the men in the room, only Lewis and his brother were unmarried, but they weren't un-henpecked; Mrs. Moore had done her duty; nonetheless, Lewis seemed to be able, no doubt with a little help from his friends, to capture the exquisite agony of the educated man's being married to a woman with a light head and a heavy hand.

I believe I have changed my mind. I'll make them a fair offer, Hilda. I will not meet him if it means just meeting him and no more. But if I'm given a free hand, I'll take charge of him again. I will take up my burden once more. But I must have a free hand. With all the time one would have here, I believe I could make something of him. . . .

Hugo Dyson rose to prevent Lewis from giving poor Robert back to the hag he'd so mercifully escaped by a timely death.

Instead of calling it *Who Goes Home?* shouted Tolkien over the laughter, why not call it *Hugo's Home!*

In this rollicking passage, the Inklings recognized themselves, and no doubt we, the MCs, can recognize ourselves in it too. Our vanity has been exposed and ridiculed for what it is. Our urn is cracked, our helmet dented, our garters crossed, and yet we continue to think ourselves perfect. And so it is with all comedy, however scabrous. It's all too obvious what we have to do. We must see to the mending.

Scriptures

"Be self-controlled and vigilant always," writes J. B. Phillips, Englishing 1 Peter 5:8–10, "for your enemy the Devil is always about, prowling like a lion roaring for its prey. Resist him, standing firm in your faith, and remember that the strain is the same for all your fellow-Christians in other parts of the world. And after you have borne these sufferings a very little while, the God of all Grace, who has called you to share his eternal splendor through Christ, will himself make you whole and secure and strong."

"Your father is the devil, and what you are wanting to do is what your father longs to do," wrote John the Evangelist in 8:44, as it appears in J. B. Phillips's rendition. "He always was a murderer, and has never dealt with the truth, since the truth will have nothing to do with him. Whenever he tells a lie, he speaks in character, for he is a liar and the father of lies."

Readings

The Screwtape Letters and *Screwtape Proposes a Toast* are short works, available in paperback. They're funny, and they're instructive. Rereading may be necessary, though, in order to keep the chiaroscuro under control. Lewis had planned to include a good angel in the work; if he had, then we'd have no trouble with a figurative meaning that's sometime elusive.

There's an audio version, somewhat abridged (four of the thirty-one chapters have been omitted), featuring John Cleese as Screwtape. Cleese's magnificent inanities in such maladventures as *Monty Python* and *Fawlty Towers* have been the perfect preparation for portraying "His Abysmal Under Secretary." Available from Audio Literature, P.O. Box 7123, Berkeley, CA 94707-1502.

The Great Divorce is also available in paperback; it's a riotous novel that reads as though it were written yesterday

A Preface to "Paradise Lost" is out of print in both hardcover and paperback, but may still be found in college and university libraries. Second-hand bookshops are a good possibility. Its scholarship has been superseded by fresher, if not better, criticism.

Leaving behind the notion of the Devil as buffoon, I'd refer you to "Wormwood," a poem that originally appeared in *The Pilgrim's Regress* and eventually found its way into *Poems* and *Collected Poems*. It's a corrosive, not a congenial, picture of the devilish presence. Lewis's last line tells all. "Lord, open not too often my weak eyes to this."

Chapter 5

Trudge

The Christian's path through life Geoffrey Chaucer described as a pilgrimage in *The Canterbury Tales*, a work that fell into Lewis's purview as a professor of medieval literature. And so it would seem appropriate for me to describe Lewis's lifelong movement from conversion to death as something of a pilgrimage.

Lewis himself was something of a Harry Bailly, the publican who ran the Tabard Inn in Cheapside, Southwark. There, in 1390 or thereabouts, a motley group of pilgrims gathered to begin their pilgrimage to Canterbury. There they'd pay their respects to Thomas à Becket, the archbishop of Canterbury who was murdered in his own cathedral by King Henry II, his friend and king, in 1170; he was canonized three years later.

On the eve of the pilgrimage, the pilgrims were welcomed by Bailly, an affable this-worldly fellow who suggested that during the to-ing and fro-ing each pilgrim should tell a tale. He'd be the arbiter of the best tale; the pilgrim who didn't tell one would have to pick up the tab for the whole trip.

I could have chosen that as the model for Lewis's Christian passage as well as the meat of this chapter. He was a cofounder of the Inklings, a group of pilgrims who met weekly from 1930 to 1949 and on Tuesday mornings in a pub until Lewis's death in 1963. Ostensibly, since they were all literary gents, they agreed to talk about the literature within their specialties, but they spent more time talking about their own literary works-in-progress and about all sorts of other things that had no relevance whatsoever.

Of all the Inklings, Lewis probably attended the weekday meetings the most, and of the evening meetings he probably hosted the most. He read from *The Lion, the Witch, and the War-*

drobe; his brother, Warren, read from *The Splendid Century: Some Aspects of French Life in the Reign of Louis XIV;* Tolkien read from *The Hobbit;* Charles Williams read a nativity play entitled *The House by the Stable*. They dissected the spiritual life. They shared the joys and sorrows in the university as well as on the home front. They told inspiring tales, and some not-so-inspiring stories, the sort Chaucer's pilgrims amused each other with on the way to and from Canterbury. The following is credited to Lewis himself in 1950.

"There was a new waiter being instructed in a hotel by an old waiter as to his duties," Lewis said, launching into a story before they could ask about his wife's health. "And the most important thing, my boy, is tact."

"How do you mean, tact?" asked the new waiter.

"Well, I'll give you an example," said the old waiter. "A few days ago I went up to the bathroom to leave a fresh cake of soap — and there was a lady in the bath, who had forgotten to lock the door. So I said, 'A fresh cake of soap, sir,' and went straight out as if nothing were wrong."

"How are you getting on," asked the old waiter a week or two later, "particularly in the matter of tact?"

"Oh, splendidly," answered the young waiter. "I'll give you an example. A few mornings ago I took a tray of tea into the bridal suite, and there were the bride and bridegroom in bed together — in the very act. So I put down the tray by the bed and said, as I turned to go, 'Your early morning tea, gentlemen.' "

A Chaucerian story if there ever was one. Perfectly inane, one of the Inklings could easily say, and then spend an hour proving his case, for even inanity has its own perfection.

Yes, I could have made Lewis into a Harry Bailly, and his life-path as a Christian into a pilgrimage to modern-day Canterbury. And I could have inserted tales from the Inklings that would both have entertained but also instructed, telling how life was the earthly pilgrimage to the heavenly Jerusalem.

But I have chosen otherwise. For Lewis as well as for other modern Christians, all life is a trudge, and the pilgrimage itself is a trudge, whether on horse or on foot, in a Bentley or a Rolls-Royce. But it's chief characteristic is drudge. In Lewis's case that meant walking, marching, steadily, laboriously.

Physical Fatigue

In 1952 Easter fell on April 13; right after that Lewis boarded the train at Oxford and headed northwest to Malvern, where he was met by a former student of his. The following day they were driven a day's march from Malvern and let out.

They began to climb the hills, switching the pack every half-hour or so. His friend did the timing; Lewis wasn't comfortable with a timepiece.

They walked and rested periodically, flopping down on the turf for a soak — a term from Lewis's childhood meaning a moment when one could rest and be thoughtful — and for a cigarette.

Up again, they moved along the ridge and talked. His friend was a Catholic, now teaching at a boys' school he once attended. But Lewis the Anglican talked quite frankly and easily about his spiritual difficulties and personal temptations and about his brother, Warren's, increasing dependency on alcohol.

When it was time for lunch, they opened the pack and fell upon the sandwiches made by his friend's wife.

After another rest and another cigarette, they continued homeward. Not much talk now, Lewis reflecting that the trek had a poetic, even an anagogical, significance.

At home again, he penned a poem and appended the title, "Pilgrim's Problem." In it he described how he and his friend were traveling what they thought was a sure path, only to find themselves lost in late afternoon. Was the map wrong, or was it the map-reader? Heaven wasn't just ahead; only earth. But by faith they both knew that at the end of the path, if they could keep tramping that long, they'd indeed find their final destination.

Spiritual Fatigue

Trinity term 1942 having ended and examinations having been graded, Lewis sat in his rooms at Magdalen College during July, writing furiously on such subjects as how Christianity made a difference and what part pleasure played in the Christian life, on prickly virtues like chastity and humility, on satiny virtues like charity and hope.

He had already given two well-received series of talks on BBC radio. When he was asked to do a third, he refused at first. "Right and Wrong as a Clue to the Meaning of the Universe," broadcast in the summer of 1941, and "What Christians Believe," broadcast in the spring of 1942, swamped Lewis with letters, letters he felt obliged to answer. Sundays he spent on this task, reading as many as thirty-five missives and scribbling his reply on each. But he didn't have the time, he told the BBC, and he didn't have the postage. But yes, he said he'd do a third series.

Emerging at intervals from his rooms in New Buildings, Lewis made friends with a rabbit, one of a colony of coneys that had been recently introduced into the deer grove surrounding the structure. He picked leaves from the chestnut tree and offered them to the rabbit, who came timorously up to the human hand and nibbled away. "Oh! the great lollipop eyes and the twitching velvet nose!"

No matter how pressed by the unforgiving deadline, Lewis still spent an hour or so most mornings dealing with his voluminous mail from England and abroad. On one, to his godchild Sarah who lived near London, he scribbled a note that included a limerick about his velvety friend:

> A funny old man had a habit
> of giving a leaf to a rabbit.
> At first it was shy
> But then, by and by,
> It got rude and would stand up to grab it.

On July 20, Lewis finished the manuscript, which was composed of eight talks; he wrapped the packet and posted it off to the BBC. He should have felt relieved; instead he was drained. Even the cool air in the colonnade of New Buildings didn't help. His rabbit friend had disappeared days before; something must have disturbed his digestion. But when he returned, he cut Lewis dead, disdaining even the fattest leaves in the outstretched hand.

The doctrines Lewis had been expounding on paper for the past month had seemed so palpable, so plausible. Now they seemed so flat, so fantastic, so full of wishful thinking.

So much for apologetics, for defending the faith, he thought as he began to scribble what he would eventually entitle "Apologist's Evening Prayer." In it he seemed to say that when he talked about the faith, audiences laughed and even applauded. That felt good at first, but then it made him uneasy, that what he was really doing was spouting hot air, making unholy sounds as if he were a morris dancer with a pig's bladder on May Day. At the end of this prayerful poem, he implored the Lord of the straight and narrow to burst this bubble, to render him thin as thread lest he not fit through the needle's eye.

Lewis was quite a successful defender of the faith, able to get the better of an atheist in a public forum and able to quash an agnostic in a pub. He didn't play sports himself — he was too clumsy — but he did approach a verbal contest with a sportsman's attitude. He asked no quarter, and gave none. He was good, and he knew he was good, but was he too good for his own trousers? *Yes* was the answer that came to him. And hence this poem is a prayer, a plea to the Godhead to take the blare from his trumpet, the trumpery from his soul. A little silence was sometimes a good thing in a noisy man's life, and being snubbed by a rabbit was better still in a proud man's life.

Rudeness

It was 1948. Revising and expanding the Clark Lectures, which he'd given at Trinity College, Cambridge, in 1944, and which would form volume 3 of the *Oxford History of English Literature,* was a slow and grueling affair for Lewis. From time to time he gave a chapter to a friend for comment or commentary. He'd given "The Close of the Middle Ages in Scotland" to John Wain, a former pupil then teaching in the university; he'd given another to Tolkien. Wain returned his without comment, but Tolkien, in a sort of *furor scribendi,* responded at length and with heat, in prose and in verse.

Lewis was offended and replied, he hoped coolly, to the criticisms.

"I regret causing pain, even if and insofar as I had the right," wrote Tolkien on January 25, "and I am very sorry indeed still for having caused it quite excessively and unnecessarily." He held the longish letter for a week before sending it the few city blocks from Merton College to Magdalen. "Do me the great generosity of making me a present of the pains I have caused," he concluded, knowing that Lewis wouldn't be resentful and that he'd offer them to the Lord, "so that I may share in the good *you* put them to."

But Lewis caused pain in others in just the same way. A former pupil, and a new tutor himself when this incident happened, sent CSL a letter in which he disputed some important points Lewis made in his writing about the Bower of Bliss in Book II of *The Faerie Queene.* "Partly out of courtesy, but partly to provoke a response in case I had actually misunderstood him, I wrote to him about it, outlining what I intended to say. . . . Very soon I received a long reply, in which he refuted my argument (I think unconvincingly) in a rather dismissive way, so that I felt completely daunted. I don't mean that it was bullying, but it was overforceful and, as quite often I think also in speech, the tone seemed wrong. Yet he was at bottom a sensitive man."

Rejection

Christianity could cost one his career, Lewis had said on more than one occasion. Hot gospeling, as he was now somewhat ruefully calling his efforts at evangelizing, certainly seemed to have turned the electors of the Merton Professorship of English Literature against him; his name hadn't been mentioned the previous year in connection with the foundation of a new chair of literature. He'd been careful never to mention religion in lectures or tutorials, nor did he ever proselytize in his professional publications. But the Socratic, a university society cofounded by him with a view to pitting a Christian speaker against an atheist speaker on a contemporary topic, had won him enemies, and the specter of Screwtape bedeviled him right from the moment of creation.

Now, as he looked at the September 8, 1947, issue of *Time* magazine, he wondered how much more his feeble commitment to Christianity would cost him. He was on the cover. "Oxford's C. S. Lewis — His heresy: Christianity" read the caption; the cover story was to be found, not in the education section, but in the religion section.

"Don v. Devil" was the title of the story; it began on page 65 and ran, interspersed with ads for products like Polident and Tampax and for a movie starring Alan Ladd and Dorothy Lamour, to page 74. "I like monotony," the anonymous magazine writer quoted him as saying; at least the magazine got that right. And he was included with a growing band of heretics — Eliot and Auden, Dorothy L. Sayers and Graham Greene — intellectuals who believed in God; not a bad paradox. There were generous quotations from the *Broadcast Talks, The Pilgrim's Regress,* and *The Screwtape Letters.* The influence of George MacDonald and Charles Williams was acknowledged. And mention of the publication by the American Macmillan of the MacDonald anthology in the spring and *Miracles* in the fall was welcome.

"One of Lewis's severest critics insists that his works of scholarship, *The Allegory of Love* (on Spenser), and *A Preface to Paradise Lost,* are 'miles ahead' of any other literary criticism in England." This was the paragraph that gave Lewis pause. "But Lewis's Christianity, says his critic, has brought him more money than it ever brought Joan of Arc, and a lot more publicity than she enjoyed in her lifetime." How much more, O Lord? prayed Lewis as he continued to read slowly. "In contrast to his tight scholarly writing [says this critic], Lewis's Christian propaganda is cheap sophism: having lured his reader onto the straight highway of logic, Lewis then inveigles him down the garden path to orthodox theology."

How costly he was to learn.

The Oxford Professorship of Poetry was a position, founded in 1708 by Henry Birkenhead, that offered a stipend for lecturing. By the 1950s that stipend was £250 a year, for which the chair holder would have to deliver three lectures, judge the final entries for two annual university prizes, and every other year orate in Latin at the Encaenia ceremony. Cecil Maurice Bowra would conclude his five-year term in February. To succeed him, candidates were nominated, and campaigning by supporters was allowed. All the masters of arts of the university were eligible to vote, perhaps as many as thirty thousand of them; only a few would make the trip to Oxford for the actual voting on February 8.

The paper nominating Lewis was signed by most of the faculty at Magdalen and by most of the heads of the other colleges. But the cry went up that a poet, not a critic, should hold the chair this time. The names of Edmund Blunden and Cecil Day-Lewis were also put into nomination.

Campaigning for Day-Lewis, and indeed the one who encouraged him to stand for nomination, was a don who loathed Lewis. During the month of January, wearing jackets and slacks in shades of red and blue, Enid Starkie of Somerville College pedaled about Oxford, gathering support for her candidate. She even encouraged Blunden to withdraw on the ground that he'd split the vote for a poet. He did so, much to the amazement of Day-Lewis.

Campaigning for Lewis was Dyson. He walked through every open door in Oxford and opened not a few doors that were closed. "If they offered you sherry, you're done; they won't vote for you," he reported to the Inklings on Tuesday, January 30; "I had lots of sherry," he said sadly, and more than one person told him that he wouldn't vote for C. Screwtape-Lewis. By month's end Starkie had been able to erode Lewis's early lead, and the outcome of the election was a toss-up.

On Thursday, February 8, 1951, the MAs in the colleges voted clearly and easily for their choice as the next Oxford Professor of Poetry, but the MAs who journeyed to Oxford that day to cast their votes were confronted with a ballot on which the candidates' names were, but for one letter, identical; the telltale hyphen was missing; some of them just had to guess which name was their candidate. By nightfall 194 had voted for C. D. Lewis, and 173 for C. S. Lewis.

The atheist-Communist bloc voted him down, blustered Warren that night. He and Jack, together with Havard, Cecil,

Dyson, and J. A. W. Bennett, a fellow and tutor at Magdalen, were about to dine at the Royal Oxford Hotel when the news arrived.

So much for publishing all those poems in *Punch* under the initials N. W., said somebody.

One consolation, said somebody else, was that all the best people voted for Jack and only the "pentecostal sweepings bearing all sorts of Slav and Balkan names" voted for the other fellow.

If only Day-Lewis didn't look like "an ageing old-time musical comedy star off the stage," said Warren, "same soigne appearance, and same ravaged gray face."

Perhaps Jack should challenge Day-Lewis to a public poetry competition, the winner to take the chair fair and square.

It was simple, said Jack; there were political issues on both sides, and the greater number of votes won.

"In spite of our defeat," wrote Warren in his diary that night, "we had a merry dinner."

Deadly Sins

Lewis was not unfamiliar with the capital sins — or as they came to be known, the deadly sins — from literature. They could be found traipsing through the medieval literature of a number of countries, especially the morality plays in which vivid personifications of them ended up as characters, and entertaining ones at that.

Some Christian writers — Cyprian, Cassian, Columbanus, Alcuin — enumerated eight such sins. Gregory the Great in the sixth century and Thomas Aquinas in the thirteenth century listed seven of them: pride (*inanis gloria, superbia*), gluttony (*gula*), lust (*luxuria*), covetousness (*avaritia*), sloth (*tristitia, acedia*), envy (*invidia*), anger (*ira*).

Aquinas defined a capital sin as a vice (the Latin word is *vitium*) that had a decidedly alluring prospect. Advancing with all deliberate haste toward that delectable destination, a person must commit a Sing Sing of sins, all of which may be said to have sprung from that original capital sin.

Lewis felt that his capital sin, if any, was sloth, and he described it in a stanza of his poem "Deadly Sins":

> Sloth that would find out a bed
> Blind to morning, deaf to waking,
> Shuffling shall at last be led
> To the peace that knows no breaking.

Lewis was made familiar with the capital, or deadly, sins again in a personal way when he took a spiritual director, a Cowley father, who made them a point of departure for examining one's conscience.

At some moment after that, Lewis adopted the habit of noting down his offenses under one of the seven categories in his pocket diary, not by writing them out but by using a code.

Lewis made his first confession to this priest in the Michaelmas term, 1940, and continued the practice — a devotional one for Anglicans — for the rest of his life.

Pain

"Are not all lifelong friendships born at the moment when at last you meet another human being who has some inkling. . . ." It was Thursday night in Michaelmas term. Lewis was reading his latest composition to a roomful of friends, who were now referring to themselves as Inklings.

During the summer of 1939 he got a letter from Ashley Sampson, an editor at Geoffrey Bles, Ltd. He'd once had a press of his own, Centenary; Bles had bought it; now both Sampson and Bles were publishing, under a dual imprint, popular theological books with the series title "Christian Challenge."

Having read and indeed relished *The Pilgrim's Regress*, Sampson invited Lewis to write a book for the series on pain. It was an unpopular subject, he acknowledged, but an important one; he thought Lewis might just be equal to the impossible task of producing an attractive book.

Lewis agreed, but on one condition, that he write anonymously; he couldn't possibly live up to the principles he'd have to enunciate. Prefaces were created for no other purpose, replied Sampson, than to reveal the author in all his nakedness.

"When I think of pain," Lewis would insert somewhere in the manuscript, "of anxiety that gnaws like fire and loneliness that spreads out like a desert, and the heartbreaking routine of monotonous misery, or again of dull aches that blacken our whole landscape or sudden nauseating pains that knock a man's heart out at one blow, of pains that seem already intolerable and then are suddenly increased, of infuriating scorpion-stinging pains that startle into maniacal movement a man who seemed half dead with his previous tortures — it 'quite o'er-crows my spirit.' If I knew any way of escape, I would crawl through sewers to find it."

He began to plan the book almost immediately. He'd have to treat such divine attributes as omnipotence and goodness and such human realities as wickedness and pain in all its varieties. He'd refer to Aquinas's *Summa Theologica* and Luther's *Theologica Germanica*, to Kenneth Grahame's *Wind in the Willows* and James Jeans's *The Mysterious Universe*, to Traherne's *Centuries of Meditations* and Laws's *Serious Call to a Devout Life*. He'd mobilize such engines of rhetoric as syllogism and dilemma, analogy and antithesis.

The connection between pain and sin would surely have to be made, but it would be difficult to make it plausible to the casual Christian. The sense of sin so essential to Christianity seemed to have slipped in the last hundred years. Virtues like kindness and mercy were in the ascendant; rocketing from the depths of the new psychology were trajectiles like repression and inhibition. Their target, after the whistling had stopped and the plunge to earth begun, was the sense of shame so essential to Christianity. Once one of the ramparts of the human spirit, it was now considered a dangerous and mischievous thing.

What about animal pain? No one had treated that subject before in a serious book with theological pretension. Would there be animals in the afterlife?

Where will you put all the mosquitoes? Dyson would surely ask.

A Heaven for mosquitoes and a Hell for men could very conveniently be combined, Lewis could certainly retort.

What about Heaven? Scripture and tradition have habitually put the joys of Heaven into the scale against the sufferings of earth, he'd argue; no treatment of the problem of pain that didn't take this into account could be called a Christian one. "There have been times when I think we do not desire Heaven, but more often I find myself wondering whether, in our heart of hearts, we have ever desired anything else."

On Thursday, November 9, most of the Inklings were present. Dinner at the Eastgate, during which Dyson became "a roaring cataract of nonsense," was followed by retirement to rooms, where Tolkien read a section from his sequel to *The Hobbit;* Williams, who'd recently moved to Oxford, read his nativity play *The House by the Stable;* and Lewis gave them another dose of *Pain*.

On Thursday, November 30, only Lewis and Tolkien were free. That evening Lewis walked up High Street, turned left at Carfax, and walked down St. Aldate's for two blocks before turning right into the gatehouse of Pembroke College, where Tolkien was now a professorial fellow. The quadrangle walls were covered with Virginia creeper, leaves aflame from a late fall. Upstairs the two men sipped gin and lime juice and read, Tolkien from his new work that would bear the title *The Fellowship of the Ring,* Lewis again from *Pain*.

All the Inklings had heard at least one of the chapters of *Pain* read aloud, except Warren; he was now at the No. 3 Base Supply Depot at Le Havre, France. Jack kept him informed of affairs at the Kilns and of the minutes of the Inklings and was pleased to tell him that he was dedicating the book on pain to Inklings both near and far.

On Thursday, February 1, 1940, the Inklings met in Lewis's rooms. Havard, the doctor of more than one person present, read "a short paper on his clinical experiences of the effects of pain." No Inkling was experiencing pain that evening, rum having been served at the outset. "Pain provides an opportunity for heroism," concluded Havard; "the opportunity is seized with surprising frequency." The paper was approved.

Illness

His own and his wife's...

Jack's Illness

On Tuesday Warren visited the Acland and found his brother still in pain. He had a streptococcus infection, said Havard, and he was receiving an injection of penicillin every three hours. If he hadn't been so exhausted, he might have been able to fight off the germ. When he recovered, he had two choices, either to take a long vacation or to get another doctor. Back to the Kilns stormed Warren, where he gave Mrs. Moore what for, extracting from her a promise that Jack could take a month's vacation when he got better.

On Wednesday Warren found his brother feeling much better and broke the news that he'd have to take a vacation and that Mrs. Moore had already agreed to it. On Thursday Warren found him sitting up and reading *Captain Margaret,* a novel by Masefield, and chattering about its good and bad points. Warren walked back to Magdalen in high spirits, where he transacted Jack's university business and attended to the mail, even rejecting an invitation to a garden party at Buckingham Palace.

One June 21 Lewis wrote to Greeves that he was going home to Belfast for a much needed period of rest and recovery.

The next day Warren started drinking uncontrollably. By Sunday Lewis and the doctor were trying to get him to enter the hospital for a few days until he straightened out. On Friday, July 1, they took him by force to the Acland; the following morning the hospital called to say that Warren was uncontrollable and would have to leave. A psychiatrist would be seeing him and, if lucky, he could be transferred to the Warneford Hospital, where the surroundings were more secure.

Thus evanesced Lewis's vacation, but he saw in the terrible interruption yet another sign of God's grace. He wondered if he could survive too many more such signs of God's favor.

"Naturally, there is no question of a later Irish jaunt for me this year," wrote Lewis on July 2 to Greeves. "Don't imagine

I doubt for a moment that what God sends us must be sent in love and will all be for the best if we have grace to use it so. My *mind* doesn't waver on that point; my *feelings* sometimes do."

Joy's Illness

When cobwebs were lace and leaves were copper, when nights were cold almost to the point of frost, people called it St. Luke's summer, the apostle's feast day being October 18. None of this did Lewis see on the following day when he sped, fast as the Cantab Crawler, as the train was called, could carry him, from Cambridge to Oxford. All he could remember was the ominous telephone call to the effect that his friend Joy Gresham, who also lived in Headington, had been rushed to the hospital that very morning in great pain.

When he arrived in Headington and found the Wingfield-Morris Orthopaedic Hospital, he saw Havard first. Preliminary X-rays revealed that her left thighbone, what was left of it, had been broken; cancer was the culprit, devouring the femur like a starving worm. Did he know she had a lump on her breast?

How would he know that? asked Lewis without humor.

A biopsy would reveal whether or not it was malignant. And how long had it been since the woman underwent a full-scale gynecological examination? Husbands were supposed to know things like that.

But he wasn't her husband! Lewis wanted to shout. He was there, if anything, *in loco spousae.* But he didn't shout. He just entered her room. She seemed in good spirits. He told her what Havard had said about the biopsy.

So much for fibrositis and rheumatism, she said wryly; Havard made a ghastly mistake and would have to be replaced.

Whatever she wanted, he said.

She proceeded to tell him the most remarkable story. She was in such discomfort the night before — it was late, eleven o'clock or so — and she was walking about the house, wondering whether she should call him in Cambridge, when she tripped on the telephone cord. Trying to keep her balance, she heard something snap, as though she'd stepped on a twig, and fell to the floor with a scream.

Next thing she knew, she heard Kay Farrer's voice, asking if she were all right. The telephone was sprawled on the floor next to her. Kay had called the very moment she tripped, fearing that something was wrong with her friend. Now wasn't that a chapter right out of his book *Miracles?*

Havard had already explained everything to her, she said wearily, the pain beginning to return; she hoped the doctor, another doctor, would be able to cure her ills, all of them this time. She was sorry she was such a burden; how was he going to pay for all of this?

The hospital would surely bill Mrs. Gresham the American, he thought out loud, but if she were Mrs. C. S. Lewis, the British citizen, the hospital would send the bill to the government. He'd worry about that when the time came. Her medication was about to be renewed; he rose to leave.

Would she like something to read?

The Problem of Pain would be nice, she said with a smile.

Jack and Joy Together

On May 4 he described Joy, now his wife, as desperately ill to Pauline Baynes, a friend and illustrator of the *Chronicles of Narnia*. On May 8 he described her as a dying woman to Sister Madeleva and worried what he was going to do with two orphan stepsons. On May 12 he was able to write to Sister Penelope that Joy was recovering her strength and her appetite.

By the end of the month, however, he himself was howling and screaming with pain in his hip. Hastily summoned, the doctor diagnosed rheumatism at the very least, a slipped disc at the very most, and prescribed deep heat and a long rest.

By June 18 the trouble in his back had been reduced to a dull ache. By July 3 Joy was in no pain at all.

But the pain in his back flared up again. The doctor ordered him to the hospital, where X-rays were taken, bone marrow sampled, anus and rectum explored. Osteoporosis was revealed, a disease of the bones. It wasn't fatal, but it wasn't curable; it afflicted women mainly and in most cases was the precursor of senility. A board under the mattress was the only prescription and a surgical belt under the shirt.

It wasn't all tragedy, he was able to write on August 1 to a friend. Comedy shone through at times.

Grief

"Tonight all the hells of young grief have opened again; the mad words, the bitter resentment, the fluttering in the stomach, the nightmare unreality, the wallowed-in tears."

After three years of marriage, an August–October romance when it began, after the physical agony of cancer on her part and the sympathetic suffering on his part, after the shared intellectual and emotional ecstasy on both their parts, Helen Joy Davidman Lewis died on July 13, 1960.

She was at peace with God, she said moments before she died, but moments after, Lewis found himself like a boat adrift. No longer moored, he was lost in the fog, and he did what Everyman did, what all the epic characters in all the epic poems he had read and taught so well had done: he railed against the universe and the god of the universe, if such a personage did exist or had indeed ever existed.

He tried to console his two stepsons, but failed; he hugged them, but he was too embarrassed to speak to them. He slept some, but his dreams were nightmares. Even when he was awake, he walked around in a dreamlike state. She was cremated, with an Anglican priest-friend presiding — no music, just some words from the Book of Common Prayer. His emotions grew cold and numb as her remains were being reduced to warm ash.

With the rest of his life, Lewis wrote and read his way into and out of everything. His grief was no exception. He picked up a notebook and, like an undergraduate undergoing the ultimate test of faith, he began to scribble God-knew-what in the pages of the quizbook. Three months and three notebooks later, Lewis found that his grief had reached full expression and complete exhaustion.

Invigilating the test was the Divine Examiner, as it were, and he found his new pupil Lewis especially eloquent in the grieving arts, and he marked him accordingly. . . .

Yawning, queasiness, sleep without rest... *Alpha,* the highest mark.

His friends hadn't called, but then he hadn't notified them of her death... *Alpha.*

No good photographs of his wife to stare at, but in the first few weeks of his grief, he could still remember that she was his daughter, his mother, his pupil, his teacher, his subject, his sovereign, his trusty comrade, his friend, his shipmate, his fellow-soldier, his everything... *Alpha.*

An American, whom he hadn't seen in ten years and whom he had indeed forgotten, visited. During the visit in the parlor at the Eastgate Hotel, Lewis found that recollection of his friend improved rapidly, like a piece of exposed film developing. With Joy the opposite was happening; as time passed, her image, her voice, her leopard-like mind and her impala-like humor were dimming... *Alpha.*

Not only was his image of Joy disappearing, but his concept of God was contracting. The Divine Attributes, so copiously described by the medieval theologian-philosophers, failed to include what was so painfully obvious now: such titles as God the Bad, the Cosmic Sadist, the Spiteful Imbecile.... *Well, maybe not Alpha — Beta.*

At the beginning of September he invited Roger Lancelyn Green to spend a few days at the Kilns. He showed his young friend and future biographer the notebooks he had filled with random thoughts. Green immediately thought of publication. Lewis didn't want that; his only purpose was to exorcise the grief that was bedeviling him. What about publication under an assumed name? asked Green. After all, Lewis already had one, N. W., Nat Whilk, Anglo-Saxon for "I know not whom," which he'd been using in *Punch* and elsewhere. The only thing Lewis would have to do with the manuscript, besides having it typed, would be to change the names. Lewis said he'd think about it.

By November his grief was no more. At 4:00 p.m. on the 24th, he left Magdalene College, Cambridge, and walked toward Milton Street. He had been invited to tea by H. C. Chang. They had corresponded when Chang was lecturer in English at the University of Malaya in Singapore; when not many months before he was appointed lecturer in Chinese at Cambridge, he renewed the acquaintance in person.

At Chang's, Lewis bowed to the family and was introduced to several guests. Ever since he heard Lewis describe himself in his inaugural lecture as old Western man, said Chang, he'd considered himself as the example of old Eastern or old Chinese man. Mrs. Chang asked that she be excused if she burst into tears; she was just recovering from a long bout of postnatal depression.

He too had been subject to fits of tears, said Lewis to comfort her. Once, when he had completed a particularly difficult examination, seemingly for no reason, he began to blubber in a most embarrassing way. Even now, he said, reaching for his handkerchief, tears seemed to come without warning....

The notebooks were published the following year by Green's publisher, Faber and Faber Limited. Entitled *A Grief Observed*, the work was authored by one N. W. Clerk; republished in 1964, the year after his death, the author was listed as C. S. Lewis.

Grief over the loss of a loved one, Lewis seems to be saying, may shatter the windows, toss the furniture, nudge the earth's plates, but if one's own faith had been built firmly, the superstructure would remain, no matter how many the aftershocks.

What It Means

Not to put too fine a point on it, Lewis's life, although rich in wit and love and prayer, was nonetheless a trudge. In a poem entitled "As One Oldster to Another," written in his fifty-second year to an American of approximately the same age, he likened the Christian path through life to a night train, screaming through the stations toward the ultimate terminus, and he not knowing yet when to take down his case from the overhead rack.

What with fatigue of body and spirit, rudeness, rejection, deadly sins everywhere he put his feet, pains physical and spiritual, debilitating illness, and eventually death, the emotion Lewis felt most in life was drudge. Prayer helped, but just. In the end he too suffered, died, and was buried; in his case, under a larch in the graveyard surrounding Holy Trinity Church, Headington.

And so it is with the MC. Discovering the Christian path comes first. Faithfulness to the pathway comes next, even if the fog rolls in and one can't see much beyond one's nose. An Ordnance Survey map would help — its palette of pale colors always pleasing to the bleary eye — but where the Christian is ultimately heading, the crown surveyors have yet to map. Weariness dogs the MC's tracks. And if it weren't for moments of prayer and acts of belief — echoing the name of Jesus in the wilderness seemed to help — the MC would end up in a ditch, there to await the merciful arrival of death.

Without religion life on this earth can be made bearable. With religion life is acceptable. With Christianity life is hopeful. Keeping hope alive is the work of prayer. But more about prayer in the next chapter.

Sentences

"Just as the Christian has his moments when the clamor of this visible and audible world is so persistent and the whisper of the spiritual world so faint that faith and reason can hardly stick to their guns," wrote Lewis in an essay entitled "Religion: Reality or Substitute?" which appeared in the September–October issue of *World Dominion*, "so, as I well remember, the atheist too has his moments of shuddering misgiving, of an all but irresistible suspicion that old tales may after all be true, that something or someone from outside may at any moment break into his neat, explicable, mechanical universe.

"Believe in God, and you will have to face hours when it seems *obvious* that this material world is the only reality: disbelieve in Him, and you must face hours when this material world seems to shout at you that it is *not* all. No conviction, religious or irreligious, will, of itself, end once and for all this fifth-columnist in the soul. Only the practice of Faith resulting in the habit of Faith will gradually do that."

Scriptures

Psalms seem to help on the holy trudge. Coverdale's paraphrase as it appears in the Book of Common Prayer was a favorite source of refreshment to Lewis. The Twenty-third seems especially appropriate, with the Good Shepherd's shadowing the grim trudger every step of the way.

*The Lord is my shepherd; * therefore can I lack nothing.*

*He shall feed me in a green pasture, * and lead me forth beside the waters of comfort.*

*He shall convert my soul, * and bring me forth in the paths of righteousness for his Name's sake.*

*Yea, though I walk through the valley of the shadow of death, I will fear no evil; * for thou art with me; thy rod and thy staff comfort me.*

*Thou shalt prepare a table before me in the presence of them that trouble me; * thou hast anointed my head with oil, and my cup shall be full.*

*Surely thy loving-kindness and mercy shall follow me all the days of my life; * and I will dwell in the house of the Lord forever.*

Readings

Illuminating fatigue, both physical and spiritual, are two of Lewis's poems, "Pilgrim's Problem" and "Apologist's Evening Prayer." A meditative reading of them will reveal what they meant to Lewis and what they may come to mean to the MC.

As a writer might do about the capital offenses in the life of the soul, Lewis summarized them in a lyric poem entitled "Deadly Sins." The poem has an opening and a closing quatrain; each sin has its own four lines. In the last stanza, Lewis portrays the Godhead as pursuing his shattered foes inexorably. Which may seem odd. According to Lewis, the seven deadly sins, for all their attractiveness, eventually come apart at the seams.

I'd also recommend "Epitaph 14," a funny sonnet found in *Poems* and *Collected Poems* about death and dying. He imagined himself in a hospital ward with only a few minutes to live. The other patients were enjoying themselves listening to the pop music roaring from a wireless. Lewis asked that it be turned off so that he could die quietly, but the other blokes in the ward refused. The majority ruled, needless to say, and hence Lewis ended his poem abruptly, stating that he died "both for, and of, democracy."

Another poem, "Evolutionary Hymn," though it was born of pain, has a joyful note about it. Lying about on single beds in the same ground-floor room at the Kilns, unable to move much, Lewis and his wife let their imaginations gambol. He came up with an idea for a tongue-in-cheek poem about evolution; each successive verse, singable to the hymnody of "Lead us, heavenly father, lead us," sent them further into laughter.

And then there's *The Problem of Pain* (1940), in which the MC will find many arresting passages among Lewis's chapter-length treatments of divine omnipotence, divine goodness, human wickedness, the fall of man, human pain, hell, animal pain, and Heaven.

Chapter 6

Festoon

"Festooning," to Lewis as well as to us poor readers, means decorating with chains or wreaths, or with garlands composed of leaves or boughs, or indeed with any other decorative object likely to enliven a festive occasion. But "festooning" wasn't a word Lewis used often in his public and private papers, nor was it a word he seems to have used frequently in his lectures and addresses. Nor did the word have any resonance in the classic works Lewis read during his lifetime search for the perfect prayer. For such an undemonstrative person, then, who lived in such undecorated digs for most of his life and wore such unadorned and ill-fitting attire, "festooning" seemed such an odd choice to describe much of anything, let alone praying.

But when one looks closely into his life, one can find any number of incidents of festoonery. Festooning a tree, a painting, an event, a text, a letter, even his own attire. A look at these will give us some insight into the part festoonery played in the development of his imagination in general and in particular how it best described, if not praying, then at least how he himself prayed.

Festooning a Tree

On Christmas eve, 1929, Lewis with Mrs. Moore and Maureen walked to Magdalen. In the great hall there was an enormous tree, a roaring fire, and green boughs festooning mantles and lintels and sconces. They saw the hundreds of candles burning upright on the branches, dappling the stately portraits on the high walls. Carols — old English, medieval, Elizabethan — the choir sang a cappella and at will. At midnight the vice president of the college sent a message to the bell tower; the ringers began their peals. Sack — dry, light, strong — was passed around in a loving cup for sipping and pledging one's blessing to others.

Festooning a Painting

It was *Encaenia* — Wednesday in the ninth week of Trinity Term, 1928 — the day on which Oxford University commemorated its benefactors and bestowed honorary degrees. The procession began at 11:30 a.m. at the college of the vice chancellor, the university's chief administrative officer, and wound its way through the streets of Oxford.

Promptly at noon the procession entered the Sheldonian, once considered the grandest room in Europe. Its ceiling was a marvel of mechanics and mathematics: it measured seventy feet by eighty feet, and provided a pillarless hall accommodating fifteen hundred people on hard seats on the floor and in tiers around the walls.

As the degrees were handed out, Lewis's eyes drifted toward the ceiling whereon was painted an allegorical pageant entitled "Truth Descending upon the Arts and Sciences." What his eye saw, his imagination festooned. The allegorical characters in the painting above were in a frenzy of activity. Logick was arguing. Chyrurgery was dissecting a brain. Theology wanted Truth to help her open the Bible. Law was parading about with Records, Patents, and Evidences.

All the while three other characters were being tossed from the heavenly ceiling; they too deserved especial *festooning,* thought Lewis. Ignorance couldn't understand why nobody liked her. Rapine, dagger in one hand, torch in the other, dared anybody to come after her. Envy, with hag's breasts and snaky tresses, just plummeted hopelessly.

Festooning a Text

Hundreds of instances come to mind, but perhaps the most entertaining appears in his book *The Allegory of Love: A Study in*

Medieval Tradition, which was published in 1936. In it he analyzed *The Faerie Queene,* an agonizingly long allegorical romance in poetic form by Edmund Spenser, which was published at the end of the sixteenth century. Lewis was comparing the garden of Adonis with the Bower of Bliss, and within his comparison he singled out for special observation, and for a blatant bit of festoonery, some naked damsels who were capering about.

"Acrasia's two young women (their names are obviously Cissie and Flossie) are ducking and giggling in a bathing-pool for the benefit of a passer-by: a man does not need to go to faerie land to meet them."

Festooning His Attire

He dressed simply, thought Peter Bayley, who was a freshman at Oxford in 1940; he later became a colleague on the university faculty. In a memoir decades later, he noted that Lewis "usually wore a slightly too small Harris tweed jacket, of a rather hot brown, with all three buttons done up over his, at this time, rather stout figure. His gray flannel trousers were baggy and unpressed. He was large, but rather narrow shouldered and shapeless."

No festoonery at the haberdashery here!

This isn't to say that Lewis didn't dress up. Formal attire was required for any number of professional occasions, and he did the appropriate sartorial thing. On at least one occasion — I refer again to that *Encaenia* in 1928 — he found himself among the best-dressed men in Oxford as he processed through the streets of Oxford to the Sheldonian Theatre.

Ambling toward the end, among the masters of arts, in black calf-length gown with crimson-lined hood, sporting a square cap, was Lewis himself, noting how "few dons' faces are fit to bear up against the scarlet and blue and silver of their robes," himself included. *Cucullus non facit monachum* (The cowl does not a monk make) went the Latin saw, but the hood and the cap and the gown and the flying sleeve, Lewis seemed to be saying by way of festoon, certainly did the Oxford don make, himself included.

Festooning His Magdalen Rooms

His university rooms in New Buildings were, as Bayley described, "bare and dully and sparsely furnished. Apart from a large sofa and two arm chairs, I recall a poor dining table and some cheap dining chairs, just like those you would find in a not very well-off undergraduate's rooms."

Bayley remembered seeing "a reproduction of the National Gallery picture *The Origin of the Milky Way* by Tintoretto. It was the only picture in Lewis's rooms.... The point is that in a dull, soulless, unaesthetic college room, which was of noble proportions and could have been beautiful, the only cheering or beautiful object, except for a coal fire, was this alluringly erotic picture." Sad to say, Lewis has left no *festoon* about the Tintoretto.

Bayley felt there was another picture somewhere in the room. Walter Hooper has suggested that it might be a reproduction of Michelangelo's "Creation of Adam" from the ceiling of the Sistine Chapel; a favorite of Lewis's, he took it from Magdalen to Magdalene, that is to say, from Oxford to Cambridge, where he moved his collegiate things in 1954.

So much for his festooning of the walls of his university rooms. As for the carpet, it had been there forever. He and his chain-smoking friends used it as the ashtray of convenience whenever the Inklings met to read bits and bobs of their own works-in-progress and bash each other whenever they felt so critically inclined. Another literary group met there also to read Icelandic literature; *Kolbitar*, as it was called, was "an Icelandic word for old cronies who sit around the fire so close that they look as if they were biting the coals." And there were the "Beer & Beowulf" parties in which dons and undergraduates read portions of the three-thousand-line epic poem in Anglo-Saxon. Ashes were good for a carpet, Lewis stoutly festooned; it was something women had been slow to discover.

✣

So much for the presence of *festooning* in Lewis's life and how it functioned, malfunctioned, and sometimes didn't function at all. Suffice it to say, he was something of a stranger to festoonery, and it therefore it was something of a surprise that when he turned to prayer, the prayer he liked most was the prayer of festoon.

Festooning a Prayer

When Lewis began to pray as an adult, he used the "ready-made" prayers of his youth, which were the prayers of the centuries. But as he repeated the petitions contained in them over a long period of time, he found that he'd expanded the prayers. That is to say, he didn't add petitions to their own quite perfect symmetry, but he did add notes or sentiments that he came to regard as wreaths, garlands, ornaments, that is to say, as *festoons*. They didn't obliterate the plain, public sense of the petitions but were merely wreathed or garlanded or festooned round about them.

Festooning the Lord's Prayer

The formulation of the Our Father was an ancient one, the New Testament actually, and praying that, Lewis felt at one with the apostles and disciples of the first century of the Christian era, and indeed with Jesus himself who prayed the prayer to his Father in Heaven.

For example, when it came to praying "hallowed by thy name," he ornamented, garlanded, festooned the words with the notion that not only was he hallowing the Lord's name but also the angels and saints were hallowing at the same time. And in the hallowing, he was praying *with*, but not *to*, the angels and saints.

"Thy kingdom come" he festooned as the kingdom's coming not only into his heart but also into his college, into his country, into the world at large.

"Thy will be done" he festooned as the divine will sending him agreeables and disagreeables and expecting not only to accept God's will but also to do it.

"Our daily bread" he festooned with the notion to mean all the things necessary not only for the soul but also for the body.

"Forgive us . . . as we forgive" he festooned with the notion that he must not only forgive someone who has bullied him but also pray for those whom he himself has bullied.

"Lead us not into temptation" he festooned with the notion of being spared "from all crises, whether of temptation or affliction."

"The kingdom" he festooned as sovereignty de jure; "the power" as sovereignty de facto; and "the glory" as, well, the glory.

This is how he festooned his prayers, he wrote to the fictional Malcolm. But he didn't recommend it to his academic friend, or to his friend's wife, Betty, or to their son George who suffered from a gastric ailment, but he very well could have. It was a homely mode of praying not only for academic folk but also for the simple bloke on the dole or the lolly.

These and other festoons, as Lewis called them, were "the private overtones" he gave to the petitions in the Lord's Prayer. They were his and no one else's. Although he could tell his festoons to somebody else, chances were that the other person would have absolutely no idea what Lewis was talking about.

The Mechanics of Prayer

For most of his personal and professional life, Lewis was in and out of churches and chapels. Many of them dated back centuries and all of them had choir stalls, two ranks facing each other. That hearkened back to the time when the holy buildings were manned by the religious orders of men, and later of women. There they met several times daily for communal prayer, reciting the Divine Office throughout the day and night, beginning with Matins and Lauds long before dawn and ending up with Vespers and Compline long after dusk. When recited, the complete Office for a day of the year took ninety minutes; when sung, it took considerably longer. Franciscans, Benedictines, Carmelites, Augustinians all did this.

But with the coming of Ignatius Loyola in the sixteenth century, that changed. He campaigned the pope and the Vatican for a new sort of monk, one who'd recite the Office daily, but not together with his brothers and perhaps not even in his home city. For the new monk Loyola wanted mobility; he was a former soldier, and hence valued a monk's being able to move effectively from one fray to another. At the same time he wanted all the spiritual perquisites that cloistered and semi-cloistered monasticism had to offer. Again, as a military man, he wanted his soldiers to be as heavily armed with things spiritual as their coifed and biretta-ed counterparts were.

The upshot of this minor revolution was that the male religious priest — a Jesuit or a member of an order modeled on the Jesuits — could pray anywhere, and he could recite the Office anywhere, with or without company, with or without accompaniment. And if a member of a religious order could do that, then a layperson, whether male or female, could do the same.

Lewis has told us his own experience.

When to Pray

In the hurly-burly of everyday life, Lewis had to pray when he could. Outside of set times in set places, such as Magdalen College Chapel and Trinity Church in Headington Quarry, he preferred early in the day; the earlier, the better. Worse was to postpone his prayers until bedtime. Worst was to find himself in a strange hotel in an uncomfortable bed as he tried to prostrate himself before the divine tribunal! "My own plan," he wrote in *Letters to Malcolm: Chiefly on Prayer*, "is to seize any time, and place, however unsuitable, in preference to the last waking moment."

Where to Pray

When at Magdalen, his order of the day featured prayers in the chapel at set times. When traveling about, whether in the city or the country, he was never far from a church. But these massive unforgiving edifices were heated only during worship services. The stone was damp, and the plaster was rank. If his senses could endure, he collapsed into a pew to compose his soul.

At that precise moment, as if by conspiracy, there'd infallibly rise up either the throaty tones of the organ (it was practice day) or the swish-swash of a wet mop being passed across the sanctuary floor by a stout woman in elastic side-boots.

The work of the ambitious keyboarder and the industrious swabber were in and of themselves of a higher order of work than his own, Lewis had no trouble acknowledging to himself—after all, wasn't work, any work, a species of worship?—but he felt that they were drowning him out.

One exception to Lewis's oft-expressed aversion to entering cold, inhospitable houses of worship was his habit, in the 1930s, of visiting a random church when on a fifty-mile hike with his friends. For example, on an April weekend in 1930, he and three friends began a three-day tramp at Luccumbe.

One afternoon, at Stoke Pero, they stopped at a pub for tea. In the tiny hamlet there was also a little gray church without a tower that held no more than twenty people. Here, according to their excellent custom, Lewis and his fellow tramps sat wearily in the pews and spread out their mackintoshes to let the steam out of the linings. Then one of them approached the brass eagle lectern and read a chapter from the open Bible.

All of which is another way of saying that Lewis prayed where he could. Sitting on a bench in the park. Pacing up and down on a back street. Jouncing about on a rackety train.

With regard to trains, he once described how a clergyman liked to pray in a railway compartment, but only if he had it to himself. It was neither quiet nor noisy, but the clickety-clack of the wheels on the rails provided just the right amount of rhythmic distraction to make the prayer possible.

How to Pray

In chapel and church, Lewis's corpus knelt, stood, and sat as the rubrics of the Anglican Communion dictated. But the body was something like a family dog; it did what it was told, sometimes; but the obedience broke down, sometimes, no matter how harsh or insistent the command. And so it was with the soul. The soul wanted to pray, but the body wanted to chase rabbits or to sleep, or to eat, or to read a book.

Home-Made Prayers

So much for ready-made prayers. What about home-made prayers?

Lewis knew the tropes and figures of English, and indeed of Latin, Greek, Icelandic, Anglo-Saxon. For him language, whatever language, was something of a trampoline by which he could bound from one level of meaning to another, from the literal to the allegorical, from the tropological to the analogical, and back again.

But when it came to prayer, and indeed after many years of consistent and insistent prayer, he came to realize that words, often the pretty words of metaphor and simile, were nice, but that they weren't always necessary. It was no longer necessary, for example, always to beseech, or to besiege, the Godhead for favors desired. At times it was enough just to utter his name. Enough, eventually, to say only "Thou."

He put this sentiment into a poem of uncertain date, "Footnote to All Prayers." In it he went on to say that there was a certain blasphemy in prayer — and this surely was hyperbole on Lewis's part — in that it used symbols of human making; that humankind has clothed the Godhead with a Tussaud of litotes, anaphora, paranomasia. And yet it was an odd blasphemy; the very symbols themselves were encouraged by the Godhead himself who had sown them like seeds into the fertile soil of all language.

For all his life a man of many words, many meanings, Lewis knew that even in his own prayer he had created idols, linguistic idols perhaps, and that even this poem in which he tried to capture the very thought of the idolatry in prayerful words was an idol itself... and a bad one at that, when he compared the one speaking with the one spoken to.

It's a commonplace of human rhetoric, dating back at least to Aristotle, that every comparison — metaphor, simile, whatever — limps. (*Omnis comparatio claudicat* is the Latin formulation of it.) Every poem is a comparison of sorts, and as such, Lewis would be the first one to admit, every poem limps. Hence, in the final rhyming couplet of this lyric poem, he prays the Godhead to translate the infirm words of humankind into divine language.

In a simple, yet profound way, then, Lewis may be seen in this poem to prostrate himself before the Divine Linguist and offer in adoration his most precious treasure, his supreme mastery of the language of humankind.

Petitionary Prayer

Jesus in the Garden of Olives, praying that the cup offered to him by his Father — the cup of suffering, death, and resurrection — is an image known and treasured by us all, in print as well as in art and film.. But in the history of petitionary prayer, it certainly has to be the low point. The Father said no, even to the Son with whom he was well pleased, and the Son dutifully said yes to the horrific, if redemptive, acts required of him. But the rest of humankind, of whom very little has been required, plods on, hopefully petitioning the Godhead for everything in sight and a fair number of things out of sight, from sparing populations from famine to sparing the spotted owl from extinction. That having been said, four questions eventually arose in Lewis's mind.

Does Prayer Work?

By 1931 Lewis had come to grips with a sensible universe, a personal God, and the divinity of Jesus Christ. Then be began to regularize these beliefs by taking them seriously and putting them into daily practice. On Sundays he went to Holy Trinity Church, Headington Quarry, and took Holy Communion. It was only a matter of time before he confronted the proposition, Prayer may be good, but does it work?

The answer he propounded was a sensible one, a philosophical one. It was both no and yes. *No*, because Providence ran the universe and everything in it; hence, prayerful petitions from respectful underlings were nice but not necessary. *Yes*, because at least on earth it was possible to alter the course of events by a variety of strategies; and one would've been rash not to include among them petitioning the Godhead.

There was a certain poignancy to these thoughts, as he expounded them in a letter, dated February 21, 1932, to his brother, Warren, a member of the Royal Army Service Corps, billeted somewhere in Shanghai, experiencing the anxiety of a potential Japanese attack on the Chinese part of the city.

That same month Lewis addressed a long letter to Arthur Greeves. In their off-again on-again correspondence, which lasted a lifetime, they discussed all sorts of topics, from art to religion and back again. In this particular rambler, Lewis again put down his burgeoning thoughts about the efficacy of prayer. The simple reason? Greeves had asked Lewis to pray for him.

"When you ask me to 'pray for you,' " he responded, "I don't know if you are serious, but, the answer is, I do. It may not do you any good, but it does me a lot, for I cannot ask for any change to be made in you without finding that the very same needs to be made in me; which pulls me up and also by putting us all in the same boat checks any tendency to priggishness."

Do Hymns Work?

It has been commonplace, since the time of Ambrose, bishop of Milan in the fourth century, that he or she who sings, prays twice. Lewis, who wasn't a bishop, just a disinterested person in the pew, thought the opposite. He or she who sings in a church doesn't pray even once.

Lewis had somewhat churlish views on the subject, but Leonard Blake, editor of *English Church Music* (he was married to Mrs. Moore's daughter Maureen), asked him to put them into writing anyway for the April 1949 issue.

"Fewer, better, and shorter hymns" was the long of it. "Especially fewer" was the short of it.

Of course, Lewis had to admit that he had no musical education in his background. Neither could he claim a lifelong attendance at a hymn-singing church. Nor was he a member of the clergy. He was only a layperson (not only *laicus* but even *laicissimus*). But he also had to admit the basic idea behind music in church.

"It glorifies God by being excellent in its own kind; almost as the birds and flowers and the heavens themselves glorify him."

In every church, however, there were highbrows and lowbrows.

The priest or the organist was generally the highbrow, a person of "trained and delicate taste," who reveled in Palestrina.

The lowbrow was the "stupid and unmusical" layperson, who at best could carry a tune in a taproom.

If the former could tone down his esthetic appetite, and if the latter could believe that the music he didn't appreciate in church did indeed give glory to God, then perhaps there was hope.

In other words, when it came to the confines of the church, Lewis was a man of the Word, not a man of the melody, no matter how harmonious or cacophonous it was. "The case for abolishing all Church Music whatever," he wrote, "seems to me far stronger than the case for abolishing the difficult work of the trained choir and retaining the lusty roar of the congregation. Whatever doubts I feel about the spiritual value of the first, I feel at least equally about the spiritual value of the second."

In other words, if hymns worked, then they worked for people other than Lewis.

His brother, Warren, shared the same view, and often mouthed off about his dislike for sung prayer. One day in 1946 he did it in the Headington barbershop. Victor Drew, a troubled man in the best of times, draped the cloth over Warren's generous form, confiding that he himself found great comfort in the hymns he and his lady wife, a very frail woman in the best of times, sang in church of a Sunday. As Drew's scissors flashed and razor swiped, he quoted couplets from hymns that were so banal, Warren had to blush in embarrassment. Never again, Warren vowed as he went under the steaming towel, lucky enough to have escaped with only a few nicks on his exposed throat, would he dogmatize in public about how everyone hated hymns!

Is Prayer a One-Way Conversation?

In 1926, Lewis tutored Alan Richard Griffiths, a poor scholar at Magdalen College, eight years his junior. Griffiths was bright and unbelieving, at least when it came to English literature and theology, but he underwent a slow conversion to Roman Catholicism that he'd describe some years later in *The Golden String*.

During Griffiths's post-graduate years, they met infrequently, but corresponded with some regularity until, wonder of wonders, Griffiths got the idea that God was calling him to be a Benedictine monk.

In 1934 Griffiths professed vows of poverty, chastity, and obedience; they were simple vows, vows that could be canceled on request by either party. That was to say, but for the paperwork, he was free to leave Prinknash Priory if he wanted.

Three more years passed, and he decided it was in his best spiritual interest to spend the rest of his life as a monk. The community assembled in chapter and voted on his admittance. He easily received the required two-thirds majority. On Tuesday, December 21, 1937, he made his solemn profession as a Benedictine monk, which included a vow of "stability, conversion of life, and obedience."

Not long thereafter, he was appointed guestmaster at the priory. Since their founding in the sixth century, the Benedictines had raised to the level of a virtue an extraordinary hospitality to their visitors. Fourteen centuries later it was Griffiths's job to extend that very same hospitality to the weekenders, a trickle in winter, a torrent in summer. With these people, who were seeking refreshment of one sort or another, Dom Bede, as he was now called, was able to talk on everything from the most superficial to the deeply supernatural. All of the visitors needed help, and the help the Benedictines offered best was prayer and spiritual direction.

The correspondence between Lewis and Griffiths during this time was friendly but crusty. Griffiths the new Catholic wanted Lewis the old Anglican to abandon the religion of Henry VIII. Lewis demurred when it came to the theological issues; instead, he wanted to talk of what they both had in common, prayer. It was on this level that they communicated best. Lewis even sent him a poem about the dynamics of prayer that had about it a whiff of mysticism.

The letter of which the poem was part wasn't dated, but it was sent probably in 1931. This wording of the poem, when it appeared in *Poems* (1964) under the title "Prayer," had undergone some revision, but the sentiment was clear, that the one who prayed prayed the prayer of the Godhead. And hence if that prayer seemed like a one-way conversation, it was that both parties were saying the same prayer.

Speaking of one-way conversations...

What Lewis and Griffiths didn't share was how the division between the Churches of England and Rome might be healed. They were like two terriers tearing at opposite ends of a treasured towel.

"I feel that whenever two members of different communions succeed in sharing the spiritual life so far as they can now share it, and are thus forced to regard each other as Christians," wrote Lewis to Griffiths on April 29, 1938, "they are really helping on reunion by producing the conditions without which official reunion would be quite barren. I feel sure that this is the laymen's chief contribution to the task, and some of us here are being enabled to perform it.

"You, who are a priest and a theologian, are a different story; and on the purely natural and temperamental level there is, and always has been, a sort of tension between us two which prevents our doing much mutual good. We shall both be nicer, please God, in a better place. Meanwhile, you have my daily prayer and good wishes."

Should One Pray to the Saints?

Lewis, like much of Protestantdom, prayed for the living and for the dead, as Ephesians admonished; but he didn't pray, directly or indirectly, to the blessed in Heaven. When he looked at the way Roman Catholicism had developed prayer to the saints, he saw only silliness and excess. He did feel he had friends in Heaven, but he didn't feel he could prevail upon them to do a personal favor, spiritual or material. And the English church, which was founded in the second century of the Christian era but de-Romanized by Henry VIII in the sixteenth century, wasn't much help. Henry chose not to continue the practice of making new saints, but rather to develop the sainthood of all the faithful. What that meant in practice was that his minions, instead of imploring the saints as the clergy were exhorting them to do, went around the country pulverizing the heads of saints as their statues stood sentinel in the churches.

In the chapel at Magdalen College, Oxford, where Lewis often prayed, there's a towering screen, or reredos, behind the altar in which there are niches for twenty-four statues; these succumbed to the hammer blows of the sixteenth century but were restored in the twentieth. If not *to* these saints as a whole or to any one in particular, Lewis did pray *with* them to the object of all prayer, the Answerer of all petitions, the Godhead.

Consolation and Desolation

On roller-coastering, a universally experienced phenomenon in the spiritual life, Lewis gave his views in two letters.

The first was in Letter VIII of *The Screwtape Letters*, in which he described the Law of Undulation.

"Humans are amphibians — half spirit and half animal. (The Enemy's determination to produce such a revolting hybrid was one of the things that determined Our Father to withdraw his support from Him.) As spirits they belong to the eternal world, but as animals they inhabit time.

"This means that while their spirit can be directed to an eternal object, their bodies, passions, and imaginations are in continual change, for to be in time means to change. Their nearest approach to constancy, therefore, is undulation — the repeated return to a level from which they repeatedly fall back, a series of Troughs and Peaks.

"If you had watched your patient carefully, you would have seen this undulation in every department of his life — his interest in his work, his affection for his friends, his physical appetites, all go up and down. As long as he lives on earth, periods of emotional and bodily richness and liveliness will alternate with periods of numbness and poverty. The dryness and dullness through which your patient is now going are not, as you fondly suppose, your workmanship; they are merely a natural phenomenon, which will do us no good unless you make good use of it."

The second was contained in a letter, dated Sunday, April 3, 1949, to his godchild Sarah, who was being confirmed and receiving her first Holy Communion in the Anglican Church on the following Saturday.

"Our Lord will give us right feelings if He wishes — and then we must say Thank you."

He had to apologize that he couldn't be present himself. Ordinarily Saturday afternoon was free time for him, but he was looking after Mrs. Moore.

Coming to the end of her life at the Kilns, Janie King Askins Moore grew more crotchety with each passing hour. During the week Lewis had a housekeeper who helped with the old woman, but on the weekend he became "nurse, kennel-maid, woodcutter, butler, housemaid, and secretary all in one."

In the letter to Sarah, he enclosed a suitable check for the grand occasion, and with it he gave some godfatherly advice. At holy moments like confirmation and Communion, one shouldn't count on — or demand — holy feelings. It was classical spiritual advice about consolation and desolation.

Nevertheless, he continued, the holy things that do happen, like confirmation and Holy Communion, are real things, whether one feels them or not. If Our Lord gives good feelings, we have to thank him; and if he doesn't, well, one can't kick him in the shins. He'll give us the good feelings when he's good and ready.

Lewis revealed a bit of himself to her. For years after he'd become a regular at the Communion rails, he felt dry as dust; no holy feelings at all; just dreary distractions. But now, some seventeen or eighteen years later, he seems able to pray at Communion time.

In closing his letter to dear Sarah, he promised to mention her in his prayers every day, and especially on the coming Saturday.

"If [Our Lord] doesn't [give us right feelings] then we must say to ourselves (and Him) that He knows us best."

Four Diabolical Delusions about Prayer

"The best thing, where it is possible," writes Screwtape to Wormwood in Letter IV, "is to keep the patient from serious intention of praying altogether."

Screwtape had deluded himself into thinking he was the great tempter of the Western world. That, if nothing more, qualified him for a tenured position at Tempters' College.

He advised his nephew Wormwood, an undergraduate at the college, who was at the time on internship in London, how to delude a patient about that most deleterious element in the spiritual life, prayer.

There were four ways.

First, and most effective, turn everything upside down. That was to say, Wormwood should encourage the young man to whom he'd been assigned to dismiss the sort of praying he was brought up with — memorized formulas mindlessly recited an infinite number of times with no visible results.

Second, encourage the man toward something mature, something moody, something mystical. When one prays, one should feel good, feel noble, feel honorable; above all, feel prayerful. But the young man will never know the difference.

In this regard the learned Lewis had his infernal collegiate professor cite Samuel Taylor Coleridge. The nineteenth-century romantic poet and opium addict, according to his own admission, didn't pray "with moving lips and bended knees"; instead, he "composed his spirit to love" and indulged "a sense of supplication." In other words, wrote Screwtape to Wormwood, and thereby Lewis to reader, this sort of prayer never failed to delude. Unfortunately, the delusion never lasted long. Hence, the next step.

Third, turn the young man's gaze away from Heaven and toward himself. Let him pray for the prayerful feelings, and he'll be praying to the person he sees in the mirror. Screwtape could have cited the story of Narcissus here, but Lewis, quite conversant with Greek mythology, didn't put the words into Screwtape's pen.

Fourth, if all else fails, fatigue will slay the dragon-slayer God. Keep the patient active, hustling about, seeing too many people, reading too many books, attending too many plays... and he'll be too tired to pray. Or if he does begin to pray, he'll fall asleep.

Screwtape made it sound so simple, and Lewis, by virtue of writing a work from the diabolist point of view and thereby presenting the angelist point of view, made it sound so entertaining. But, as paradox, that handy figure of thought in the writer's trade, would have it, it's a deadly game.

"It is funny how mortals always picture us as putting things into their minds," wrote Screwtape in summary; "in reality our best work is done by keeping things out."

That's how it happened in Lewis's life....

What It Means

So much for Lewis's prayer life. What does it boil down to for us?

The MC can pray anywhere, anytime, in any position. That seems so obvious, but it bears repeating many times. And if one follows the advice, then one will find himself or herself praying in the oddest places.

Some prayers, ready-made prayers, have words, and the petitions in these prayers may be festooned with spiritual ornaments of one's own making; the way one festoons a Christmas tree; the way a daydream festoons an actual event; a drawing festoons a letter; a suit, a man; a rug, a floor; a tablecloth, a dinner table.

Other prayers have no words. They consist in affections of the soul; that is to say, they are acts of love, not words; the lover communing with the beloved. In a manner of speaking, they're festoons of the soul, adornments without the material things adorned. And it's but a hop, skip, and jump from adornment such as this to adoration.

Does prayer work? That's the powerful question all prayerful practitioners must ask themselves virtually every time they pray. When Jesus prayed for others, lepers leaped, paralytics pranced, the possessed smiled and made new friends, the newly dead arose from their cold sleep and asked for a nice warm meal. But when he prayed for himself, nothing happened. Does prayer work?

As in the natural life, so in the spiritual life, a little rain must fall. Things aren't better when one feels good about them; and they're not necessarily worse when one feels bad about them. And it's certainly all right if one has no feelings one way or the other.

The classical terminology of prayer denominates these ups and downs as consolation and desolation. And the spiritual masters have consistently said — and our spiritual experience has consistently proven to be true — that the one follows the other as night follows the day, and day follows the night.

But what about the volcanoes and hurricanoes? Can such irruptions and conniptions be considered a good for the geological part of creation and, at the same time and under the same aspect, as a devastating evil for that part of humankind who got caught camping out in the wrong place? Lewis hasn't a prayerful answer to that, nor indeed have the masters and mistresses of prayer before him.

Last of all, Lewis turns our minds to distraction in prayer, and distinguishes four kinds. There's no prayer without it if the one praying is of humankind. It's a natural flaw in a supernatural act, a brownish vein in the whitest cup, which shows that it's been used by humans and has suffered in the process. Screwtape made a game of it for Wormwood, but his awkward nephew was a slow learner. When all is said and done, temptation was, and is, a very deadly game.

One good thing about festoonery in prayer is that it's a mechanism, albeit a clumsy one, for turning the inevitable distractions in a highly active intellect and imagination like Lewis's into the very fabric of prayer itself.

Time was, in the history of prayer, when distractions were considered imperfections. Stories abound in ascetical literature about holy people being bedeviled by distractions during time of meditation. Such distractions inevitably had something to do with the problems they faced in everyday life. These men and women retaliated by ignoring such solutions as were presented during the meditation time. A noble strategy perhaps, but how many tactics in the turbulent history of the church have come a cropper because solutions were presented, willy-nilly, during prayer!

In fact, Lewis's notion of festoonery just might make sense to contemporary Western society when it comes to pray. The distractions are the prayer, and the pray-er can offer these distractions to the Lord much as the intellectually challenged lay brother in ascetical lore juggled oranges in front of the statue of Mary the mother of Jesus. It was what he did best, and Mary the mother of Jesus acted accordingly.

Sentences

"The prayer preceding all prayers," Lewis wrote in *Letters to Malcolm,* "is 'May it be the real I who speaks. May it be the real Thou that I speak to.' Infinitely various are the levels from which we pray. Emotional intensity is in itself no proof of spiritual depth. If we pray in terror, we shall pray earnestly; it only proves that terror is an earnest emotion. Only God Himself can let the bucket down to the depths in us. And, on the other side, He must constantly work as the iconoclast. Every idea of Him we form, He must in mercy shatter. The most blessed result of prayer would be to rise thinking 'But I never knew before. I never dreamed....' I suppose it was at such a moment that Thomas Aquinas said of all his own theology, 'It reminds me of straw.'"

Scriptures

"Be strong — not in yourselves but in the Lord, in the power of his boundless resource," wrote the Apostle Paul to the Ephesians in 6:10–18. "Put on God's complete armor so that you can successfully resist all the Devil's methods of attack. For our fight is not against any physical enemy: it is against organizations and powers that are spiritual. We are up against the unseen power that controls this dark world, and spiritual agents from the very headquarters of evil. Therefore you must wear the whole armor of God that you may be able to resist evil in its day of power, and that even when you have fought to a standstill you may still stand your ground. Take your stand then with truth as your belt, righteousness your breastplate, the gospel of peace firmly on your feet, salvation as your helmet, and in your hand the sword of the Spirit, the Word of God. Above all be sure you take faith as your shield, for it can quench every burning missile the enemy hurls at you. Pray at all times with every kind of spiritual prayer, keeping alert and persistent as you pray for all Christ's men and women."

Readings

Write about prayer always, Lewis could say, adapting the Apostle Paul, for one can find passages about prayer in most of Lewis's books and a great deal of his correspondence.

The best of what he's written is contained in *Letters to Malcolm: Chiefly on Prayer,* which was published in 1964, the year after his death. That the work has become something of a classic obscures the fact that, for at least a decade before, he'd attempted to begin just such a work.

"I am trying to write a book about private prayers for the use of the laity," he wrote to Don Giovanni Calabria on January 5, 1953, "especially for those who have been recently converted to the Christian faith and so far are without any sustained and regular habit of prayer. I tackled the job because I saw no doubt very beautiful books written on the subject of prayer for the religious but few which instruct tiros and those still babes (so to say) in the Faith."

The form seemed to be something a problem, until he thought of his own *Screwtape Letters.* An epistolary novel it was then, and the ink flowed almost in a continuous stream during March and April 1963.

"However badly needed a good book on prayer is," he wrote to Malcolm in Letter XII, "I shall never try to write it. Two people on the foothills comparing notes in private are all very well. But in a book one would inevitably seem to be attempting, not discussion, but instruction. And for me to offer the world instruction about prayer would be impudence."

Letters to Malcolm proved to be the perfect conveyance for his entertaining and instructive thoughts about prayer.

Reflections on the Psalms is, admittedly, short on the biblical scholarship of not only the twentieth century, but also the sixteenth. Lewis wanted to comment on the poetry of the Psalms; specifically, he wanted to comment on Miles Coverdale's rendition ("translation" is too strong a word) of the Psalms as it was found in the Anglican Book of Common Prayer.

"Even of the old translators he is by no means the most accurate," wrote Lewis in his introductory remarks; "and of course a sound modern scholar has more Hebrew in his little finger than poor Coverdale had in his whole body. But in beauty, in poetry, he, and St. Jerome, the great Latin translator, are beyond all whom I know."

For more about Coverdale, the reader may want to consult *English Literature in the Sixteenth Century, Excluding Drama,* Lewis's volume in the Oxford History of English Literature.

If not of scholarship, *Reflections on the Psalms* is a work of piety, full of the sort of festoonery that he described so well in *Letters to Malcolm.*

Chapter 7

Business

"Nasty business, this!"

That's how one detective chief inspector in Lewis's time greeted a particularly messy crime scene.

"This is a pretty piece of business!"

That's how another chief inspector hallooed the very same crime scene, what with "pretty" meaning "nasty."

And that's what many a Christian has yoicked when faced by the unpleasantness in his own life.

An example from Lewis's life presents itself.

As 1942 wound down, Lewis could look back at a year's worth of rheumatism, neuralgia, sinusitis. And what did the doctor recommend but Friar's Balsam, an inhalant composed of a bowl of boiling water from the kettle, doused with some powder. For twenty minutes a day, the patient had to bend over the bowl, his head tented by a towel, and breathe the offending fumes for as long as he could hold out. It'd clear his nasal passages, but at the same time it'd make him gag. And all the while Lewis's family, knowing he couldn't respond, had a field day with their farcical comments.

Nasty, yes, but nasty in the sense of Friar's Balsam's being a necessary medicament, whose application was sometimes hard, sometimes long.

When he was feeling better, Lewis would even go so far as to say the necessary nastiness was joyful. Joy was the central story of his life, he wrote in *Surprised by Joy.* It wasn't to be confused with Happiness or Pleasure or indeed with his wife, Helen Joy Davidman. It was as though his connection with the God Above was umbilical, not in the anatomical sense, although it did deliver nourishment and remove waste, but in a musical sense; it was a cord which, when plucked from above, sent shivers of satisfaction below.

So much for joy in this life, but he went further. "Joy," he had the temerity to write in *Letters to Malcolm*, "is the serious business of Heaven." That's as it may be for Lewis and Aldous Huxley and John F. Kennedy, all of whom died on November 22, 1963; they know for sure what the serious business of the afterlife is.

But what's the serious business here on earth?

What does it take for the Christian to scrape his soul?

Among the things that Lewis found spiritually helpful, especially when practiced regularly if not always enthusiastically, were ten bits of *nasty* or *pretty* — that is to say, *serious* — business: church-going, Bible-reading, and almsgiving; spiritual friendship, spiritual direction, and spiritual reading; confession and defending the faith; smuggling theology and good works.

SERIOUS BUSINESS #1
Church-Going

As a lifelong member of, first the Church of Ireland, then the Church of England, Lewis was never obliged to attend church. As a child his parents and elders made him go, but he stopped first chance he had. During the laborious process of conversion, which took more than a decade, he resumed his church-going, slowly, surely, finally taking Holy Communion. It was a personal choice both times, first not to attend, and then to attend and even participate.

The specific churches he attended in his adult life were the Magdalen Chapel in Oxford, Holy Trinity in Headington Quarry, and Magdalene Chapel in Cambridge. Much that went on inside these buildings — the liturgiology and the hymnology, for example — didn't please him.

With regard to the latter, or so he pretended, Lewis never heard a hymn that he liked.

With regard to the former, an article in the May 6, 1949, issue of the *Church Times* set him off. It argued that the liturgy might conveniently be lengthened for such things as "devotions to the Mother of God and to the hosts of heaven." He had to write a response. To lengthen a service by as much as ten minutes could throw out of whack the whole congregation's order of the day. As for the devotions, they weren't so much a matter of liturgiology as of doctrine; hence, they should be debated and accepted before being slipped in without notice.

And then there was the preaching. Lewis was rarely happy with what he heard from the Anglican pulpit, and I daresay the Anglican pulpit wasn't all that happy with him. His portraits of the Anglican clergy—Mr. Broad in *The Pilgrim's Regress* and Fr. Spike in *The Screwtape Letters*—were most unflattering. And in *Who Goes Home?* a.k.a. *The Great Divorce*, he sent an Anglican bishop who didn't believe in a literal Heaven or Hell to Hell.

But that really was Lewis's point. He'd heard Anglican priests preaching doctrine that wasn't Christianity, let alone Anglican Christianity; often what they were saying was either Roman or so broad, liberal, modern that it excluded the supernatural and thus ceased to be Christian. Boundary lines had to be drawn; priests who went to either extreme, however honestly they arrived there, should abandon their Anglican ministry.

When Lewis was invited to address some junior clergy in the Anglican Church at a meeting in Wales, he offered a few suggestions about what he'd like to hear from the pulpit.

First, people should be told about Christianity because it was true, not because it was likable or good for society.

Second, parishioners should be told that they had to face up to all of the elements of original Christianity, even the obscure and repulsive ones; "do not attempt to water Christianity down."

Third, the divinity of Christ should be preached even before going into the existence of God; odd sequence, it would seem, only that Lewis had it on good authority that thoroughgoing atheists were hard to find.

If Lewis didn't always find his three churches hospitable to his tastes, he could have sampled more. But that was a trap, as he had Screwtape explain to Wormwood. "If a man can't be cured of churchgoing, the next best thing is to send him all over the neighborhood looking for the church that 'suits' him until he becomes a taster or connoisseur of churches."

What meaning for the MC does Lewis's own experience have?

Liturgiology, hymnology, sermonology aside, Lewis would advise something like the following. Attendance in church is better than non-attendance. Regular churchgoing is better than irregular churchgoing. Participation in the services in whatever manner is best of all. But bad hymns and bad sermons? Better none at all.

Choose, Lewis would say. Choose to attend church. Choose to participate in the service, whatever that service is. Why? I'd answer for Lewis by asking, Why would a MC want to limit the occasions that God could cozy up to a soul?

The same advice would apply to those MCs for whom Sunday observance is mandatory. Go, Lewis would say, and don't act like a cabbage.

SERIOUS BUSINESS #2
Bible-Reading

According to Guigo II, a twelfth-century Carthusian monk who was prior of the Grande Chartreuse in France, there was a device by which "monks . . . [were] lifted up from earth to heaven." It was a long ladder with but four rungs, the first of which was reading the Scriptures.

"I hear the words read: 'Blessed are the pure in heart, for they shall see God,'" he wrote. "This is a short text of Scripture, but it is of great sweetness, like a grape that is put into the mouth filled with many senses to feed the soul."

Second rung was meditating on the scriptural text; that is to say, ruminating on the meaning of the text to see if there is some relevance to the reader.

Third was praying the scriptural text; that is to say, asking for the grace of the text as a means to draw closer to God.

Fourth was contemplating the scriptural text; that is to say, fixing one's gaze on the text as though it were a window through which as the breeze parts the curtain one might get a glimpse at the Divine; or, as though it were a mirror in which one saw oneself, through which God saw you.

So much for the four rungs on the one ladder. In practice,

there is but one rung on the ladder, all the activity — reading, meditating, praying, contemplating — taking place at the same time, and barely if at all discernible the one from the other.

But what kind of ladder is it that has two side rails but only one rung?

A mystical ladder.

In the thirteenth century Dominicans and Franciscans established houses of study in Oxford and chanted the Divine Office. That is to say, they sang, or read, the Scriptures, Psalms, and a variety of traditional prayers virtually all day and all night, with suitable intervals for the necessities of life and the teaching of theology. At the Reformation the Anglican Church condensed the Divine Office into Morning and Evening Prayer. This was how Lewis began his prayer life as an adult. This was what his devotional reading of the Scriptures consisted of.

His particular devotional favorite was the Psalms. During the course of a month, the Psalter would be recited in its entirety. As for reading the Psalms himself — they were honied poems to him in the Coverdale rendition — he paused where he willed, entertaining a word here, a phrase there, until suddenly he found himself in deep prayer. *Lectio divina* the fathers of the church called it; praying through reading.

It wasn't surprising, then, that he should put his devotional observations into book form. *Reflections on the Psalms* was published in 1958, the same month the archbishop of Canterbury invited him to become a member of the Commission to Revise the Psalter. T. S. Eliot was also a member, and no doubt when the commission met, they prayed together.

As for the validity of the Bible as a revelational document, Lewis could make himself quite clear, as he did on July 19, 1943, during a panel discussion recorded for broadcast on July 22. *The Anvil,* as the program was called, was a sort of Christian "Brains Trust," a BBC program to which listeners could write the sort of questions they felt reluctant to ask the clergy. Lewis was one of four guests. The host's fourth question exercised him the most. Wasn't the Bible partly fiction?

He didn't know this to be true, replied Lewis, but, of course, he wasn't a biblical scholar.

"All I am in private life is a literary critic and historian;

that's my job. And I'm prepared to say on that basis, if anyone thinks the gospels are either legends or novels, then that person is simply showing his incompetence as a literary critic.

"I've read a great many novels, and I know a fair amount about legends that grew up among early people, and I know perfectly well the gospels are not that kind of stuff. They're absolutely full of the sort of things that don't come into legends."

As for what language to read the Bible in, Lewis was quite flexible. He read the New Testament in the Septuagint Greek and the Vulgate Latin. He relished Miles Coverdale's rendition of the Hebrew Old Testament into sixteenth-century English. And of course, professionally as well as personally, he was soaked in the Authorized King James version, which debuted at the beginning of the seventeenth century.

But what about the twentieth century for himself and others? He admired the Bible translations of the Church of Scotland's James Moffatt and the Church of Rome's Ronald Knox. Moffatt taught briefly at Oxford in 1913 and 1914 as his New Testament was being published. Knox was educated at Balliol in the first decade of the century and spent a number of years as chaplain to the student body, first as an Anglican then as a Roman; his Englishing of the New Testament appeared serially in the early 1940s; in its entirety, in 1945; the Old Testament, in 1949. And so Lewis was quite prepared for the piece of mail that arrived one morning in 1943.

In the packet he found a letter-cum-manuscript from J. B. Phillips, vicar of the Church of the Good Shepherd in London. He didn't know the man, but the vicar said some nice things about his books and broadcasts. As for the enclosed manuscript, well, with bombs falling and sirens wailing and buildings collapsing all about, London was not unlike first-century Rome, at least for Christians. Paul's epistles seemed right to the point. Trouble was, however, that the young people in his parish couldn't understand the Authorized Version. What they needed was something just a little easier to read. Hence, his own attempt at Colossians. What did he think?

Lewis thought he knew Colossians pretty well, but the paraphrase, for that was what it was, seemed to hit it right on the nail. He then read the Phillips version from beginning to end.

It was like seeing a painting in the Tate or the National Gallery after it had been restored to its original luster, Lewis wrote on August 3 to Phillips, and he encouraged the vicar to continue his work through the rest of the epistles and to ignore the attacks that would be sure to come from the devotees of the Authorized Version, defenders to their death of an antique literary document; these were the same people who complained about the contemporaneity of the dialogue in Dorothy L. Sayers's *The Man Born to Be King,* a play cycle based on the gospels and broadcast on BBC radio.

Phillips sent him each epistle as he finished it. Once the twenty-one epistles were completed, Lewis suggested a title for the work, *Letters to Young Churches,* and cadged Geoffrey Bles into publishing the work by offering to write an introduction.

"It would have saved me a great deal of labor if this book had come into my hands when I first seriously began to try to discover what Christianity was."

What does Lewis's experience with the Bible mean to the MC of today?

Reading the Bible is praying. Reading the Bible is listening. How much easier can it possibly be for the MC to hear the word of God? And there's just the possibility that a conversation may strike up.

But the MC can't pray in this way unless he or she can read and understand what's been read. When it came to reading a complex work like the Bible, the easier it was to read, the better. Which is another way of saying that both blighters and blokes need a paraphrase that appeals to their sensibilities as well as the collegians and academicians need an annotated translation. Fortunately for all, at the end of the twentieth century there are more than enough of each to suit the finickiest taste.

A caustic question.

Which church does the Bible more and which church does the Bible better, the liturgy-oriented one or the Bible-oriented one?

A cautionary answer.

Wherever read, wherever reverenced, the Bible gives Screwtape the hives.

A candid question.

Isn't Bible reading really distinct from Bible study?

A careful answer.

Bible study peruses the Scriptures with a view to the reader's mastering the text, underlining, highlighting, consuming the text in the way that Cicero thought one should read any book; that is to say, by masticating and ultimately digesting the text, by making it one's own. That's also what the Collect for the Second Sunday in Advent, the Book of Common Prayer, says: "Read, mark, learn, and inwardly digest." Bible reading, on the other hand, has just the opposite effect; thoughtfully read, prayerfully read, the text masters the reader, sometimes with astonishing results.

Lewis prayed in the most prosaic places, and so in the most prosaic places he read the Bible. And so can the MC.

SERIOUS BUSINESS #3
Almsgiving

"Believe me, anyone who gives even a drink of water to these little ones, just because he is my disciple, will by no means lose his reward."

That's the way Matthew put it in 10:42; that's the way J. B. Phillips rendered it; and that's what Lewis tried to do.

For each of his BBC talks on Christianity, which he was delivering regularly on the radio during World War II, Lewis was paid ten guineas and offered vouchers for the train. The vouchers he took; the fees he asked the BBC to send to a number of worthy and needy people.

One of these was a woman who'd read *The Problem of Pain* and found herself in it. She wrote Lewis, advising him of this, and telling him that she was a Christian, had read English at Oxford, and was now living in Buckinghamshire on a very small income. He sent her books from time to time; money from the BBC was posted to her at his instruction.

In disposing of income over and above his modest university salary, Lewis was just following the gospel imperative, but when he got a royalty check for *The Screwtape Letters* in the amount of £2,003, and with the prospect of more such checks with each reprinting, he thought with horror of the Inland Revenue. Was it usual, he wrote to his friend and solicitor Barfield, that he had to pay £2,003 in taxes?

Only when that man had been giving money away without at the same time declaring it as income, replied Barfield. If Lewis wanted to continue making donations to the Home for Retired Professors of Ichthyosophy and not be taxed for them, he'd need some legal instruments.

That was precisely what Lewis wanted; he named it the Agape Fund.

Barfield then made arrangements with Lewis's bank concerning tax withholdings from his account; then he opened an account for the trust; finally he was ready to write checks for Lewis's charities and send them off with gracious letters.

"He is certainly a fool and perhaps a lunatic, but he seems very miserable." It was August 22, 1949; Lewis was forwarding to Barfield a letter from a person who might be a candidate for the Agape Fund. "I *think* he means he is poor."

In 1952 a female acquaintance of Lewis's stood accused of slander; she was going to fight back. She asked him to testify as to her good character if the court proceedings required it. He agreed and offered her some money for the coming legal expenses. She'd accept it as a loan. He insisted that it was a gift from the Agape Fund.

On Friday, April 9, 1954, the Lewises and the Greshams motored to Whipsnade, where they visited the zoo. Warren walked ahead with the boys, pointing out the general layout and the best way to attack the exhibits and habitats. The boys seemed to be happy, said Joy, but she was not. Her husband, William Lindsay Gresham, had promised, when they separated, to send $60 a month for the support of the boys. Most months the money didn't arrive; now the spring-term fees and tuitions were due at Dane Court. The Agape Fund would take care of that, said Lewis as they arrived at the bears.

Lewis knew what almsgiving meant in his own life, albeit in a jolly, offhand sort of way, but what can the MC learn from his experience?

Lewis never knew how much money he had in his bank account and never really learned how to read a bank statement. But he did feel that he should give a fair amount to the chronically poor and to that emerging sociological group, the middle-class poor. He gave money, books, tuitions to those he knew personally as well as to those he didn't know from Adam. He even gave away hams, tinned hams from American admirers of his works who felt that the meager British diet of the late 1940s and early 1950s needed supplementing. All the "poor" had to do was ask.

At tax time the MC tots up his or her contributions to worthy causes, spiritual as well as temporal, and the amount can sometimes be astonishingly high. And the church-tithers among us may well see Jesus himself when they contribute. Screwtape himself would approve. He'd even pose for a smiling photograph, with the MC on one side and the tither on the other; at the same time he's doing his damnedest to get one or the other of them to crow about it, to greet the day cockadoodling about the wonderfulness of him- or herself.

SERIOUS BUSINESS #4
Spiritual Friendship

For Marcus Tullius Cicero, two people were company and three a crowd, or so he opined in his essay *De amicitia* ("On friendship"), written in 44 B.C. Cicero's was the definitive word on the subject until well into the twelfth century when Aelred, a Cistercian monk in the Abbey of Rievaulx, Yorkshire, penned a Latin essay of his own. For him also two made friendship, but three made something better, a spiritual friendship. The third party was Jesus Christ, who was the source from which the friendship sprang, the framework on which it grew, and the final end at which it aimed.

"Here we are then, you and I, and with us, as we've come to hope, although we can't see, is Christ. Just the three of us. No one to drown us out, no one to dagger our friendly chats. Nothing captious, nothing bumptious, just this very pleasant mood. You can talk to me now, my beloved brother in Christ. Unlock your heart. Feel free to say what you want. And let's not be ungrateful for the spot, the time, and the leisure."

Lewis had read the Ciceronian essay, maybe even the Cistercian dialogue. But the sort of friendship he had with several people certainly fitted Aelred's description.

Sister Penelope Lawson, CSMV

Lewis made the acquaintance of Sister Penelope Lawson, member of the Congregation of St. Mary the Virgin, an Anglican sisterhood, when she wrote to him in 1939, asking if he'd recommend some light reading for some sick nuns.

He'd asked her to pray for him when he responded on April 10, 1943.

Between winter and spring terms he was spending most of his time at the Kilns. Mrs. Moore's ulcer wept without stop. Muriel, a lady gardener, went into hysterical rages, putting off an operation she surely ought to have. Margaret, a mentally deficient young girl who'd been hired as a maid, was subject to fits of anger and misery. There were times when all three women were caterwauling, but never a time when all three were purring. And yet Lewis came to feel during this bad time that a visitor had come to stay at the house, albeit a mystical visitor: Jesus Christ. Lewis was glad of the new company, but sad that he couldn't share the news with the rest of the household.

"It was a bad time, but I almost venture to say I felt Christ in the house as I have never done before," wrote Lewis to Sister Penelope, now signing himself as Brother Ass, "but alas, such a house for him to visit!"

Lewis continued corresponding with his "elder sister in the faith" for the last twenty-four years of his life.

Dom Bede Griffiths, OSB

In December 1935 Lewis got a letter from Bede Griffiths (whom we've already met), inviting him to visit Prinknash Priory. He told Lewis he was completing his term as novice and would become a full-fledged Benedictine monk on December 21 when he professed vows of poverty, chastity, and obedience.

Lewis accepted. At the priory door he was welcomed by Griffiths, a huge dark Celt in a magnificent white habit.

That was a *himation*, wasn't it?

A tunic, said Griffiths.

A *chlamus?*

A scapular; since professing his vows a few days before, he was allowed to wear a cowl, a heavy outer garment with long sleeves that was the choir dress of a monk.

What should Lewis call him now? When clothed as a novice Griffiths had taken the name of Bede, after the seventh-century monk who wrote the *Ecclesiastical History of England.*

"Bede" it was then, and he led the way to the midday meal. Silence reigned in the refectory full of white-robed figures, the sole voice being that of a monk reading from the pages of a book, that the spirit might also be refreshed while the body was receiving its sustenance. After the meal, the community processed to the chapel, Lewis in tow, chanting an anthem or psalm, for yet another word of thanksgiving.

The afternoon belonged to the tutor and his pupil. Was the life hard enough for him? Lewis reminded Griffiths that in his Oxford days he had never used tobacco, ate meat rarely, and avoided hot baths because they were voluptuous, enervating, and led to an effeminate love of the clean.

Life in the monastery wasn't an easy one, said Griffiths, but it was "far less austere" than he'd expected. "The meals were simple but they were generous, and though there was no meat, there was an abundance not only of fruit and vegetables but also of cheese and eggs and fish and cereals." He was used to wooden beds with straw mattresses. A chair and a desk in his cell served his intellectual needs. But he had to admit that the community's "hot baths and central heating and other luxuries of that kind" took some getting used to.

The correspondence between the two men continued until Lewis's death. Griffith favored haggling over the ultimate rightness of the Roman positions. Lewis preferred to talk about prayer, the Christian life, and so on. Griffiths favored talking about the schism; Lewis, about what they had in common.

So much for two of the spiritual friendships in Lewis's life, but what can they possibly tell us about ours?

Both spiritual friendships endured and prospered because they had in common Jesus Christ. Haggling about historical positions only recreated the centuries of schisms past. As Aelred wrote, echoing Bernard of Clairvaux, "Spiritual friendship . . . is desirable not because we can think up some way to squeeze the juice out of it, but because we can see it has a stature of its own. It needs no apology. Its fruit is itself, and our admiration is reward enough."

SERIOUS BUSINESS #5
Spiritual Direction

Maps may be wrong, even maps about the spiritual journey. That's why spiritual directors have been so necessary in the history of prayer. Even the experienced may be wrong on occasion, and one would have to change. But what kind of director is the right kind? To this perennial question, and to the perennial possibilities, the answer has seemed to be either a holy person without a whiff of wordliness or a worldly person with a discreet but nonetheless discernible scent of holiness. Teresa of Avila picked the latter. Whom did Lewis choose?

Father Walter Adams, SSJE

Right from the start Lewis confessed his sins in the Communion Service as it appeared in the Book of Common Prayer. That was the way the Anglicans did it, and that way was tolerable to a Protestant. But he felt drawn to do something more. Roman Catholics confessed their sins directly into a priest's ear, not because they wanted to but because their church law required them to. And that ear wasn't the priest's; it was the ear of Jesus one poured one's sins into, and it was Jesus who gave the absolution. Anglicans, of course, could do the same, but it wasn't required. Accordingly, Lewis, when he felt an overwhelming desire for an auricular confession, sought out an Anglican priest.

Cowley was the industrial center of greater Oxford. Morris Motors had been established about a mile from the Kilns in 1934. Its factory buildings occupied ninety acres of what was once prime agricultural land. From its assembly line, fourteen and three-quarters miles long, rolled five hundred Morris Eights every working day.

In Cowley also was the Church of St. John the Evangelist. Staffing it were the members of a religious community of Anglican priests known as the Society of St. John the Evangelist. Fr. Walter Adams was the one who answered Lewis's knock, and didn't think it so odd that an Anglican wanted to go to confession in the Roman way.

When Lewis decided to make his first confession, he made an appointment with Fr. Adams. Then he wrote a letter to Sister Penelope, lest he renege on his appointment with the Devil (or so Screwtape had made him think), and lest she upbraid him for being weak of heart.

Then he did the dirty deed!

He survived, he wrote to her on October 24, 1940. Everything he'd feared about the experience turned out to be true to some extent, but he discovered much good that he hadn't anticipated and would try to adopt confession as a regular practice.

Having survived the first encounter, Lewis visited Adams once a week, not only confessing his sins but also receiving manifold directions in the mapless world of spirituality.

Don Giovanni Calabria, PSDP

On Boxing Day 1951 Lewis was in his rooms at Magdalen College, Oxford, attending to the mail. He found an unopened envelope with Italian postage. The letter was from Don Giovanni Calabria, a Roman Catholic priest in Verona with whom he was having an interesting correspondence, conducted not in Italian or English, but in Latin.

Don Giovanni had founded the Casa Buoni Fanciulli in Verona, Italy, an orphanage for boys, in 1907–8. He also founded a religious congregation, the Poor Servants of Divine Providence, which was approved by his bishop in 1932 and by the pope in 1947. He died in 1954 at age eighty-one and was beatified by Pope John Paul II in 1988.

Calabria first wrote to Lewis in 1947. *The Screwtape Letters* had just been published in Italian, and the good father expressed his thanks for the book and urged Lewis to write more such books. The subtext was, to the experienced eye, an appeal for funds to support the overburdened charity.

Beginning his reply, Lewis took the date from the liturgical calendar, St. Stephen's Day. In the course of the letter, he revealed to his Italian friend that in the past eight months he found particular spiritual joy in a practice that had been going on now for a decade, that of confessing his sins to a priest.

On St. Mark's Day, April 25, he'd been overcome by the realization that sins might be cicatrices on the body spiritual but they could be, and actually were being, forgiven each and every day. Of course, his intellect had perceived this decades ago, but his deepening faith on the topic just dazzled him one day when he was least expecting it.

Naturally, perhaps supernaturally, enough, he wanted to share this soul-warming insight with Don Giovanni. It seemed that the priest, as saintly persons were wont to do, had a tendency to perceive his own sins, faults, imperfections as larger than they might be in the sight of God. It was as though a scientist magnified the pores in the skin until they appeared to be the size of moon craters.

But Lewis cautioned Calabria not to let his humility harden into anxiety or soften into sadness. The New Testament prescription for what ailed them both was Rejoice, and Rejoice again.

"Jesus has wiped the slate clean of the charges against us. Hearts up!

"Pray for me, dear Father, that I won't be too brassy or too rabbity; that I don't do something I should or that I do something I shouldn't.

"I pray every day for both you and your congregation. While we're on the trudge, we meet only on the printed page. But I look forward to the time, in our soul's true home, when we may meet face to face."

So much for Lewis's scarifying experiences as he progressed down the garden path of the spiritual life. What meaning can it possibly have for the MC?

Because Lewis took Christianity more seriously than most, he required direction. He asked for and received help from two experienced men, Adams and Calabria. For decades his own parish priest at the Anglican church of Holy Trinity, Headington Quarry, Fr. Ronald Head, stout in the Catholic tradition as well as the Anglican, provided him with all sorts of books and biblical commentaries when he needed them.

If one needs help — that is to say, if one needs a spiritual director — Lewis would say, Ask. As one would proceed in getting a doctor, ask for recommendations. What are friends for? It's a simple task. Maybe it'll take a short time; maybe a long time. Patience will help over the short haul; impatience, over the long haul. Persist, pray while you persist, and your prayer'll be answered.

A trial period for the new director would seem to be in order. If he or she's holier than thou, watch out; especially if the first piece of advice is "Embrace a leper"; and the second piece, "Well, if you can't embrace a leper, just finding one would do."

If the director is worldlier than thou, you may think you've won the Irish Sweepstakes; but be doubly careful; especially if the first piece of advice is, "What a sweetie Jesus is! He smoked and drank and messed around just like the rest of us!" Common sense is a rare commodity in everyday life; even rarer in the spiritual life.

SERIOUS BUSINESS #6

Spiritual Reading

Spiritual reading is an extension of spiritual direction. That is to say, most of what the spiritual masters and mistresses of the past have had to say about the care and cultivation of the soul has been put into books. Lewis seemed to have read most of the classics of Western spirituality and enough of the classics of Eastern spirituality to form the concept of the Tao. He read everything, and he remembered everything he read. Putting it into action was the problem.

"There is a strange idea abroad that in every subject the ancient books should be read only by the professionals, and that the amateur should content himself with the modern books."

Old books, Lewis was fond of arguing, were better than new

books. That was to say, the reason one read a new book about an old author was to admit beforehand that one couldn't possibly understand the classic without help. Hence, one had to read a commentary on Plato before one could read Plato himself.

But even the amateur or the student reader quickly came to discover that often one couldn't make head or tail of the dreary, driveling commentary and had to give up on the possibility of ever reading the philosopher himself.

The same might be said of Athanasius's treatise "On the Incarnation." The fourth-century theologian's part in the Council of Nicea was crucial to the ultimate definition of Jesus as the son of God, but few of the faithful since that time, theologians excluded, had ever read it.

When Lewis learned that his friend Sister Penelope had translated and edited the work and that she'd been having trouble convincing a publisher, the Society for the Promotion of Christian Knowledge, to bring the work out, he offered to write the introduction, which he began with the previously quoted sentence.

Her Englishing of the Athanasian treatise *"De incarnatione verbi Dei,"* she dedicated "To C.S.L., Witness and Teacher."

What Lewis was saying in his introduction to her work was that whether one was a seasoned reader or just a casual reader, one could get a great deal out of Plato and Athanasius on a first reading. That wasn't to say there weren't dark patches in these works that needed a second reading or indeed a second opinion to understand. But such first readings often gave unexpected pleasure, bringing, as they did, the reader face to face with the writer. And who knew what conversation might spring up across the centuries between the two?

What, if anything, can this possibly mean to the MC today?

If the choice were to read old books or new books, the amateur reader should choose the old books, for the new books often distorted as they interpreted. But many of the old books, long out of print, have been republished and may be read now as new books, Sister Penelope's among them.

The publishing cycle is continually being enriched by both old and new books. And of course Lewis's books were among the new books, and surely he wasn't counseling readers not to read them. Fact is, his ideas, new as they may appear to the great unread, are merely recycled ideas of the ancients with new twists, new metaphors for new readers.

Which is another way of saying, a good idea is good in itself, regardless of whether the author, ancient or modern, was the first or last one who proposed it, and may be relished as such. The reader just has to recognize it as such. And one can judge that only after doing what Lewis did, reading everything in sight, old and/or new.

SERIOUS BUSINESS #7

Confession

Confession was good for Lewis, as we have already seen, but was it any good for anybody else? The subject seemed to surface during the many invitations he had to ascend the pulpit.

For example, on the fourth Sunday of Lent, March 31, 1946, Lewis was preaching at evensong at his own parish church, Holy Trinity in Headington Quarry, just up the hill from Oxford proper, just down the road from Shotover Hill, site of the Kilns.

He was attempting to clarify some phrases in the General Confession, which was made at Holy Communion. There, the burden of sins was described as "intolerable." He looked up from his text and his eye caught his brother, Warren, who cringed at the thought that he was about to be singled out. Lewis knew that his brother always left this phrase out when he recited the General Confession; he didn't find his emotions exercised by the burden of sins.

"Unbearable" would be a better choice of words, said Lewis, if one were writing the *Prayer Book* today.

It wasn't so much that the burden of sins was emotionally unbearable as that the burden was like a heavily laden truck about to cross a lightly constructed bridge. Cross it, and the bridge, instead of bearing the load, would collapse into rubble below.

"I wonder if this is what the *Prayer Book* means; that there is on each of us a load which, if nothing is done about it, will in fact break us, will send us from this world to what ever happens afterward, not as souls but as broken souls."

Next Sunday, April 7, 1946, preaching in St. Matthew's Church, Northampton, some forty miles north-northwest of Oxford, Lewis brought up the subject of confession again.

"I wonder, would I be safe in guessing that every second person has in his life a terrible problem conditioned by some other person?" That other person had a "fatal flaw," which seemed to wreck all those who tried to reach it. But one had only to look within his or her own life to discover the presence of such a flaw. But once discovered, what should one do about it?

One good thing, Lewis suggested, was confession to a priest. If not to a priest, then one should confide one's sins to a tablet of paper, enumerating the transgressions in no particular order. Then one should meditate on the sinfulness of each item on the list and then express prayerfully one's sorrow and repentance.

A caution.

Some items on the list might appear elephantine; others, pismirical. But lest one be overcome by the one or scoff at the other, a priest or spiritual director will eventually have to be consulted. If after mature consideration you found nothing worth putting on your list, then you're in the greatest trouble of all.

So much for Lewis's recommendations about confession for others. What meaning does it have for the MC? Lewis tells us himself.

In 1953 he found himself trying to encourage a woman who was staggered at the prospect of having to confess her sins to a priest; she'd undergone a conversion, and in her first fervor was thinking of joining a religious order.

After reciting general confessions in a church service, many people don't feel forgiven or believe in forgiveness. But uttering the sins to a priest can lead an MC to a new appreciation of forgiveness. It helped Lewis, and Lewis felt it would help her; and so he told her in a letter in April.

A further cautionary word.

All Christians are obligated to confession. Some to particular confession; some to general confession; some to biblical confession. And all Christians are required to be charitable about what the Christians of other denominations do in this regard. Anything less would require immediate confession.

SERIOUS BUSINESS #8

Defending the Faith

On October 11, 1521, Pope Leo X conferred on Henry VIII the title of Fidei Defensor, Defender of the Faith. The occasion was Henry's pamphlet *Assertio septem sacramentorum adversus Martinum Lutherum* (Declaration of the seven sacraments against Martin Luther). Some years later, when England broke from Rome, the pope withdrew the title, but Parliament restored it, and every sovereign since that time has borne the title. From the time of George I, the letters *Fid. Def.* or the initials *F.D.* have regularly appeared on the irregularly sized coinage, the side with the sovereign's profile together with the initials *D.G.* (*Deo gratia*, Latin for "by the grace of God").

Defending the faith had its moments. For Lewis some of them occurred at meetings of the Socratic. Its intention was to allow atheists and agnostics to present their views and Christians to respond. Three episodes come to mind.

The first occurred in 1944 with the Philosopher, who taught philosophy at the University of London. His reputation as an outspoken agnostic, pacifist, popular philosopher, and radio personality was well known.

The night was bitterly cold, but the steam was whistling inside Lady Margaret Hall. Two hundred fifty people packed the room. As the heat of argument rose, the Philosopher asked leave to remove his jacket. That the agnostic mightn't have the advantage, the chair whispered to Lewis to remove his. He couldn't, he whispered back; he had a large hole in his shirt and would have to sweat it through to the dripping end.

The second occurred in 1946 with the Physicist. "Is progress possible without religion?" was the announced topic. The speaker identified himself as a Roman Catholic and a liberal. That Nazism and communism, both of which promised progress, had failed miserably, was his point. He was witty and humorous at first, but his presentation against religionless ideologies deteriorated into a political invective. Members of the Rationalist Society and the Socialist Club, who were cosponsoring the event with the Socratic, began to heckle.

Responding, the Physicist, who described himself as a dialectical materialist, had a sunnier interpretation of history. He claimed that the years since the revolution had produced both change and progress in Russia and that in England it was a socialist, G. B. Shaw, who'd championed most of the progressive causes. Members of the Student Christian Movement as well as the Socratic hooted at that.

Chairing the meeting that night was Lewis, who had to remind the audience several times that catcalls and rude remarks weren't in the spirit of rational exchange. At the end, in an attempt to draw some clarity, he defined progress and religion to the satisfaction of neither speaker.

The third occurred in 1948 with the Geneticist, who agreed to deliver a paper entitled "Atheism." Lewis had used him, everyone was convinced, as the remote inspiration for the character of Weston, the mad but loquacious scientist in *Out of the Silent Planet* and *Perelandra.* It would be a contest of giants this November night; one of them would have to emerge the victor.

The Geneticist appeared at ease on the stage of the lecture room, which was large enough to be a small theater. Atheism, he said, was the only intellectually honest position to take. Theism, he was sure they would have to agree, was founded on insufficient evidence. The existence of evil could never be reconciled with the concept of a good god. Religious people — a statistical study could easily verify this — led worse lives than nonreligious people. In fact, by a happy sort of inverse ratio, the closer one got to the pope, the worse one's life seemed to grow.

Lewis could hardly contain himself. He was president of the club and could, of course, speak whenever he wanted, but he had to let a philosophy tutor at Wadham College give the official reply.

"Atheism may encounter fewer intellectual difficulties," waffled the tutor, "but that is because it is not a hypothesis but a refusal to look for explanations of a certain type."

Commenting briefly on the reply and sensing that the audience was lusting for his blood, the Geneticist didn't wait for the questions from the floor. Edging from the podium, he made "an impressive running panegyric of atheism," his last words being spoken as he went off the stage and out of the building.

So much for Lewis's defending the faith. What do these three episodes have to reveal to the MC?

Whenever the faith's attacked, the MC should defend. Sometimes by a discreet comment. Sometimes by a letter to the newspaper. Sometimes by a public display of rhetoric. Something. Anything. All the way to, but not including, fisticuffs, no matter what encouragement the famous hymn gives to the Christian soldier.

As these three episodes illustrate, defending the faith can be unglamourous. There'll be good nights and bad nights, the latter outnumbering the former by at least two to one, and one never knew what was to come when one stood up for the faith. Just standing up at all was a good start. And the ultimate consideration for the Mere Christian isn't how many times one gets knocked down; it's how many times one gets up.

SERIOUS BUSINESS #9

Smuggling Theology

"It is not easy to find the right type of story book for sisters who are resting or convalescing after illness," wrote Sister Penelope Lawson on August 5, 1939, to Lewis. She was librarian at the convent of the Anglican community of St. Mary the Virgin at Wantage, some fifteen miles southwest of Oxford.

"At ordinary times we do not read novels at all, as you may imagine; but the right novel at the right moment can have a real spiritual value."

She had read Mascall's review of *Out of the Silent Planet* in the April issue of *Theology*, ordered the book for the library, and was the first in her convent to read it. "All along the line it provokes thought in just the directions where I have always wanted to think; and wherever it is most delightfully suggestive, one senses the most profound scriptural basis. . . ."

Enclosed with the letter was a copy of a book of hers, *God Persists*, a short survey of world history in the light of the Christian faith, which had just been published by Mowbray's in Oxford.

Out of sixty reviews of Lewis's novels, only two adverted to the idea that Lewis, whatever the literal level of the novel, might just be writing about the fall of Lucifer; and so he told her in a letter dated August 9, 1939. He went on to add, rather whimsically, that theology could easily be smuggled into fiction, and the readers would never know, at least directly, that it had actually happened.

"You will be both grieved and amused to hear," wrote Lewis on August 9 in reply to Sister Penelope, "that out of about sixty reviews [*Out of the Silent Planet*] only two showed any knowledge that my idea of the fall of the Bent One was anything but an invention of my own. But if there only was someone with a richer talent and more leisure, I think that this great ignorance might be a help to the evangelization of England; any amount of theology can now be smuggled into people's minds under cover of romance without their knowing it."

That was in 1939. This was in 1950.

"Go quickly," read aloud Lewis's mercurial friend Dyson one Thursday morning. "Summon all our people to meet me here as speedily as they can," he read, now standing up, the better to be heard at the Bird and Baby. "Call out the giants and the werewolves and the spirits of those trees who are on our side." It was June 22; Inklings were assembling for a morning pint and an hour's conversation. "Call the Ghouls and the Boggles, the Ogres and the Minotaurs!" Lewis had brought with him the first proof of *The Lion, the Witch, and the Wardrobe;* from the parcel Dyson had snatched a galley and was orating the White Witch's call for help before finally confronting the Gold Lion. "Call the Cruels, the Hags, the Specters, and the people of the Toadstools! We will fight! What?" The noontime regulars were beginning to arrive at their local and looked toward the hubbub in the back parlor. "Have I not still my wand? Will not their ranks turn into stone even as they come on?" Someone pulled Dyson back into his seat and pushed a glass into his hand. "Be off quickly! I have a little thing to finish here while you are away."

An allegory, said an Inkling; the story was an allegory.

Of course, it wasn't an allegory, said Lewis with a smile; it was just a story for children.

This wasn't the first time the Inklings had heard the story. The manuscript was read to them in the past months, but as they perused one galley or another, they looked beyond the details of the narrative toward its meaning. Aslan had to be a Christ-figure in lion's clothing. Edmund was obviously a young Adam who erred, betrayed his primal trust. That White Witch, insisted Dyson, had to be Screwtape, but in alarming costume with ghastly cosmetic. Deep magic was original sin and its human consequences. The deeper magic was the redemption by, and the resurrection of, the golden-maned character. The lion's visiting the witch's castle at the end to revivify the petrified figures was nothing else but the harrowing of Hell. And so on.

So much for Lewis's life. Here's what it means.

Smuggling theology was one thing Lewis did well, and he was rather smug about it. Truth to tell, a fully formed MC who's read the right books and had the right education is something of a living reproach when he or she commingles in secular society. The secularists they meet often feel they must unload their prejudices against Christian practices. Christianity seems to act as a poultice, drawing the poison out. But by their Christian demeanor and behavior the MCs often present Christianity in an attractive way. They even might be said to be smuggling Christianity into the enemy's camp by their very presence.

SERIOUS BUSINESS #10

Good Works

"Good works" in the plural was, according to Lewis, an expression much more familiar to modern Christianity than "good work."

That was how he began the article he was writing in 1959 for the *Catholic Art Quarterly*. Great works of art and good works of charity had better also be good work: that was the conclusion he wanted to reach, the principle he wanted to enunciate, but the road to it was tortuous, and he was having a hard time not going right off the cliff.

There were good works like almsgiving and helping in the parish....

There was also good work, objects of utility and not a little beauty that were produced by cabinet makers, cobblers, and sailors....

There was never enough of the former; the number of the latter was decreasing at an alarming rate....

The villain of the piece, or so Lewis theorized, was industrialized society with its diabolical stepchild, built-in obsolescence. In the nineteenth century a horse-drawn carriage was made to last a lifetime; but in the twentieth century the car with all its horsepower was made to last two years. The centuries-old button, because it always worked, was being ruthlessly replaced by a twentieth-century zipper that always snagged.

Another serpentine offspring of industrialization was advertising, the sort that was plastered on a hoarding to broadcast for sale what people didn't need but were made to feel they had to have....

Redecoration as a Good Work

Some of the products of industrialization he feared had invaded the Kilns when Joy, his wife of less than a year, went on an orgy of spending. Repair and refurbishing — the first in at least thirty-five years — were her motives, but he couldn't help but feel that she had bought more than the household needed.

The fact that Joy had approached the job with foreknowledge, that she had bought much of the stuff at bargain prices, learned from one medium of advertising or another, was no consolation to him....

And it was no consolation to her — his intellectual and emotional peer — to learn that he considered her time and effort to have produced neither "good work" nor "good works."

If the Kilns were a tenement in the Bronx, it would have been torn down a long time ago! Feet had plunged through floorboards; ceilings had crashed onto furniture; walls would surely have caved in long before if it hadn't been for the bookcases all over the house! No wonder his friends called it the Midden! The Dungheap!

But Lewis knew that already, and he'd even made his checkbook available to her. Before she could use it, however, she had to reconcile the account against the bank statements in order to discover the correct balance; that, he assured her, was a process that had been wanting for some time. Credits outweighed debits by thousands of pounds, she discovered; she instructed him to put some of the funds into savings accounts and other banking investments where they would earn interest.

From the windows she tore down the blackout curtains that had been hanging since 1939; when they hit the tub, they turned to ink. The carpets were in tatters; some of them she replaced. In danger from eating on chipped dishes and drinking from cracked glasses, she invested in new china and crystal.

When Lewis asked her how much she had finally spent, she gave a good round figure.

Things had gone up since he last bought anything like that, he admitted, but wasn't there anything cheaper on the market?

Only half that was the cost, she told him laughingly, having shopped about to buy as much as she could on sale, the sort of sale that had been advertised on the hoardings that he so studiously abhorred.

Although bewildered at the cost of repairing and refurbishing the Kilns, he finally had to admit that Joy had done both good works and good work at one and the same time. From that moment on he relished the dinners she served on the tablecloth she'd crocheted. Game on china, wine in crystal, candles on sconces. *Philia, eros, agape.*

So much for Lewis's argumentation. Here's what it means in Lewis's own words.

"When our Lord provided a poor wedding party with an extra glass of wine all around, he was doing good works. But also good work; it was a wine really worth drinking."

Lunch as a Good Work

"After Priggery — What?" asked Lewis in an article of his that appeared in the December 7, 1945, issue of *The Spectator.*

But before answering the question of what came after, it was necessary to develop a definition.

Priggery seemed to be a better-than-thou-ness, a moral effrontery, a spiritual superiority laid like a cane across the back of a presumed inferior. A horrid prospect that recalled the Lucan Pharisee belaboring the publican in the synagogue or the Dickensian beadle railing against the orphans in the workhouse. If unchecked, such priggery became only more horrid.

Then Lewis instanced what he meant by a horrid priggery when he described in this article an imaginary lunch between a friend of his and a journalist of dubious reputation named Cleon.

Now Lewis's friend was a prig; perhaps it was better to describe him as a reformed prig; that is to say, he'd been one of those who didn't hesitate to speak cuttingly against a sin that was a sin. But in a society increasingly more tolerant of the sinner, Lewis's friend had to check his priggery at the restaurant door when he joined the guttersniping journalist at the table.

Now Cleon was the sort of columnist that specialized in calumny. He dished out detritus on a daily basis; and he made a good living at it besides. Over lunch he seemed a nice enough fellow, kempt and couth, but morally he was a leper. In a well-ordered and spiritual society, even in a priggish or self-righteous society, he'd have had to ring a bell to announce his presence and to ward off the unwary.

But here Cleon was, enjoying his lunch, nice as you please, wolfing his food, sloshing his drink, dabbing his lips daintily with his napkin. Lewis's friend, no longer fearing contagion by association with the leprous, was engaging Cleon in all sorts of pleasantries, and Cleon was regaling him with newsy tidbits of all sorts about his fellow man that weren't so pleasant.

What was a prig — or former prig — to do? Revert to an earlier state of priggery and pillory the yellow journalist in front of the noonday crowd? No, Lewis couldn't do that. That wouldn't be civilized, or indeed an appropriate way to respond in a society that tolerated moral inferiority rather than tromped on it. But Lewis's friend did feel that, without his razor-sharp priggery, he was addressing a particularly tough piece of meat without a knife and a fork.

Like a good friend, Lewis had some suggestions.

Lewis suggested that his friend hadn't risen above priggery so much as he'd slipped below it.

He suggested also that it wasn't incumbent upon his friend to approach Cleon in the same way a missionary approached an aborigine; it wasn't necessary to convert the morally fuzzy-wuzzy, to put the fear of God into him, to bludgeon him to the point of baptism.

Lewis also had some recommendations for his friend.

First, avoid Cleon like the moral pariah he was, but don't pronounce against him publicly.

Second, don't buy Cleon's newspaper or indeed any other newspaper that slings the sort of mud Cleon's did; the profit would disappear, and the publication would implode.

Third, get others to elude Cleon's presence and not to buy his paper. After five years, the number of Cleons practicing the mudslinging journalism would necessarily diminish, perhaps even disappear.

So much for Lewis's life. Here's what it means.

Sometimes it's better to ignore than to insult, Lewis seemed to be saying; to deflate than to deflower, to boycott than to picket.

Moreover, Jesus did much of his own good work — and indeed good works — over lunch, and Lewis didn't fail to notice. But what Jesus called pharisaism, Lewis exposed as priggery, a moral vice often at its most virulent at a modern power lunch, where the MC is sometimes the host, sometimes the guest, sometimes even the entrée.

Finally, with regard to lunch, in a book about Lewis's spirituality, it should be said somewhere that there's no way to underestimate how much a good lunch can do to keep a spirituality well in kilter, whether it's a paper-napkined sort of ploughman's lunch at the Trout or a starched-napkin sort of affair in the dining room at the Randolph Hotel.

Mustard as a Good Work

No doubt the seasoned veteran of spirituality will look at Lewis's spirituality, or my attempt to derive a spirituality from

Lewis's own, as amusing, even interesting, but, ultimately, it just doesn't cut the mustard. . . .

And indeed it doesn't cut the mustard, at least in the way that Bernard and Bruno, Dominic and Francis, Ignatius and Alphonsus, Teresa and John cut it with their own spiritualities. Supposedly, because they've been developed by ordained men and vowed women in the clerical and religious life, they're considered superior, the knife's edge, as it were, on just how laymen and laywomen should design their own spiritual lives.

But what I'd like to suggest is that, when it comes to spirituality for the MC, it's not the knife that counts; it's the mustard.

May I explain?

In 1921 Dorothy L. Sayers was hired at Benson's, a London advertising agency, as "an idea man and copywriter," and for the next nine years she contributed enormously to the success of a now-famous campaign for Colman's mustard. A declining ad budget and the essential dullness of mustard were the problems to be solved. A club was invented, characters concocted, situations devised, and soon members of the Mustard Club and the message of "mustard for the masses" were appearing on posters and billboards, in newspapers and magazines, all over England.

In a like manner she and others revivified Christianity by writing plays, novels, and essays; most notable in this regard is her "The Dogma Is the Drama." And even as Lewis swiped Colman's onto his own game pies and roast beef, so he virtually re-metaphorized Christianity in his imaginative, scholarly, and doctrinal works. In a word, he as well as Sayers made believing *believable*, acceptable, to the masses.

No, it's not the knife that counts when the blade hits the mustard; it's the mustard itself, for the mustard is for the masses.

But be it known that Colman's is not a dull mustard; it's a sharp one, a hotter-than-hot, one whose rising fumes make the sinus membranes quaver like the drawn strings of a viol da gamba.

Two questions.

Is it just a coincidence that the initials of both Mere Christianity and the Mustard Club are the same?

May Colman's reasonably be considered the official mustard of Mere Christianity?

What It Means

Early Sunday evening, June 8, 1941, Fred Paxford, the gangling gardener, sometime cook, and general factotum at the Kilns, drove Lewis down Headington Road and St. Clement's, over Magdalen Bridge and up the High. Lewis alighted at St. Mary the Virgin's. Solemn evensong was approaching; the vicar had asked him to speak. By the time Paxford parked the car and returned to the church, he had to fight his way in. The seats, the benches, the galleries, even the window ledges were hung about with undergraduates.

The vicar presiding, the organist intoned, the congregation sang, Lewis winced. How Screwtape hated the mewlings humans called music! How Lewis himself dreaded that in Heaven there would almost certainly be an organ with sweating pipes and hooting bellows!

When quiet descended on the nave, Lewis ascended the pulpit — the very pulpit from which began not only Methodism but also the Tractarian movement — and placed his manuscript on the lectern. "The Weight of Glory," it was entitled. He began to read, his voice deep, his tone serious, his appearance cheerful.

Reward for Christians was Heaven, he stated, but he quickly pointed out how like a siren the wail of worldliness had been for the last hundred years, leading people to believe that man's true home was on earth, that earth could be made into a sort of Heaven, or that if there were a heavenly Heaven, it was a long way off. Philosophies like progress and creative evolution promised happiness, but a happiness they couldn't seem to deliver.

Even if they could deliver, Lewis countered with a little logic, such happiness would die when we died, a sorites of linked arms, a daisy-chain of generations, the last arm left unlinked, when there would be nothing else left to die, except the philosophies themselves.

He went on to articulate the spiritual longings of humankind. He paid special attention to desire; a wanderlust without compass or sextant throughout the natural world in search of happiness; a happiness that, no matter how long the day's trudge, was no closer to the horizon itself.

"Meanwhile," he said at the end, "the cross comes before the crown, and tomorrow is a Monday morning." He wanted the undergraduates to leave the church, not thinking about celestial glory, which would come at some unknown point in the future, and then not for everyone in the church, but about practical charity toward one's immediate neighbor.

Sometimes that sort of charity was like the hard labor of the hod carrier, toting the leaden gray mortar of his neighbor's shortcomings, a load lightened only by humility, a load that if not lightened tumbled the proud shoulders into the sopping trough.

As Lewis stepped down from the pulpit, the organ swelled, the congregation sang "Bright the vision that delighted," and the preacher beat a hasty exit onto the High.

As tomorrow for Lewis was a Monday morning, so tomorrow for us is the beginning of the week. But, as Lewis assured us and the Scripture reveals to us, the bearing of the cross is followed by the wearing of the crown as surely as the trudge from Monday through Saturday is followed by a stroll on Sunday.

In the meantime, it seems the week will never end. . . .

Sentences

"The schoolboy beginning Greek grammar cannot look forward to his adult enjoyment of Sophocles as a lover looks forward to marriage or a General to victory. He has to begin by working for marks, or to escape punishment, or to please his parents, or, at best, in the hope of a future good which he cannot at present imagine or desire. . . .

"The Christian, in relation to Heaven, is in much the same position as this schoolboy. Those who have attained everlasting life in the vision of God doubtless know very well that it is no mere bribe, but the very consummation of their earthly discipleship; but we who have not yet attained it cannot know this in the same way, and cannot even begin to know it at all except by continuing to obey and finding the first reward of our obedience in our increasing power to desire the ultimate reward."

Scriptures

Throughout the holy trudge that is life, the MC must hold fast, as the evangelist Luke told us in his gospel (8:22–25).

"It happened on one of these days that [Jesus] embarked on a boat with his disciples and said to them, 'Let us cross over to the other side of the lake.' So they set sail, and when they were under way, he dropped off to sleep. Then a squall of wind swept down upon the lake, and they were in grave danger of being swamped. Coming forward, they woke him up, saying, 'Master, master, we're drowning!' Then he got up and reprimanded the wind and the stormy waters, and they died down, and everything was still. Then he said to them, 'What has happened to your faith?' "

Who ever heard Paul the Apostle preach knew he was a clever, well-educated man. But whenever he preached, he pointed out that, although he had the smarts, his preaching relied totally on the power of the Holy Spirit (1 Corinthians 2:1–5).

"When I came to proclaim to you [the Christians at Corinth] God's secret purpose, I did not come equipped with any brilliance of speech or intellect. You may as well know now that it was my secret determination to concentrate entirely on Jesus Christ himself and the fact of his death upon the cross. As a matter of fact, in myself I was feeling far from strong; I was nervous and rather shaky. What I said and preached had none of the attractiveness of the clever mind, but it was a demonstration of the power of the Spirit! Plainly God's purpose was that your faith should rest not upon man's cleverness but upon the power of God."

Lewis's life, as well as the life of MCs everywhere, was crowded, overcommitted, resistant to scheduling. Hence, the advice that he adopted was that of the Apostle James in his letter to the Jews in the diaspora (1:2–5).

"When all kinds of trials and temptations crowd into your lives, my brothers [and sisters], don't resent them as intruders, but welcome them as friends! Realize that they come to test your faith and to produce in you the quality of endurance. But let the process go on until that endurance is fully developed, and you will find you have become men [and women] of mature character with the right sort of independence. And if, in the process, any of you does not know how to meet any particular problem, he [or she] has only to ask God — who gives generously to all [humankind] without making them foolish or guilty — and he [or she] may be quite sure that the necessary wisdom will be given. . . ."

Readings

Much of Lewis's best advice about how to accomplish the serious business of living on this earth as a Mere Christian may be found in his letters. A casual browsing through any of the following will provide some helpful suggestions:

Letters of C. S. Lewis, edited, with a memoir, by W. H. Lewis (1966); revised and enlarged edition edited by Walter Hooper (1988).

Letters to an American Lady [Mary Willis Shelburne] (1971).

Letters to Children, edited by Lyle W. Dorsett and Marjorie Lamp Mead (1985).

Letters [*to*] *Don Giovanni Calabria,* translated and edited by Martin Moynihan (1988).

Afterword

The main reason Dom Giovanni Calabria wrote to Lewis in 1947, and indeed to many other famous contemporaries, was to solicit his aid in solving what Calabria felt was a great contemporary problem, that of the dissenting Christian brethren, of which Lewis as an Anglican would be one. The priest's concern was for their return to the unity of the body of Christ, which for him would be the Roman Church.

Of course, Lewis had been doing just that, urging, especially in *Mere Christianity,* that Christians of all communions believe the basic tenets of Christianity. But Lewis didn't want to engage Calabria in a kindly disputation about the root causes of the Reformation and Counter-Reformation in the sixteenth century.

"Disputations aggravate schisms," he wrote; "they don't heal them."

He granted that sins were committed by both sides. He even placed Henry VIII and perhaps Luther, in Hell, but he also consigned to that unhappy place the Catholics Tetzel and perhaps Pope Leo X. Yet in the cases of Luther and Leo, he felt that a lighter sentence might be passed by a human judge.

But, Lewis mused, there was also virtue on both sides. He pointed to the Protestant William Tyndale and the Catholic Thomas More. He'd read the books of both and found them illuminating and edifying. That, in the face of the fact that their writings were often at variance doctrinally. The divine judge would no doubt look more favorably upon these two men.

One thing was sure, Lewis wrote to his saintly Catholic friend, he felt unworthy to undo the shoes of either of them.

"A comparable way of doing things and praying for things, together with strength and perseverance throughout the trudge, and at the end a comparable way of dying for Christ, God willing, all these will make us one."

So much for schism. But what about ecumenism?

"I believe we are very near to one another, but not because I am at all on the Romeward frontier of my own communion."

Among the many Americans who took it upon themselves to write a letter to their favorite British author was a woman who lived in Washington, D.C. Indeed she wrote so many letters (seventy or so) that she received just as many in return; most, if not all, of them have been published under the title *Letters to an American Lady*.

"I should need to be either of angelic humility or diabolical pride not to be pleased at all the things you say about my books," wrote Lewis on October 26, 1950, in response to her first letter.

If his letters to her were any indication, she not only liked Lewis's books but also suffered a great number of grievous ills, financial (she represented herself as a widow with few means) as well as familial (she didn't like being dependent on her daughter and son-in-law). To relieve the former, Lewis sometimes sent monetary help; to relieve the latter, well, he could send only letters of condolence.

"May I assure you of my deep sympathy in all the very grievous troubles that you have had. May God continue to support you; that He has done so till now, is apparent from the fact that you are not warped or embittered. I will have you in my prayers."

On November 10, 1952, he replied to Shelburne, who'd just left the Church of England in America to join the Church of Rome. He was tempted to let the correspondence take a controversial turn. Instead he chose, once again, to celebrate what was common between the Church of England and the Church of Rome, not what was different.

He pointed out how much more both had in common with a real Jew or a real Muslim than with a wretched liberalizing, occidentalized specimen of the same category. Fervor, not torpor, was the only thing that could sustain a believer. Praying for each other — that was the only form of "work for reunion" that ever did anything good and lasting.

"I believe that, in the present divided state of Christendom, those who are at the heart of each division are all closer to one another than those who are at the fringes."

So much for ecumenism. But what about Mere Christianity?

Lewis's spiritual legacy, if it's anything, is to believe oneself, and to encourage others to believe, the basic doctrines of Christianity and to put into action the basic practices of Christianity as they are taught by one's denomination. All Christians are included; none excluded. It doesn't require hopping, skipping, and jumping to another denomination. Oddly, the merer the MC's Christianity becomes, the closer the MC moves to the center of his or her own denomination and the warmer the MC feels toward members of all the other denominations. Presumably, that's where Jesus may be found discoursing on one thing or another. That one denomination should crow its supposed superiority over others in this regard is lamentable. It would be sheer knavery to prefer one nave to another. They're all one to Screwtape, the knave of naves, and they're all trouble to him.

That's not to say that denominationalism is unimportant; indeed, it may even be necessary. But Lewis would never encourage a Christian to denounce one denomination for another. He'd say that ecumenism, however broadly or badly one defines it, is a historical movement, and hence will require inventions as revolutionary as the wheel and the passage of many eons before it's accomplished.

Mere Christianity, on the other hand, can begin on a Monday morning....

Readings

As the MC continues the holy trudge, he or she may find refreshment in Lewis's words as they are found in the following collections: Walter Hooper's *The Business of Heaven: Daily Readings from C. S. Lewis* and *C. S. Lewis, Readings for Meditation & Reflection;* my own *The Joyful Christian, 127 Readings; George MacDonald: An Anthology* edited by Lewis himself.

Notes

Many of Lewis's works, since their *original* publication in the United Kingdom and the United States, have undergone new editions, and some of them have acquired new publishers; some of his longer works now appear in two or more editions; some of his shorter works appear in more than one volume; a few of his works have new titles.

Profusion, yes, but in order to avoid confusion for readers holding different editions of a work, I've decided to add, to the usual bibliographic reference, a sort of universal system referring to, instead of page numbers, chapter titles and/or numbers and paragraph numbers.

Epigraph

5 *Man... cherry:* cited by Lewis on the last page of "Friendship," a chapter in *The Four Loves* (London: Geoffrey Bles; New York: Harcourt, Brace & World, 1960). Dunbar was a Middle Scots poet (1460/65–before 1530) treated at great length and with great affection by Lewis in his *English Literature in the Sixteenth Century, Excluding Drama,* Oxford History of English Literature 3 (Oxford: Clarendon Press, 1954).

Introduction

12 *That litany... their weight:* Adam Fox, "At the Breakfast Table," *C. S. Lewis at the Breakfast Table* (San Diego: Harcourt Brace Jovanovich, 1992 [1979]), 93; paragraph 13.

14 *Night, ghosts, a castle... affection slipping away:* "Hamlet: The Prince or the Poem?" *Selected Literary Essays,* ed. Walter Hooper (Cambridge: Cambridge University Press, 1969), 104; paragraph 22.

17 *Thank God that... Respectable and innocent:* "In Praise of Solid People," *Spirits in Bondage: A Cycle of Lyrics,* ed. Walter Hooper (San Diego: Harcourt Brace Jovanovich, 1984), 42.

17 *I had always . . . blade of grass: Surprised by Joy: The Shape of My Early Life* (New York: Harcourt, Brace & World, 1956), 10; chapter 1, paragraph 8.

17 *Give me a number . . . me the line:* quoted in Stephen Schofield's *In Search of C. S. Lewis* (South Plainfield, N.J.: Bridge Publishing, 1983), 6–7; the undergraduate was Kenneth Tynan.

18 *One must take . . . rather like this:* letter dated May 15, 1941, to Sister Penelope Lawson, CSMV; as it appears in *Letters of C. S. Lewis,* edited, with a memoir, by W. H. Lewis, 1st ed. (New York: Harcourt, Brace & World, 1966), 193–94.

18 *literary, classical, serious . . . popular, common, commercial:* see "High and Low Brows," *Selected Literary Essays*, 266–79.

19 *redskinnery:* "On Stories," *On Stories and Other Essays on Literature,* ed. Walter Hooper (San Diego: Harcourt Brace Jovanovich, 1982), 4; paragraph 2.

19 *Church-History . . . of Bishops:* it has generally been thought that the source of "mere Christianity" was *The Saints' Everlasting Rest;* it was confirmed in Walter Hooper's admirable *Companion and Guide;* but in a missive to me, dated December 15, 1997, he has offered this correction.

19 *The style is . . . often spoken arrogantly: English Literature in the Sixteenth Century, Excluding Drama*, 451–52; in it Lewis cited passages in Richard Hooker's sermon "Of Justification."

20 *Hooker had never . . . and one Baptism:* same, 454; in it Lewis cited passages from Richard Hooker's multi-volume work, *Of the Laws of Ecclesiastical Polity.*

21 *The only safety . . . their proper perspective:* Introduction to *St. Athanasius, On the Incarnation* (New York: Macmillan, 1946), xii–xiii; paragraph 3.

21 *Ever since I . . . at all times:* "Preface," *Mere Christianity: Anniversary Edition,* ed. and with an introduction by Walter Hooper (New York: Macmillan, 1981), xxxviii; paragraph 2.

22 *It is at . . . the same voice:* same, xli; paragraph 8.

23 *All the hormones . . . like messenger boys:* Philip Hoare, *Noël Coward: A Biography* (New York: Simon & Schuster, 1995), 249.

24 *I love the . . . I welcome changes:* Anthony Sampson, "The Crusading Intellect," *Church of England Newspaper*, October 4, 1946.

24 *Things are pretty . . . all the time:* letter dated December 20, 1943, to Arthur Greeves; as it appears in *They Stand Together: The Letters of*

C. S. Lewis to Arthur Greeves (1914–1963) (New York: Macmillan, 1979), 499.

25 *You look very... had no importance:* Nevill Coghill, "The Approach to English," as it appears in *Light on Lewis,* ed. Jocelyn Gibb (New York: Harcourt Brace Jovanovich, 1965), 60–61.

28 *A little comic... most sincere conversations: Reflections on the Psalms* (New York: Harcourt, Brace & World, 1958), 90; chapter 9, paragraph 1.

29 *quot homines:* see *Studies in Words,* 2d ed. (Cambridge: Cambridge University Press, 1967 [1960]), 138.

29 *God, in his... his own sons:* this and other renderings by J. B. Phillips have been taken from *The New Testament in Modern English* (New York: Macmillan, 1960).

1. Diversion

32 *I am a... under the tiles: Surprised by Joy,* 10; chapter 1, paragraph 8.

33 *from Divine protection... cad, a snob:* same, 68; chapter 1, paragraph 16.

33 *These, and many... the sounding blast:* Henry Wadsworth Longfellow, *The Poetical Works of Longfellow* (Boston: Houghton Mifflin, 1975), 222.

34 *I heard a... sunward sailing cranes:* same, 111.

34 *God of the... all the Gods:* same.

34 *floated far away... the misty sea:* same.

34 *I had never... or terrestrial twilight: Surprised by Joy,* 72–73; chapter 5, paragraph 4.

34 *I read in... of the gods:* same, 74; paragraph 5.

35 *To a boy... like a thunderbolt:* same, 75; paragraph 6.

35 *to be the... few fathoms deeper:* same, 75–76; paragraph 7.

36 *All religions... much as Loki: They Stand Together,* 135; letter 44, paragraph 2.

37 *Rum thing... had happened once: Surprised by Joy,* 223–24; chapter 14, paragraph 15.

38 *a zoo of... of fondled hatreds:* same, 226; paragraph 19.

38 *I think the... non-existent address: They Stand Together,* 398–99; letter 155, paragraph 9.

39 *How we roared . . . with renewed seriousness:* same, 372; letter 146, dated July 29, 1930, paragraph 9.

39 *feeling rather . . . your damned dilettanti:* same.

40 *propitiation . . . shocking:* same, 427; letter 172, October 18, 1931.

40 *real things:* same.

41 *A myth working . . . it really happened:* same.

41 *translations into . . . language more adequate:* same, 428.

41 *the most . . . of meaning:* same.

41 *I have just . . . do with it:* same, 425; letter 171, October 1, 1931.

44 *They were not . . . the Blue Flower: Surprised by Joy,* 7; chapter 1, paragraph 4.

47 *philosophical theorem . . . living presence:* same, 227; chapter 14, paragraph 20.

47 *a bright red . . . in the war: The Lewis Papers: Memoirs of the Lewis Family, 1850–1930,* unpublished work, 8:121; May 29, 1923.

47 *There's going . . . accidennnnnt:* same, 8:151; September 12, 1923.

47 *I am . . . I am: Surprised by Joy,* 227; chapter 14, paragraph, 20.

48 *I gave in . . . in all England:* same, 228–29; chapter 14, paragraph 23.

48 *unmatchable tea things: Brothers and Friends: The Diaries of Major Warren Hamilton Lewis,* ed. Clyde S. Kilby and Marjorie Lamp Mead (San Francisco: Harper & Row, 1982), 71; October 20, 1930.

49 *All right . . . drenched in joy:* "Man or Rabbit?" as it appears in *God in the Dock: Essays on Theology and Ethics,* ed. Walter Hooper (Grand Rapids: Wm. B. Eerdmans, 1970), 112; paragraph 10.

2. Blues

52 *that hot whore:* from John Heath-Stubbs's "Maria Aegyptica" in *The Swarming of Bees* (London 1950), 15; as it is quoted in Benedicta Ward, SLG, *Harlots of the Desert: A Study of Repentance in Early Monastic Sources* (Kalamazoo, Mich.: Cistercian Publications, 1987), 26.

54 *with his pension . . . commemorate his discharge:* Hoare, *Noël Coward: A Biography,* 80.

55 *He was last . . . more definite information: They Stand Together,* 225; letter 82, July 17?, 1918; note.

55 *Sharp, smart, elegant . . . next two decades:* Hoare, same, 90–91.

56 *close-fitting scarlet . . . straps and belt:* same, 80.

57 *dignified and fairly ... rather a bitch: The Lewis Papers,* 9:79.

57 *It is as ... wouldn't be eyes:* same, 9:90; May 12, 1926.

57 *The pretty ones ... are ugly: Letters,* 108; June 5, 1926.

58 *There's a time ... let you know:* Hoare, *Noël Coward: A Biography,* 38.

58 *nearly amoral ... divorce and adultery:* same, 114.

59 *their angular limbs ... dry metallic noises: Surprised by Joy,* 8; chapter 1, paragraph 6.

59 *I was in ... on to other topics: They Stand Together,* 391; September 15, 1930.

61 *decided to let ... young married man: The Pilgrim's Regress: An Allegorical Apology for Christianity, Reason, and Romanticism* (Grand Rapids: Wm. B. Eerdmans, 1958 [1943, 1933]), 72; book 5, section 2, paragraph 2.

61 *a nice mountain apple:* same, 73.

61 *And then — you ... to her mind:* same, 73–74.

61 *the sin of Adam:* same, 74.

62 *a Man came ... in the darkness:* same, 140; book 8, section 5.

62 *Your life has ... Landlord after all:* same.

63 *a sweetness and ... could scarcely resist:* same, book 8, section 2.

63 *the wanting, though ... else we experience:* same, 178; book 10, section 3.

63 *hear the horns of elfland: They Stand Together,* 452; March 25, 1933.

63 *confusion ... contradictions:* same, 445; November 4, 1932.

63 *passages where one ... make the difference:* same, 446; December 17, 1932.

63 *idiomatic and racy:* same, 445.

64 *One of the ... cause of atheism:* same, 447; December 17, 1932.

64 *The intellectual side ... was not simple:* same.

64 *I suppose you ... than anyone else:* same, 452; March 25, 1933.

65 *complete chaos:* Noël Coward, *Play Parade* (New York: Garden City Publishing Company, 1933), 179.

65 *I thought it ... at a debauch: They Stand Together,* 455; August 17, 1933.

65 *angular and strange: Play Parade,* 178.

65 *oddly discordant:* same.

65 *Why is it ... Twentieth Century Blues:* same, 178–79.

66 *Iron will eat . . . were a god: The Pilgrim's Regress*, 186–87; book 10, section 6.

67 *a big room . . . nearly all window:* same, 37; book 3, section 1.

67 *Drinking what looked . . . of their voices:* same.

67 *They were all . . . hair and beards:* same.

67 *the poetry of:* same.

67 *the swamp literature:* same, 39; book 3, section 2.

67 *the gibberish literature:* same, 41; book 3, section 3.

67 *a red shirt . . . like burning coals:* same, 39; book 3, section 2.

67 *very tall and . . . in her face:* same, 40; book 3, section 3.

67 *Globol . . . gloo:* same, 41.

67 *ended by pursing . . . in their nurseries:* same.

70 *I cannot praise . . . dust and heat:* John Milton, *Areopagitica, A Speech for the Liberty of Unlicensed Printing, to the Parliament (1644),* as it appears in *Milton's Prose Writings,* introduction by K. M. Burton (London: Dent, 1958), 158.

70 *new policemen . . . obstructing traffic:* Hoare, *Noël Coward: A Biography,* 160.

71 *In the New . . . self or temperament:* "Christianity and Literature, *Christian Reflections*, ed. Walter Hooper (Grand Rapids: Wm. B. Eerdmans, 1967), 6–9.

74 *Apparently . . . all come out: A Preface to "Paradise Lost"* (New York: Oxford University Press, 1942), vi.

74 *a common chastitute: Letters,* 178; March 3, 1940.

3. Broadcasts

75 *I write to . . . Problem of Pain: Mere Christianity,* x; introduction by Walter Hooper.

78 *Everyone has heard . . . things they say:* same, 3; book 1, chapter 1, paragraph 1.

79 *A controlling power . . . a Guide:* same, 21; book 1, chapter 4, paragraph 4.

80 *Dear Mr. Lewis . . . Jehovah: They Stand Together,* 492; December 23, 1941.

81 *beautifully, delicately made: Poems,* ed. Walter Hooper (New York: Harcourt, Brace & World, 1964), 135.

81 *Enemy-occupied territory...campaign of sabotage: Mere Christianity,* 40; book 2, chapter 2, paragraph 12.

82 *this process of...full speed astern:* same, 49; book 2, chapter 4, paragraph 7.

82 *droppeth as...from heaven:* act IV, scene 1.

83 *baptism, belief...the Lord's Supper: Mere Christianity,* 53; book 2, chapter 5, paragraph 3.

83 *I do not...on our side:* same, 56; book 2, chapter 5, paragraph 9.

84 *what man...to play:* same, 61; book 3, chapter 1, paragraph 5.

85 *the only plain...and conceited manner: Pride and Prejudice,* chapter 6, paragraphs 23–24.

86 *our warped natures...propaganda for lust: Mere Christianity,* 85; book 3, chapter 5, paragraph 10.

86 *monstrosity:* same, 88; book 3, chapter 6, paragraph 2.

88 *when Christ told...to lay eggs:* same, 116; book 3, chapter 10, paragraph 6.

89 *And that is...come to life:* same, 136; book 4, chapter 1, paragraph 16.

91 *the nice, kind...believe in Christ:* J. B. Phillips, *Plain Christianity, and Other Broadcast Talks* (New York: Macmillan, 1956), 15–16.

92 *Are you the...mind of man:* "What Are We to Make of Jesus Christ?" *God in the Dock,* 158; paragraph 3.

93 *I think all...further than mine: Mere Christianity,* 126–27; book 3, chapter 12, paragraph 9.

95 *A kind of...the word 'love': Plain Christianity,* 13.

4. Buffoon

96 *a power...all eternity: The Screwtape Letters* (New York: Macmillan, 1943); references are from the Macmillan paperback edition, 1962; vii; "Preface to the Paperback Edition," paragraph 10. Included at the end of this edition, beginning on p. 151, is "Screwtape Proposes a Toast."

96 *I believe in...to us:* same.

96 *It agrees with...at most times:* same, paragraph 11.

97 *In fourteenth-century...sinner to mastication:* see *Inferno,* 34:28.

97 *Treble confusion . . . his head: Paradise Lost,* 1:209.

99 *He tempts you . . . the Lord's Prayer: Martin Luther: Selections from His Writings,* ed. with an introduction by John Dillenberger (Garden City, N.Y.: Doubleday & Company, 1961), 225–26.

99 *Imagine you see . . . horror and terror:* Karl Rahner, SJ, *Spiritual Exercises,* trans. Kenneth Baker, SJ (New York: Herder and Herder, 1965), 171.

99 *Consider how he . . . individual is overlooked:* same, 172.

99 *Consider the address . . . all other vices:* same, 172–73.

100 *Marlborough in his . . . Battle of Blenheim: Blenheim Commemorative Booklet,* 24.

100 *the sovereign and . . . Christ Our Lord:* Rahner, *Spiritual Exercises,* 176.

100 *Behind the grenadier . . . of the enemy: Booklet,* 24.

100 *It is Faust . . . evil is liberating: Screwtape Letters,* ix; paragraph 15.

101 *friend . . . discretion:* Roger Lancelyn Green and Walter Hooper, *C. S. Lewis: A Biography* (New York: Harcourt Brace Jovanovich, 1974), 196.

102 *The idea would . . . point of view: Letters,* 188.

102 *something like the . . . raise their voice": Screwtape Letters,* x, paragraph 17.

102 *Our Father Below:* same, 160; paragraph 18.

104 *Dear Wormwood . . . is humor:* Stephen Schofield, "Congratulations — You Have Done It," *The Canadian C. S. Lewis Journal,* September 1979, 5–6.

105 *The best way . . . cannot bear scorn: Screwtape Letters,* 5.

105 *The Devil . . . to be mocked:* same.

106 *self-dependent: Preface,* 97.

106 *The quality of . . . or a turnip:* same, 97–98.

107 *Consider . . . his true condition: Screwtape Letters,* 26–27; letter 5, paragraph 2.

107 *There is nothing . . . happen to them:* same, 28; letter 6, paragraph 1.

107 *Never forget that . . . He has forbidden:* same, 41–42; letter 9, paragraph 2.

107 *No doubt he . . . easy to do:* same, 46; letter 10, paragraph 2.

107 *Your patient has . . . go to bed:* same, 63; letter 14, paragraph 2.

108 *One of the . . . Gluttony of Excess:* same, 76; letter 17, paragraph 1.

108 *A good many... simply as biography:* same, 106–8; letter 23, beginning paragraph 3.

109 *Mr. Principal... and Gentledevils:* same, "Screwtape Proposes a Toast," 153.

109 *There was real... got it down:* same, 154; paragraph 5.

110 *Is the dullness... is petering out?* same, 158, paragraph 14.

110 *Oh, they have... avant-garde stuff:* Nevill Coghill, "The Approach to English," 64.

110 *Your Imminence... and the College:* "Screwtape Proposes a Toast," 172; last paragraph.

110 *Some have paid me... of the ungodly: Screwtape Letters,* xiii, paragraph 24.

111 *You will see... austerity of Hell:* same, 50; letter 11, paragraph 2.

112 *Fun is closely... many other evils:* same, paragraph 3.

112 *A thousand bawdy... lack of humor:* same, 51–52.

112 *Flippancy is the... who practice it:* same, 52; letter 11, paragraph 6.

114 *Vanity of... is vanity:* Ecclesiastes, 1:2.

114 *a depression... public affairs:* as quoted in "The Criterion," *The Oxford Companion to English Literature,* 5th ed., ed. Margaret Drabble (Oxford: Oxford University Press, 1985), 241.

114 *If Mr. Eliot... in the Restoration: Preface,* 137.

116 *I should not... something of him: The Great Divorce* (New York: Macmillan, 1946), 84–89; chapter 10, paragraph 2.

5. Trudge

121 *There was a... morning tea, gentlemen:* "In the Evening" by Roger Lancelyn Green as it appears in *C. S. Lewis at the Breakfast Table, and Other Reminiscences,* comp. and ed. James T. Como (New York: Macmillan, 1979), 212.

123 *A funny old... to grab it: C. S. Lewis, Letters to Children,* ed. Lyle W. Dorsett and Marjorie Lamp Mead (New York: Macmillan, 1985), 21.

125 *I regret causing... excessively and unnecessarily: The Letters of J. R. R. Tolkien,* selected and ed. Humphrey Carpenter (Boston: Houghton Mifflin company, 1981), 126.

125 *Do me the... put them to:* same, 127.

125 *Partly out of . . . a sensitive man:* Peter Bayley, "From Master to Colleague," *C. S. Lewis at the Breakfast Table,* 81.

126 *One of Lewis's . . . to orthodox theology: Time,* September 8, 1947, 72.

127 *If they offered . . . lots of sherry: Brothers and Friends,* 239; January 30, 1951.

128 *pentecostal sweepings . . . Balkan names:* same, 239; February 8, 1951.

128 *an ageing old-time . . . ravaged gray face:* same; January 28, 1951.

128 *In spite of . . . a merry dinner:* same, 240; February 8, 1951.

128 *pride . . . anger:* see *S. Thomae Aquinatis Summa Theologica,* I–II, q. 84, a. 4.

128 *Aquinas defined . . . original capital sin:* see same, q. 153, a. 4.

129 *Sloth that would . . . knows no breaking: Poems,* ed. Walter Hooper (New York: Harcourt, Brace, 1964), 91.

129 *Are not all . . . has some inkling: The Problem of Pain* (New York: Macmillan, 1943), 134; chapter 10, paragraph 2.

130 *When I think . . . to find it:* same, 93; chapter 6, paragraph 16.

130 *Where will you . . . conveniently be combined:* same; see chapter 9, paragraph 9.

131 *There have been . . . desired anything else:* same, 133; chapter 10, paragraph 1.

131 *a roaring . . . of nonsense: Letters,* 170; November 11, 1939.

131 *a short paper . . . effects of pain:* same, 176; February 3, 1940.

131 *Pain provides . . . surprising frequency: Problem of Pain,* 145; Appendix, paragraph 4.

132 *Naturally, there is . . . feelings sometimes do: They Stand Together,* 513–14.

135 *Tonight all the . . . wallowed-in tears: A Grief Observed* (San Francisco: Harper & Row, 1989), 69; part 3, paragraph 45.

138 *Just as the . . . gradually do that:* "Religion: Reality or Substitute?" *Christian Reflections,* ed. Walter Hooper (Grand Rapids: Wm. B. Eerdmans, 1967), 41–42, paragraph 9.

6. Festoon

143 *Acrasia's two young . . . to meet them: The Allegory of Love: A Study in Medieval Tradition* (London: Oxford University Press, 1936), 331.

143 *usually wore a . . . shouldered and shapeless:* Peter Bayley, "From Master to Colleague," *C. S. Lewis at the Breakfast Table,* 78.

143 *few dons' faces... of their robes: Letters,* 62; June 27, 1921.

144 *bare and dully... undergraduate's rooms: C. S. Lewis at the Breakfast Table,* 78.

144 *a reproduction of... alluringly erotic picture:* same, 77.

144 *an Icelandic word... biting the coals: They Stand Together,* 298; January 26, 1927.

146 *the private overtones: Letters to Malcolm* (San Diego: Harcourt, Brace & Company, 1964), 24; letter 5, paragraph 1.

147 *My own plan... last waking moment:* same, 16–17; letter 3, paragraph 7.

151 *When you ask... tendency to priggishness: They Stand Together,* 438–39; February 1932.

151 *Fewer, better... of the second:* "On Church Music," *Christian Reflections,* 95–96.

154 *I feel that... and good wishes:* unpublished letter in the Wade Collection, Wheaton College, Wheaton, Ill., and the Bodleian Library in Oxford.

155 *Humans are amphibians... use of it: Screwtape Letters,* 36–37; letter 8, paragraph 2.

156 *Our Lord will... knows us best: Letters to Children,* 25–26.

157 *The best thing... keeping things out: Screwtape Letters,* 19–20; letter 4, paragraph 2.

160 *The prayer preceding... me of straw: Letters to Malcolm,* 82; letter 15, paragraph 17.

161 *I am trying... in the Faith: Letters, C. S. Lewis, Don Giovanni Calabria: A Study in Friendship,* trans. and ed. Martin Moynihan (Ann Arbor, Mich.: Servant Books, 1988), 73.

161 *However badly needed... would be impudence: Letters to Malcolm,* 63; letter 12, paragraph 4.

162 *Even of the... whom I know: Reflections on the Psalms,* 7.

7. Business

164 *Joy is the... business of Heaven: Letters to Malcolm,* 93; letter 17, last sentence.

164 *devotions to the ...hosts of heaven:* referred to in "The Church's Liturgy," a letter to *Church Times* (May 20, 1949), as it appears in *God in the Dock,* 332.

165 *do not attempt . . . water Christianity down:* "Christian Apologetics," *God in the Dock*, 99.

165 *If a man . . . connoisseur of churches: Screwtape Letters*, 72; letter 16, paragraph 1.

166 *monks . . . feed the soul:* Guigo II, *The Ladder of Monks and Twelve Meditations*, trans. with an introduction by Edmund Colledge, OSA, and James Walsh, SJ (Garden City, N.Y.: Doubleday Image Books, 1978), 82–83.

167 *All I am . . . come into legends: Mere Christianity*, 209; Appendix C.

169 *It would have . . . what Christianity was:* as it appears in "Modern Translations of the Bible," *God in the Dock*, 231.

171 *He is certainly . . . he is poor:* unpublished letter in the Wade Collection, Wheaton College, Wheaton, Ill., and the Bodleian Library in Oxford.

172 *Here we are . . . and the leisure: Aelredi Rievallensis Opera Omnia*, vol. 1: *Opera Ascetica*, ed. A. Hoste OSB and C. H. Talbot (Turnholti: Typographi Brepols Editores Pontificii, 1971), 289; book 1 of *De Spiritali Amicitia*, section 1; a volume in the Corpus Christianorum series; English translation mine.

173 *It was . . . to visit:* unpublished letter dated October 5, 1943; Wade Collection, Wheaton College, and Lewis papers, Bodleian Library, Oxford.

174 *far less austere . . . of that kind:* Bede Griffiths, *The Golden String: An Autobiography* (Springfield, Ill.: Templegate Publishers, 1954, 1980), 134.

175 *Spiritual friendship . . . is reward enough: Aelredi*, section 45; English translation mine.

177 *Jesus has wiped . . . Hearts up: Calabria*, 68; December 26, 1951. English translation mine.

177 *Pray for me . . . face to face: Calabria*, 72; January 5, 1953. English translation mine.

178 *There is a . . . the modern books:* "Introduction," *St. Athanasius on the Incarnation*, trans. and ed. Sister Penelope Lawson, CSMV, with an introduction by C. S. Lewis, with a foreword by Walter Hooper (New York: Macmillan, 1981), xi.

180 *intolerable . . . broken souls:* " 'Miserable Offenders': An Interpretation of Prayer Book Language," *God in the Dock*, 120–21; paragraphs 2–3.

181 *I wonder . . . some other person:* same, 121; paragraph 4.

183 *Atheism may encounter . . . panegyric of atheism:* Walter Hooper, "Oxford's Bonny Fighter," *C. S. Lewis at the Breakfast Table,* 166.

184 *It is not . . . profound scriptural basis:* unpublished letter in the Wade Collection, Wheaton College, Wheaton, Ill., and the Bodleian Library in Oxford.

185 *You will be . . . their knowing it:* same source, different letter.

185 *Go quickly . . . you are away: The Lion, the Witch, and the Wardrobe,* chapter 13.

186 *Good works . . . good work:* see "Good Work and Good Works," *The World's Last Night, and Other Essays* (New York: Harcourt Brace Jovanovich, 1960), 71–81.

188 *When Our Lord . . . really worth drinking:* same, 71; paragraph 1.

188 *"After Priggery — What?"* See *Present Concerns,* ed. Walter Hooper (San Diego: Harcourt Brace Jovanovich, 1986).

193 *Meanwhile . . . Monday morning: The Weight of Glory, and Other Addresses,* revised and expanded edition, ed. with an introduction by Walter Hooper (New York: Macmillan, 1980), 18; last paragraph.

193 *The schoolboy beginning . . . the ultimate reward:* same, 4–5; paragraphs 2–3.

Afterword

196 *Disputations . . . heal them: Calabria,* 38; letter 5, November 25, 1947; English translation mine.

196 *A comparable way . . . make us one:* same.

197 *I believe we . . . my own communion: Letters to an American Lady* (Grand Rapids: Wm. B. Eerdmans, 1971 [1967]), 11; November 10, 1952.

197 *I should need . . . in my prayers:* same; October 26, 1950.

197 *I believe that . . . at the fringes:* same; November 10, 1952.

Bibliography

For a comprehensive bibliography of Lewis's writings, which includes not only books but seven other categories of publication, the reader is referred to Walter Hooper.

His first masterful compilation appears in *C. S. Lewis at the Breakfast Table, and Other Reminiscences,* ed. James T. Como (New York: Macmillan, 1979), 245–88.

It appears again "revised and enlarged" in a subsequent edition of the same book (San Diego: Harcourt Brace Jovanovich, 1992), 245–319.

His latest compilation appears in his own *C. S. Lewis: Companion and Guide* (San Francisco: HarperSanFrancisco, 1996), 799–883.

What follows is a chronicle only of Lewis's books (originals) and Lewis books (anthologies) as they have been published in England and the United States.

The format of the bibliography illustrates that not all publications originated in England or were published simultaneously in both England and the United States, and that some publications were published in only one country.

1919 *Spirits in Bondage: A Cycle of Lyrics.* London: William Heinemann. Published under the pseudonym Clive Hamilton.

1926 *Dymer.* London: J. M. Dent. New York: E. P. Dutton. Published under the pseudonym Clive Hamilton.

1933 *The Pilgrim's Regress: An Allegorical Apology for Christianity, Reason, and Romanticism.* London: J. M. Dent.

1935 *The Pilgrim's Regress.* London and New York: Sheed and Ward.

1936 *The Allegory of Love: A Study in Medieval Tradition.* Oxford: Clarendon Press.

1938 *The Allegory of Love.* London: Oxford University Press. Reprinted with corrections.

Out of the Silent Planet. London: John Lane, The Bodley Head.

1939 *Rehabilitations, and Other Essays.* London: Oxford University Press.

The Personal Heresy: A Controversy. London: Oxford University Press. Coauthored with E. M. W. Tillyard.

1940 *The Problem of Pain.* London: The Centenary Press.

1942 *The Screwtape Letters.* London: Geoffrey Bles.

A Preface to "Paradise Lost." London: Oxford University Press. "Being the Ballard Matthews Lectures, delivered at University College, North Wales, 1941." Revised and enlarged.

Broadcast Talks. London: Geoffrey Bles and The Centenary Press. "Reprinted with some alterations from two series of Broadcast Talks ('Right and Wrong: A Clue to the Meaning of the Universe' and 'What Christians Believe') given in 1941 and 1942."

1943 *The Pilgrim's Regress.* Third edition. London: Geoffrey Bles. "With the author's important new Preface on Romanticism, footnotes, and running headlines."

Out of the Silent Planet. New York: Macmillan.

The Problem of Pain. New York: Macmillan.

The Screwtape Letters. New York: Macmillan.

The Case for Christianity. New York: Macmillan. American edition of *Broadcast Talks.*

Christian Behaviour. London: Geoffrey Bles and The Century Press. New York: Macmillan. "A further series of *Broadcast Talks.*"

Perelandra. London: John Lane, The Bodley Head.

The Abolition of Man, or Reflections on Education with Special Reference to the Teaching of English in the Upper Forms Schools. London: Oxford University Press. "Riddell Memorial Lectures, Fifteenth Series."

1944 *The Pilgrim's Regress.* Third edition. New York: Sheed and Ward.

Perelandra. New York: Macmillan.

Beyond Personality: The Christian Idea of God. London: Geoffrey Bles and The Centenary Press.

1945 *Beyond Personality: The Christian Idea of God.* New York: Macmillan.

That Hideous Strength: A Modern Fairy-tale for Grownups. London: John Lane, The Bodley Head.

The Great Divorce: A Dream. London: Geoffrey Bles and The Centenary Press.

1946 *The Abolition of Man.* London: Geoffrey Bles and The Centenary Press.

The Tortured Planet (That Hideous Strength). New York: Avon Books. "A paperback specially abridged by the author with a different Preface."

The Great Divorce: A Dream. New York: Macmillan.

That Hideous Strength. New York: Macmillan.

George MacDonald: An Anthology. Ed. C. S. Lewis. London: Geoffrey Bles.

1947 *Miracles: A Preliminary Study.* London: Geoffrey Bles and The Centenary Press.

The Abolition of Man. New York: Macmillan.

George MacDonald: An Anthology. Ed. C. S. Lewis. New York: Macmillan.

Essays Presented to Charles Williams. Ed. with a preface and chapter by C. S. Lewis. London: Oxford University Press.

1948 *Arthurian Torso.* London: Oxford University Press. "Containing the posthumous fragment of 'The Figure of Arthur' by Charles Williams and 'A Commentary on the Arthurian Poems of Charles Williams' by C. S. Lewis."

1949 *Transposition, and Other Addresses.* London: Geoffrey Bles. New York: Macmillan; published as *The Weight of Glory, and Other Addresses.*

1950 *Dymer.* New York: Macmillan.

The Lion, the Witch, and the Wardrobe: A Story for Children. Illustrations by Pauline Baynes. London: Geoffrey Bles. New York: Macmillan.

1951 *Prince Caspian: The Return to Narnia.* Illustrations by Pauline Baynes. London: Geoffrey Bles. New York: Macmillan.

1952 *Mere Christianity.* London: Geoffrey Bles. "A revised and amplified edition, with a new introduction, of the three books 'Broadcast Talks,' 'Christian Behaviour,' and 'Beyond Personality.' "

Mere Christianity. New York: Macmillan. "A revised and enlarged edition, with a new introduction, of the three books,

'The Case for Christianity,' 'Christian Behaviour,' and 'Beyond Personality.' "

The Voyage of the "Dawn Treader." Illustrations by Pauline Baynes. London: Geoffrey Bles. New York: Macmillan.

1953 *Voyage to Venus (Perelandra).* London: Pan Books.

The Silver Chair. Illustrations by Pauline Baynes. London: Geoffrey Bles. New York: Macmillan.

1954 *The Horse and His Boy.* Illustrations by Pauline Baynes. London: Geoffrey Bles. New York: Macmillan.

English Literature in the Sixteenth Century, Excluding Drama. Volume 3 of the Oxford History of English Literature. Oxford: Clarendon Press. "The Completion of 'The Clark Lectures,' Trinity College, Cambridge, 1944."

1955 *That Hideous Strength.* London: Pan Books. British edition of *The Tortured Planet*, abridged version of *That Hideous Strength.*

The Magician's Nephew. Illustrations by Pauline Baynes. London: Geoffrey Bles. New York: Macmillan.

Surprised by Joy: The Shape of My Early Life. London: Geoffrey Bles.

1956 *The Last Battle: A Story for Children.* Illustrations by Pauline Baynes. London: The Bodley Head, 1956. New York: Macmillan; published as *The Last Battle.*

Till We Have Faces: A Myth Retold. London: Geoffrey Bles.

Surprised by Joy. New York: Harcourt, Brace & World.

1957 *Till We Have Faces.* New York: Harcourt, Brace & World.

1958 *The Allegory of Love.* New York: Oxford University Press.

Miracles. The Association Press. "An abridgment with a specially written preface by the author."

Reflections on the Psalms. London: Geoffrey Bles. New York: Harcourt, Brace & World.

1960 *Miracles.* With revision of chapter 3. London: Collins–Fontana Books.

The Four Loves. London: Geoffrey Bles. New York: Harcourt, Brace & World.

Studies in Words. Cambridge: Cambridge University Press.

The World's Last Night, and Other Essays. New York: Harcourt, Brace & World.

1961 *The Screwtape Letters, and Screwtape Proposes a Toast.* London: Geoffrey Bles. "With a new and additional Preface."

A Grief Observed. London: Faber and Faber. Published under the pseudonym N. W. Clerk. Reprinted in 1961 under C. S. Lewis.

An Experiment in Criticism. Cambridge: Cambridge University Press.

1962 *They Asked for a Paper: Papers and Addresses.* London: Geoffrey Bles.

The Screwtape Letters, and Screwtape Proposes a Toast. New York: Macmillan.

1963 *A Grief Observed.* Greenwich, Conn.: Seabury Press. Published under the pseudonym N. W. Clerk.

Beyond the Bright Blur. New York: Harcourt, Brace & World. "*Beyond the Bright Blur* is taken from *Letters to Malcolm: Chiefly on Prayer* (chapters 15, 16, 17) by C. S. Lewis, which will be published in the year 1964. This limited edition is published as a New Year's greeting to friends of the author and his publisher."

1964 *Letters to Malcolm: Chiefly on Prayer.* London: Geoffrey Bles. New York: Harcourt, Brace & World.

The Discarded Image: An Introduction to Medieval and Renaissance Literature. Cambridge: Cambridge University Press.

Poems. Ed. Walter Hooper. London: Geoffrey Bles.

1965 *Screwtape Proposes a Toast, and Other Pieces.* With a preface by J. E. Gibb. London: Collins-Fontana Books.

Poems. New York: Harcourt, Brace & World.

1966 *Studies in Medieval and Renaissance Literature.* Collected by Walter Hooper. Cambridge: Cambridge University Press.

Letters of C. S. Lewis. Edited, with a memoir, by W. H. Lewis. London: Geoffrey Bles. New York: Harcourt, Brace & World.

Of Other Worlds: Essays and Stories. Ed. Walter Hooper. London: Geoffrey Bles.

1967 *Studies in Words.* 2d ed. Cambridge: Cambridge University Press. Three additional chapters.

Of Other Worlds. New York: Harcourt, Brace & World.

Christian Reflections. Ed. Walter Hooper. London: Geoffrey Bles. Grand Rapids: Eerdmans.

Spenser's Images of Life. Ed. Alistair Fowler. Cambridge: Cambridge University Press.

Letters to an American Lady. Ed. Clyde S. Kilby. Grand Rapids: Eerdmans.

1968 *A Mind Awake: An Anthology of C. S. Lewis.* Ed. Clyde S. Kilby. London: Geoffrey Bles.

1969 *Letters to an American Lady.* London: Hodder and Stoughton.

Narrative Poems. Ed. Walter Hooper. London: Geoffrey Bles.

Selected Literary Essays. Ed. Walter Hooper. Cambridge: Cambridge University Press.

1970 *God in the Dock: Essays on Theology and Ethics.* Ed. Walter Hooper. Grand Rapids: Eerdmans.

1971 *Undeceptions: Essays on Theology and Ethics.* London: Geoffrey Bles. British edition of *God in the Dock.*

Arthurian Torso as it appears in *Taliessin Through Logres* [and] *The Region of the Summer Stars by Charles Williams and Arthurian Torso by Charles Williams and C. S. Lewis.* Introduction by Mary McDermott Shideler. Grand Rapids: Eerdmans.

1972 *Narrative Poems.* New York: Harcourt, Brace & World

1975 *Fern-seed and Elephants, and Other Essays on Christianity.* Ed. Walter Hooper. London: Collins-Fontana Books.

1977 *The Dark Tower, and Other Stories.* Ed. Walter Hooper. London: Collins. New York: Harcourt Brace Jovanovich.

The Joyful Christian: 127 Readings from C. S. Lewis. With a foreword by William Griffin. New York: Macmillan.

1978 *Miracles.* With revision of chapter 3. New York: Macmillan.

1979 *God in the Dock: Essays on Theology.* Ed. Walter Hooper. London: Collins-Fontana Paperbacks. Abridgement of *Undeceptions.*

They Stand Together: The Letters of C. S. Lewis to Arthur Greeves (1914–1963). Ed. Walter Hooper. New York: Macmillan. London: Collins.

1980 *The Weight of Glory.* Revised and expanded edition, with a new introduction by Walter Hooper. New York: Macmillan.

1981 *Mere Christianity.* Anniversary edition edited and with an introduction by Walter Hooper. New York: Macmillan.

The Lion, the Witch, and the Wardrobe. Illustrations by Michael Hague. New York: Macmillan.

The Visionary Christian: 131 Readings from C. S. Lewis. Selected and edited by Chad Walsh. New York: Macmillan.

1982 *On Stories, and Other Essays in Literature.* Ed. Walter Hooper. New York: Harcourt Brace Jovanovich.

The Grand Miracle, and Other Selected Essays on Theology and Ethics from God in the Dock edited by Walter Hooper. New York: Ballantine Books.

1984 *The Business of Heaven: Daily Readings from C. S. Lewis.* Ed. Walter Hooper. London: Collins; San Diego: Harcourt Brace Jovanovich.

Spirits in Bondage: A Cycle of Lyrics. Ed. Walter Hooper. San Diego: Harcourt Brace Jovanovich.

1985 *Boxen: The Imaginary World of the Young C. S. Lewis.* Ed. Walter Hooper. London: Collins; San Diego: Harcourt Brace Jovanovich, 1985.

First and Second Things: Essays on Theology and Ethics. Ed. Walter Hooper. London: Collins Fount Paperbacks.

Letters to Children. Ed. Lyle W. Dorsett and Marjorie Lamp Mead. New York: Macmillan. London: Collins.

1986 *Mere Christianity.* New York: Collier Books.

The Seeing Eye, and Other Essays from "Christian Reflections." New York: Ballantine Books.

Present Concerns. Ed. Walter Hooper. London: Collins.

1987 *Timeless at Heart: Essays on Theology.* London: Collins Fount Paperbacks.

Present Concerns. Ed. Walter Hooper. San Diego: Harcourt Brace Jovanovich.

1988 *Letters, C. S. Lewis, Don Giovanni Calabria: A Study in Friendship.* Trans. and ed. Martin Moynihan. Ann Arbor, Mich.: Servant Books.

1989 *Letters, C. S. Lewis, Don Giovanni Calabria: A Study in Friendship.* Trans. and ed. Martin Moynihan. London: Collins.

1990 *Christian Reunion, and Other Essays.* Ed. Walter Hooper. London: Collins Fount Paperbacks.

1991 *All My Road before Me: The Diary of C. S. Lewis, 1922–1927*. Ed. Walter Hooper. London: HarperCollins.

1992 *All My Road before Me: The Diary of C. S. Lewis, 1922–1927*. Ed. Walter Hooper. San Diego: Harcourt Brace Jovanovich.

Daily Readings with C. S. Lewis. Ed. Walter Hooper. London: HarperCollins.

1994 *The Collected Poems of C. S. Lewis*. Ed. Walter Hooper. London: HarperCollins.

1996 *C. S. Lewis: Readings for Meditation and Reflection*. San Francisco: HarperSanFrancisco. Originally published in England in 1992 under the title *Daily Readings with C. S. Lewis*.

The Spiritual Legacy Series

Spiritual Legacy is a series designed to make available the ideas of the greatest spiritual masters the West has ever known. The wisdom of the spiritual guides, treasured and passed down through the centuries, is a rich resource for personal growth and insight into the human condition. Now there is a way, not only to have the great texts on one's bookshelf, but to learn from them and make them part of one's life. Each volume provides the reader with a brief history of the subject, the world in which he or she lived and wrote, selections of his or her key writings, and commentary on the application of the writings to life today.

Benedict J. Groeschel
AUGUSTINE
Major Writings
0-8245-2505-1; $13.95

Joan Chittister
THE RULE OF BENEDICT
Insight for the Ages
0-8245-2503-5; $12.95

Regis J. Armstrong
ST. FRANCIS OF ASSISI
Writings for a Gospel Life
0-8245-2501-9; $12.95

The Spiritual Legacy Series

Wendy M. Wright
FRANCIS DE SALES
Introduction to the Devout Life and Treatise on the Love of God
0-8245-2508-6; $12.95

Renate Craine
HILDEGARD
Prophet of the Cosmic Christ
0-8245-2510-8; $14.95

Joseph A. Tetlow
IGNATIUS LOYOLA
Spiritual Exercises
0-8245-2500-0; $12.95

Tessa Bielecki
TERESA OF AVILA
Mystical Writings
0-8245-2504-3; $12.95

Robert Barron
THOMAS AQUINAS
Spiritual Master
0-8245-2507-8; $14.95

Harvey Egan
KARL RAHNER
Mystic of Everyday Life
0-8245-2511-6; $16.95

crossroad

Of Related Interest

Robert Ellsberg

All Saints

Daily Reflections on Saints, Prophets, and Witnesses for Our Time

Winner of the 1998 Christopher Award

"A richly imagined collection of mediating figures in a spiritual communion of many faiths."

—Kenneth L. Woodward, Religion Editor, *Newsweek,* and author of *Making Saints*

"Robert Ellsberg expands our understanding of holiness through the lives of 365 saints, mystics, and seers. What is most compelling about *All Saints* is the inclusion of nontraditional figures and persons from outside the Catholic faith, such as Anne Frank, Gandhi, and Raoul Wallenberg, whose very lives are the greatest testimony to what human beings can be. All saints shows that we can learn the most about goodness from the stories of good people."

—*On Spirit Review*

"This book should be in every home, on every shelf, in every library. It raises the standards of life. It is the kind of book which, if read to our children, would change the tone of the next generation."

—Joan Chittister, author of *The Seasons of Life* and *The Psalms*

0-8245-1679-6; $19.95

Of Related Interest

Christian Feldman

MOTHER TERESA: LOVE STAYS

Foreword by Brother Roger of Taizé

A unique and complete biography,
composed of eye-witness reports, photographs,
and her own lasting words.

0-8245-1738-5; $12.95

GOD'S GENTLE REBELS

Great Saints of Christianity

Adventurous stories of men and women who turned the world upside down quite simply by living differently. Chapters include:
The Crazy Dropout: Francis of Assisi,
The Charming Mystic: Catherine of Siena,
The Torn Christian: Augustine of Hippo,
The Emancipated Nun: Teresa of Avila,
Martyr of Conscience: Thomas More.

0-8245-1519-6; $14.95

We hope you enjoyed
C. S. Lewis.
Thank you for reading it.